THE SACRIFICE OF AFRICA

THE EERDMANS EKKLESIA SERIES

Editors

Michael L. Budde
Stephen E. Fowl

The Eerdmans Ekklesia Series explores matters of Christianity and discipleship across a wide expanse of disciplines, church traditions, and issues of current and historical concern.

The Series is published in cooperation with the Ekklesia Project, a network of persons for whom "being a Christian" is seen to be the primary identity and allegiance for believers — superseding and ordering the claims on offer by the modern state, market, racial and ethnic groups, and other social forces. The Ekklesia Project emphasizes the importance of the church as a distinctive community in the world, called to carry into contemporary society the priorities and practices of Jesus Christ as conveyed in the Gospels.

The Ekklesia Series will draw from the broad spectrum of the Christian world — Protestantism of many traditions, Roman Catholicism, Anabaptism, Orthodoxy — in exploring critical issues in theology, history, social and political theory, biblical studies, and world affairs. The Series editors are Stephen E. Fowl, Professor and Chair, Department of Theology at Loyola College in Baltimore; and Michael L. Budde, Professor of Political Science and Catholic Studies and Chair, Department of Political Science, at DePaul University in Chicago.

Additional information about the Ekklesia Project, including submission guidelines for the Eerdmans Ekklesia book series, may be found at www.ekklesiaproject.org.

THE SACRIFICE OF AFRICA

A Political Theology for Africa

Emmanuel Katongole

WILLIAM B. EERDMANS PUBLISHING COMPANY
GRAND RAPIDS, MICHIGAN / CAMBRIDGE, U.K.

Published 2011 by

Wm. B. Eerdmans Publishing Co.

2140 Oak Industrial Drive N.E., Grand Rapids, Michigan 49505 /

P.O. Box 163, Cambridge CB3 9PU U.K.

Printed in the United States of America

17 16 15 14 13 12 11   7 6 5 4 3 2 1

Library of Congress Cataloging-in-Publication Data

Katongole, Emmanuel, 1960-

The sacrifice of Africa: a political theology for Africa / Emmanuel Katongole.

p.   cm.   — (The Eerdmans Ekklesia series)

ISBN 978-0-8028-6268-6 (pbk.: alk. paper)

1. Christianity and politics — Africa, Sub-Saharan — History.

2. Political theology — Africa, Sub-Saharan.   I. Title.

BR1430.K38   2011

261.70967 — dc22

2010023292

www.eerdmans.com

To the memory of my father Anthony,
who taught me some of the best lessons of life.
Because he was a late convert to Christianity,
he taught me to be passionate about the Christian faith.
Because he was illiterate,
he taught me to value education.
Because he died young,
he taught me to see life as a gift
and never to take anything for granted.

Contents

vii

III: The Sacrifice of Africa

Acknowledgments

In the process of writing this book I have received many gifts for which I am extremely grateful. In the first place, *The Sacrifice of Africa* is itself a gift. Of course this is *my* book, and I have spent many hours, months, and years working on it, but that I have had the time, resources, and ability to read and write is an incredible gift that I can never take for granted. That is why my first debt of gratitude is to my late father, Anthony, to whom the book is dedicated, who himself did not have an opportunity for literate education, but who encouraged — nay demanded — that I take the gift of education and literacy seriously. I hope what I have tried to communicate in these pages reflects what he himself would have said had he had the chance and ability to do so in his short life. I am also grateful to all my teachers, mentors, and benefactors, who made possible, formed, and shaped my education.

There is another sense in which *The Sacrifice of Africa* is a gift. The argument of this book began to take shape in the spring of 2002, out of a course on "Nation-State Politics and Theology in Africa," which I was then teaching as a visiting professor at Duke Divinity School. By the fall of 2003, I had the argument pretty worked out, and submitted the manuscript for consideration to two publishers with the working title *Church and State in Africa: Towards a Constructive Social Imagination.* Even though one of the publishers came back to me with a very positive assessment of the manuscript and the promise of publication, I was not very happy with the manuscript, as I felt that its argument was still overly theoretical and still too "academic." Moreover, whereas the manuscript set out a compelling argument for the need for a fresh social imagination in Africa, it lacked the necessary evidence through stories and other practical displays of what a constructive social reimagination of Africa might look like. I was still trying to figure out how to overcome this shortcoming when I was invited in the fall of 2004 by Dean Gregory Jones to work with Chris Rice to shape a vision for a Center for Reconciliation at Duke Divinity School. This required me to put on hold a number of projects I was working on, including the manuscript, so as to give time and energy to birthing the Center for Reconciliation, which was launched in the spring of 2005, with Chris and myself as founding co-directors. Over the next few years, as the Center took off, we established a number of programs and initiatives, including the Great Lakes Initiative, which brings together Christian leaders in the East African region for rest, renewal, and theological reflection on the theme of peace and reconciliation. It was through these meetings and gatherings of the Great Lakes Initiative that I had an opportunity to meet and interact with so many impressive Christian leaders, and to learn about their various programs and ministries. This is how I first came in contact with Maama Angelina Atyam, Bishop Paride Taban, and Maggy Barankitse. Their lives, stories, and ministries not only made real and concrete the truth of Paul's claim of a "new creation" (2 Cor 5:17); they offered the practical, concrete, and narrative demonstration of the social reimagination of Africa for which I was desperately searching.

I am therefore grateful to Angelina Atyam, Paride Taban, and Maggy Barankitse, and other Christian leaders like them, without whom the argument of this book remains only a theoretical possibility. I am grateful to them for their willingness to share their stories, as well as for their patience and gracious responses to my many inquiries and requests for interviews. One of the greatest gifts of my work at Duke, particularly with the Center for Reconciliation, has been the opportunity to know and become friends with leaders like Maggy, Taban, and Angelina. That is why I am also grateful to Dean Greg Jones for his leadership, and his invitation to me to serve as founding co-director for the Center. I also thank him for his continued support and encouragement for the type of "systematic practical theology" that is pursued and exemplified in this book. Chris Rice is not only a colleague and co-director of the Center for Reconciliation, but a dear friend and trusted companion in the work and journey of reconciliation. To him and the rest of the staff of the Center I am grateful for the gift of friendship and community. The Center is for me truly an oasis of fellowship and support in the often lonely and competitive world of the academy that characterizes the modern university, even in a place like the Duke Divinity School.

I am also extremely grateful to my friend Mike Budde, who kept encouraging me to publish *The Sacrifice* (even in its original version) and invited me to submit it for consideration as part of the Eerdmans Ekklesia series. Mike also introduced me to the DePaul Center for World Catholicism and Intercultural Theology. The latter, under its Director, Professor Peter Casarella, offered me a four-month sabbatical, and named me its First Senior Research Fellow. It was during this time of sabbatical at De Paul that I thoroughly revised the earlier manuscript, tightened its argument, added new content, and rewrote it in a fresh style. I am therefore grateful to Peter and the staff of the DePaul Center for World Catholicism and Intercultural Theology for the generosity of the sabbatical grant and for their hospitality and support.

During the time of sabbatical, I was very warmly received by the community of St. Clement Parish near Lincoln Park, which became my "home" and my "church" for four months. I am grateful to Fr. Ken Simpson, the wonderful pastor, to the other priests of the parish — Frs. Vince and Ramil, and "Deacon" Many — and to the parish staff and community of St. Clement for their hospitality.

The final version of *The Sacrifice of Africa* has benefitted from the editorial assistance of many people, to whom I am indebted. I am particularly grateful to Amanda Rooker, Judith Heyhoe, and Susan Bond, who spent many hours of meticulous work correcting my grammar and readjusting my clumsy constructions and expressions. The same debt of gratitude extends to the editors at Eerdmans for their work in getting the manuscript ready for publication.

I am grateful to all my colleagues at Duke Divinity School for their unwavering support and encouragement to me, and am particularly grateful to Stanley Hauerwas, who read a draft of the manuscript and offered a number of helpful suggestions for revision.

Cardinal Wamala in Uganda, now the emeritus archbishop of Kampala, remains an exceptional mentor and a steadfast friend. I am amazed at, but extremely grateful for, his love for me and his unwavering support and interest in my work.

Finally, I am grateful for the love of my family, particularly my mother, and other friends in Uganda, in the U.S., and around the world, whose love and friendship keeps me both humble and joyful.

Entebbe, Bethany House
June 28, 2010
On the 23rd Anniversary of priestly ordination

On Being Saved from King Leopold's Ghost

Has the Savior you tell us of any power to save us from rubber trouble?

Adam Hochschild, *King Leopold's Ghost*

A fresh conversation about Christian social ethics in Africa is long overdue. Christianity continues to grow and thrive in Africa, but so too grow the realities of poverty, violence, and civil war. Perhaps because of this fact, in the last twenty years, we have witnessed a renewed interest in Christian social ethics, which has resulted in a number of recommendations regarding Christianity's role in the search for peace, democracy, and development in Africa. But while these practical recommendations confirm Christianity's social relevance, they do not explain why war, tribalism, poverty, corruption, and violence have been endemic to Africa's social history. Neither do these recommendations and suggestions get to the heart of the Christian story, which is a fresh vision for the world in which we live.

There are a number of reasons for these shortcomings, not least of which are deep-seated assumptions about the relationship between Christianity and the social, political sphere. One assumption is that the task of ensuring peace, democracy, and development — in a word, the social and material conditions of life — properly belongs to the jurisdiction of politics. Christianity, which belongs to the realm of religion, can only make a helpful contribution to the field of politics. Closely connected to this un-

derstanding of the relation between religion and politics is the assumption
that politics in Africa — particularly the institution of the nation-state —
have not worked very well. Therefore, the most urgent task for Christian
social ethics is to make politics work better, that is, become more democratic and transparent, with the expectation that properly functioning
nation-state politics in Africa will ensure peace and stability and thus advance development.

Yet these recommendations do not pay sufficient attention to the
possibility that politics in Africa, and the nation-state in particular, have
not been a failure, but have worked very well. Chaos, war, and corruption
are not indications of a failed institution; they are ingrained in the very
imagination of how nation-state politics works. To put the argument differently, while Christian social ethics in Africa have focused on providing
strategies for revising, improving, or managing a failing institution, they
have paid very little attention to the story of this institution: *how* it works
and *why* it works in the way it does.

It is at this narrative level that a fresh conversation about Christian
social ethics must take place. *The Sacrifice of Africa* is about this new conversation. Therefore, this is a book of stories, specifically, the story of
nation-state politics in Africa. The study investigates what sort of difference, if any, the Christian story can make in relation to nation-state politics in Africa.

At the heart of this study is a conviction that all politics are about
stories and imagination. Stories not only shape how we view reality but
also how we respond to life and indeed the very sort of persons we become.
In other words, we are how we imagine ourselves and how others imagine
us. But this imagining does not take place as an abstraction in the world of
fantasy or as the unbounded free play of a mental faculty called the imagination. The idea that we can be anything we wish to be is one of the most
insidious lies we can ever entertain. Who we are, and who we are capable
of becoming, depends very much on the stories we tell, the stories we listen
to, and the stories we live. Stories not only shape our values, aims, and
goals; they define the range of what is desirable and what is possible.
Stories, therefore, are not simply fictional narratives meant for our entertainment; stories are part of our social ecology. They are embedded in us
and form the very heart of our cultural, economic, religious, and political
worlds. This applies not only to individuals, but to institutions and even
nations. That is why a notion like "Africa" names not so much a place, but

2

a story — or set of stories about how people of the continent called Africa are located in the narrative that constitutes the modern world.

But if stories are essential to the way we live, they, like the air we breathe, often remain invisible. This does not mean their hold on us is any less powerful. On the contrary, to the extent that the stories that form our imagination remain invisible, they hold us more deeply in their grip. This is what makes the institution of the nation-state in Africa even more powerful than has been acknowledged. Although much has been written about the nation-state in Africa — its ironic contradictions and the madness of leaders like Mobutu, Bokassa, Amin, and Mugabe — none of these accounts have made a conscious attempt to connect to the foundational stories of modern Africa.[1] Yet doing so might reveal that the Mobutus, Amins, Bokassas, and Mugabes of Africa are not exceptional but simply radical examples of predictable performances within the script of modern Africa.[2]

This is why Christian social ethics in Africa must shift its exclusive focus on strategies for fixing the structures of democracy and development and get into the business of stories. Christian social ethics must uncover the underlying stories of the key social institutions in Africa that affect both their performance and the types of characters they produce. Shifting the focus from strategies to stories provides a fresh way to talk about politics: politics as dramatic performance grounded in a particular story that requires, and in the end shapes, particular characters. But this way of thinking about politics in Africa also provides a way to view Christianity as itself a form of politics, a unique performance grounded in a different set of stories that shape unique expectations and characters. Accordingly, the focus on stories and performance not only opens up a fresh conversation about the relationship between Christianity and politics (or Christianity as politics) in Africa; it is a way to highlight the type of politics Christianity can shape, and the new future it can produce.

---

1. A number of journalistic accounts well depict the madness of nation-state performances in Africa. David Lamb's *The Africans* (New York: Random House, 1982) comes to mind here. More recently, see Keith Richburg, *Out of America: A Black Man Confronts Africa* (New York: Basic Books, 1997).

2. I use the word "performance" in this book to signify the performance of the imagined script.

A Personal Journey: Two Stories

In part, this study is a reflection on my own life lived at the intersection of two institutions: nation-state politics on the one hand, and Christianity and church life on the other. In fact, when the idea of a book-length study on the issues involving politics and theology in Africa first occurred to me, I thought of writing it as an autobiographical account titled "How Christianity Saved Me from the Politics of Uganda." I eventually decided against that title for two reasons. First, I saw that a title like "how Christianity saved me from politics" might reinforce the misleading impression that the type of "salvation" at stake is solely a "spiritual" salvation.

Second, and even more important, I feared that such a title might project Christianity as an alternative to politics that has nothing to do with the politics of Uganda, or any nation for that matter. The challenge is not so much one of being "saved from" the realities of nation-state politics, but of having resources and skills to engage that politics from a more determinative account of reality. My life and ministry as a Catholic priest has not only led me to engage more clearly the story of nation-state politics in Africa; it has led me to appreciate how deeply political the Christian gospel is.[3] As I share the stories of Scripture and celebrate Mass and other sacraments, I find myself located in a far more determinative form of political engagement than I ever would have hoped for if I had joined nationalist politics. I am not engaged in some esoteric form of "spiritual" ministry, but in a dynamic (sometimes contested) narration and imagination of life that has as much to do with the soul, prayers, and meditation as it has to do with the entire gamut of what constitutes life: sex, money, food, the bearing and raising of children, digging pit latrines, constructing wells, planting cabbages, attending to the sick, and so on.

However, to claim that Christianity has saved me from nation-state politics is more than a figure of speech. For having been born in 1960, just two years before Uganda's independence from Britain, I have shared the dreams of independence (from colonialism) and of the political and eco-

---

3. This way of framing the issue might be misleading, as it could give the impression that Christianity has contributed nothing to the rise of the modern nation-state. But, as William Cavanaugh has noted, a key feature of the modern nation-state is its claim for total allegiance, which tends to absorb, sap, and reshape all other loyalties, including religious loyalties. See Cavanaugh, "A Fire Strong Enough to Consume the Whole House: The Wars of Religion and the Rise of the State," *Modern Theology* 11, no. 4 (1995): 397-420.

nomic well-being of my generation. Yet the fact that many of my generation are already dead is an indication of the tragic waste of life, as well as the ongoing frustration of these hopes and dreams at the hand of nationalist politics. What is particularly telling is that the few of my generation who are still alive have lived through (or, more accurately, *survived*) not only many regimes but also a series of "liberation" struggles, each promising an end to, but instead only exacerbating, the political nightmare.

I was providentially saved from waging one such futile war in the beginning of 1979 when, in the wake of the liberation war that ousted Idi Amin from power, I, together with my elder brother Gabriel, sneaked through the government-controlled area to the front line with the intention of enlisting with a faction of the United National Liberation Front (UNLF) fighting alongside Tanzanian troops in a final push towards Kampala. Now I realize that it was only providence that saved me from being drafted into this war to "liberate" Uganda. It is not that I am a timid individual who shies away from any commitment that requires personal sacrifice; rather, it is the futility of sacrificing oneself for a cause that is neither true nor worthy that I now find totally tragic. As it turned out, the providence that saved me from this futile liberation was in the form of a serious lung infection, which, given the state of total collapse of the health infrastructure during Amin's regime (the hospitals had completely run out of drugs and many doctors had already fled the country and were living in exile), could be neither diagnosed nor treated. Accordingly, when my brother and I offered to join the "liberation war," I was declared too weak to fight. Gabriel enlisted, received military training, and fought along a brigade of Tanzanian troops that eventually ousted Idi Amin. Gabriel later became a commissioned officer in the Uganda National Liberation Army (UNLA), but eventually was decommissioned when Museveni's National Resistance Army (NRA) took power in 1986. He found himself out of work, and for many years he was almost literally out on the streets of Kampala. He contracted AIDS, and died from it in 2003.

For my part, having been declared too weak to join the military, I joined the seminary in the latter part of 1979. At this time, I really had no serious intention of becoming a priest, but because there seemed to be few good opportunities for a sickly young man like me, I thought the seminary would be a good place to wait it out until I got better and conditions normalized a bit in Uganda. At the seminary, I was soon referred to a mission hospital run by the Medical Mission Sisters from Ireland. Here, my medical condition was diagnosed and I was kept for over a month in the hospital receiving treatment. At the end of this time, having missed more than a month of classes and still feeling too weak to study, I could not go back to the seminary, but spent the rest of the year at home recovering. It was then that I had time to think about my life and about the call to the priesthood — and actually decided to become a priest. So, at the end of the year, having fully recovered from sickness and regained my strength, I rejoined the seminary, this time with a better focus and sense of call to priestly ministry. For seven years I went through the seminary program, first at Katigondo and then at Gaba. I was ordained a priest and celebrated my first Mass on the feast day of Saints Peter and Paul on June 29, 1987.

All the time, though, I continued to follow, with increasing frustration, the events of Uganda's political life. The 1979 "liberation" was soon over; Amin was out of power, but bitter factions and acrimony developed between various groups within the UNLF. Successive coups ushered in one regime after another; a bogus and rigged election saw the return of Obote to power and the start of a new civil war. As a result, throughout the early part of the 1980s, the country experienced nothing but mock democracy and state brutality at the hands of the second Obote regime. During this time, my home, in what came to be known as the Luweero Triangle, was attacked by government soldiers in the hunt for "rebels" launching surprise attacks on government soldiers from the neighboring forests. We lost everything. My mother and other relatives living with her barely survived as they fled. Others were not so lucky: over forty-six people were killed in my and neighboring villages on just that one day.

In 1986, the rebels took power, and Museveni became president. To Museveni's credit, there has been relative peace in the central and southern parts of the country, and the economy has grown a bit since. However, throughout these years of Museveni's rule, much of northern Uganda, particularly the districts of Gulu and Kitgum, have been living through a nightmare, with Joseph Kony's Lord's Resistance Army killing, maiming, and terrorizing the population and abducting over 26,000 children. The government's counterattacks and policy of forcing everyone to live in congested camps for internally displaced persons (IDPs) have left many more dead and condemned the survivors to a hopeless life of mere survival in the IDPs.

But even in the southern part of Uganda where there has been relative peace, Museveni's political and economic reforms notwithstanding, the rural poor have been increasingly marginalized, official and state corruption is rampant, and all indicators point to the institutionalization of a one-party dictatorship. Apparently, all these things have been set up to ensure the well-being and continued power of a few individuals and their cronies.

It was against this background of frustration with nationalist politics that I began to wonder about the difference that Christianity makes — or can make — in Africa. At the seminary, a course in moral theology introduced me to Catholic social teaching. As I studied the official documents of Catholic social teaching as well as the pastoral letters of the Uganda Catholic bishops, I discovered that these offered a number of beautiful suggestions and recommendations to ensure stability, peace, and development.[4] I was, however, frustrated that none of these seemed to have deeply challenged or offered a viable and concrete alternative to the endless cycle of violence, plunder, and poverty. In a word, it was as if these recommendations and pronouncements did not matter one way or the other. What added to my sense of frustration was the realization that even though in many parts of Africa the church, at least numerically, was a strong and powerful institution, it did not make much difference to Africa's social history of violence, corruption, and poverty.

Thus, by the time I enrolled in my graduate studies at Leuven, Belgium, in 1991, my frustration regarding Africa's social history was not only heightened; it was directed equally at nation-state politics and Christianity. At Leuven, I was interested in social and political philosophy. And so as I studied modern European philosophy, I was not only able to understand the social, religious, and cultural contexts that had given rise to the birth of the particular political arrangement of the nation-state institution; I was able to get a clear sense of its operative assumptions (through the works of Hobbes, Locke, Hume, Kant, and others), as well as its limitations (through the works of Foucault, Marx, and others). All this clearly connected to the way the institution of nation-state politics operated in Africa. But only when I began to study the theologian Stanley Hauerwas did I see the deep connections between stories, politics, and identity.[5] I began to understand that behind the problematic state of poli-

---

4. See Emmanuel Katongole and John Mary Waliggo, *The Social Teaching of the Church by the Catholic Bishops of Uganda 1962-2003*, CACISA Monograph series (forthcoming).

5. I tell the story of my initial introduction to Hauerwas and of eventually being

tics in Africa are stories that carry assumptions about Africans and African societies, which in turn shape Africans and African societies. By this time, I had begun to see the full impact of colonialism by attending to the stories that legitimated it. Of course, I had already read philosophers like Kant and Hegel and their views on Africa, and realized the extent to which these philosophers provided the framing script for early European contacts with Africa. But I had also started to read the writings of Frantz Fanon and his depictions of the effects of colonial violence on the colonized,[6] as well as the writings of scholars like Mudimbe, who were helping me to see that Africa was to a large extent the way it was (is) as imagined by Europe, with concepts like "chaos," "tribe," and "primitive" integral to that imagination — if only as a way to confirm the European imagination of Europe as civilized and developed.[7]

All these ideas and lessons were running through my mind, still in very disjointed ways, when the genocide in Rwanda happened in the spring of 1994. I sat many evenings in silence and utter shock in the salon of the Heliege Geest College where I stayed, watching the news from Rwanda and seeing pictures of the dead bodies of Rwandans and unable to believe what had happened in this otherwise beautiful and peaceful country. Even though I could not articulate the reasons behind such horrific events, I rejected the easy explanations of "age-old animosities" between the Hutu and Tutsi tribes.[8] This tragic event not only made me angry at the callousness with which the lives of so many people could easily be wasted; it shattered any naïveté I had about the church and Christianity in Africa. For the Rwanda genocide not only happened in one of the most Christianized nations in Africa; the churches themselves often became killing fields, with Christians killing fellow Christians in the same places they had worshipped together. This not only raised many questions about the

---

"hooked" by him in "Hauerwasian Hooks and the Christian Social Imagination," in *God, Truth, and Witness: Essays in Conversation with Stanley Hauerwas,* ed. L. Gregory Jones et al. (Grand Rapids: Brazos, 2005).

6. See Frantz Fanon, *The Wretched of the Earth,* trans. Constance Farrington (New York: Grove, 1968).

7. See particularly V. Y. Mudimbe, *The Invention of Africa* (Bloomington: Indiana University Press, 1988); and Mudimbe, *The Idea of Africa* (Bloomington: Indiana University Press, 1994).

8. See Emmanuel Katongole and Jonathan Wilson-Hartgrove, *Mirror to the Church* (Grand Rapids: Zondervan, 2009).

famed African sense of community and sacredness of life, but also filled me with deep anger and restlessness about the status of Christianity in Africa. I kept wondering whether Christianity in Africa had become so interwoven into the story of violence that it no longer had a vantage point from which to resist the violence. At any rate, Rwanda became a watershed event — after this, there could be no carrying on as usual. No simple formulas would do. On the contrary, the event of the Rwanda genocide laid open the need to reassess the assumptions and forms of knowledge that I had hitherto taken for granted.

On returning to Uganda at the end of my studies, I made a pilgrimage to Rwanda. And as I listened to the stories of what had happened during the genocide and visited some sites of genocide, I was led to see that Christianity was part and parcel of the political imagination of Tutsi and Hutu as distinct races or tribes, and that Christianity had been unable to resist or interrupt that story and its effects. I began to see Rwanda not only as a mirror to Africa, but to the church in general.[9] There was no course on Rwanda on the syllabus at the seminary where I was assigned to teach. I offered to design and teach one, but the academic dean told me that the syllabus was full and "could not accommodate any new courses." I had been assigned to teach a course on African Thought, which mostly consisted of a stale discussion of whether there is a distinctive African philosophy, and what was distinctive about that philosophy. I revised the course and smuggled into it discussions of African social history, and tried to push some questions about African politics, stories, and the imagination. In the course, I pointed to the ubiquity of war and violence in Africa and wondered whether there might be something like an imaginative landscape of Africa — a kind of script — that the key institutions in Africa, including Christianity, simply took for granted and unwittingly performed. If so, what is the story or the underlying stories within this script? I must admit, however, that even though I was raising these and similar questions, it was not until I read Adam Hochschild's *King Leopold's Ghost* that I was able to see clearly the interconnection of story, politics, violence, and the challenge that Christianity faces in Africa. That was in the summer of 2000.

---

9. For more detail on this conclusion, see Katongole and Wilson-Hartgrove, *Mirror to the Church.*

On Facing "King Leopold's Ghost"

King Leopold's Ghost is the story of personal ambition, greed, and violence set in the context of colonial history. In this masterfully woven narrative, Adam Hochschild recounts the ambitions of King Leopold II of Belgium: his obsession with, and eventual acquisition and brutal plundering of, his Congo colony. In numerous descriptions drawn from historical reports and eyewitness accounts, Hochschild provides horrifying glimpses of the terror and brutal savagery that accompanied Leopold II's occupation of the Congo Free State. This is how, for instance, one Tswambe remembers Léon Fiévez, one of the state officials responsible for enforcing Leopold's rubber-harvesting policies:

> All blacks saw this man (Fiévez) as the Devil of the Equator. . . . From all the bodies killed in the field, you had to cut off the hands. He wanted to see the number of hands cut off by each soldier, who had to bring them in baskets. . . . A village which refused to provide rubber would be completely swept clean. As a young man, I saw [Fiévez's] soldier Molili, then guarding the village of Boyeka, take a big net, put ten arrested natives in it, attach big stones to the net, and make it tumble into the river. . . . Rubber caused these torments; that's why we no longer want to hear its name spoken. Soldiers made young men kill or rape their own mothers and sisters.[10]

What is particularly telling about this and similar accounts of brutality and violence is the realization that they were not isolated incidents of an overambitious state official. Such punishments as the burning of villages, dismemberment, and other forms of punishment were part of official state policy. In 1899 the American Presbyterian missionary William Sheppard stumbled on one of the grisliest evidences of this policy carried out by Leopold's Force Publique. One day when Sheppard reached the marauders' camp,

> his eye was caught by a large number of objects being smoked. The chief "conducted us to a framework of sticks, under which was burning a slow fire, and there they were, the right hands, I counted them, 81

---

10. Adam Hochschild, *King Leopold's Ghost: A Story of Greed, Terror, and Heroism in Colonial Africa* (Boston: Houghton Mifflin, 1998), 166.

in all." The chief told Sheppard, "See! Here is our evidence. I always have to cut off the right hands of those we kill in order to show the State how many we have killed." He proudly showed Sheppard some of the bodies the hands had come from. The smoking preserved the hands in the hot, moist climate, for it might be days or weeks before the chief could display them to the proper official and receive credit for his kills.[11]

The stories are numerous and horrifying in their detailed depictions of the violence and brutality that decimated villages and left anywhere between five to eight million Congolese dead. As I read these accounts, and the full impact of Hochschild's *King Leopold's Ghost* sank in, I began to connect the dots. I was now able to see more clearly the five most critical challenges facing Christian social ethics in Africa.

1. Colonial Impact, Social Memory, and Forgetfulness

First, reading *King Leopold's Ghost* allowed me to see the significance of social memory. Hochschild notes that as Leopold's rubber policies "spread throughout the rain forest, [they] branded people with memories that remained raw for the rest of their lives."[12] Moreover, it was also clear that such violent memories were not limited to King Leopold's Congo, but they were the sort of memories that accompanied colonialism in other parts of Africa. For as Hochschild remarks, "what happened in the Congo could reasonably be called the most murderous part of the European Scramble for Africa."[13] But it is just that — "the most murderous part." For "the sad truth is that the men who carried it out for Leopold were no more murderous than many Europeans then at work or at war elsewhere in Africa."[14] *King Leopold's Ghost* helped me to see that the violence and brutality in Leopold's Congo were not simply isolated or pathological exceptions committed by a few overzealous colonial agents; they were part and parcel of the rubber economy, which was very rational and modern both in its design and implementation. As a modern phenomenon, it required the reorganization of

11. Hochschild, *King Leopold's Ghost*, 164-65.
12. Hochschild, *King Leopold's Ghost*, 165.
13. Hochschild, *King Leopold's Ghost*, 280.
14. Hochschild, *King Leopold's Ghost*, 283.

Congo society under new rational modalities that ensured efficient admin-istration and economic production. Thus, large areas of the forest were cleared, villages were resettled, quotas were assigned, compliance was re-corded, and slackers were punished. And since the entire project of the civi-lization of the Congo was tied up with the rubber economy, the Congo was giving me a glimpse into the story of Africa's initiation into modernity.

Thus, *King Leopold's Ghost* ceased to be a book about the Congo and became a metaphor for Africa, raising the key issues not only of founda-tional narratives but of the transmission and reproductions of social memory. Since I knew that such memories do not simply go away or die with the initial victims, I was anxious to know how and in what ways those memories live on. In fact, the more I thought about this connection, the more obvious it became that the key actors of Africa's post-independence history — Idi Amin, Bokassa, Mobutu, and Mugabe — were but colonial "types," that is, mimetic reproductions of colonial actors like Kurtz, Leopold, and Ian Smith. One cannot understand these actors without lo-cating them in a social history.

Thus it became clear that if Christian social ethics in Africa was to provide a way forward in Africa, it would have to engage the layers of memory through which the performance of the colonial imagination con-tinues to live in the present. Moreover, *King Leopold's Ghost* also led me to see that the sources for exploring the issues of social memory may not lie in public records, but in cultural patterns as well as other unofficial texts. For even as Hochschild notes that the rubber terror "branded people with memories that remained raw for the rest of their lives," he also notes that from "African voices within this time there is largely silence."[15] What this crucial observation suggested is that the task of engaging social memory also has to do with questioning and interrogating cultural forms of forget-fulness in order to uncover the patterns of performances through which the memory of history lives on.[16] In this connection, I found a Congolese song reported by a Swedish missionary in 1894 telling of the general sense of desperation that the terror of King Leopold's policies was shaping for the Africans:

15. Hochschild, *King Leopold's Ghost*, 5.

16. See, e.g., Emmanuel Katongole, "Remembering Idi Amin: On Violence, Ethics, and Social Memory in Africa," in *A Future for Africa: Critical Essays in Christian Social Imag-ination* (Scranton: University of Scranton Press, 2005).

We are tired of living under this tyranny
We cannot endure that our women and children are taken away
And dealt with by the white savages
We shall make war . . .
We know we shall die, but we want to die
We want to die.[17]

Christian social ethics would have to engage not only official texts, but also songs, poetry, and fiction to get a fuller sense of the story of modernity in Africa.

2. The Lies of Noble Ideals

One thing that makes Hochschild's *King Leopold's Ghost* such a shocking but revealing account is that so much of its evidence flies in the face of the usual image of Leopold as a "philanthropic monarch," the great emissary of civilization in Africa that I, and I am sure many others in Africa, remember from our history classes. Many Europeans still have this image of Leopold. Of course, the fact that many Europeans still regard Leopold as a great humanitarian king may simply indicate the lengths to which Leopold, and the colonial officials who came after him, went to erase incriminating evidence from public record. As Hochschild shows, shortly before he turned over the colony to Belgium, Leopold burned all the state archives. "The archives burned for eight days, turning most of the Congo state records to ash and smoke in the sky over Brussels. 'I will give them my Congo,' Leopold told Stinglhamber, 'but they have no right to know what I did there.'"[18]

But there seems to be another reason why Europe never got a chance to hear about the true King Leopold and his brutal plunder of the Congo. This other reason has to do with the noble ideals of "civilization" and "humanitarian" concern for the "poor Africans" — notions that not only framed the Europeans' vision of Africans as savage and primitive, but shaped their own identity and vision of themselves as noble and civilized. Given the power of these noble ideals and how deeply they have shaped

17. Hochschild, *King Leopold's Ghost*, 172-73.
18. Hochschild, *King Leopold's Ghost*, 294.

European culture, the true story of Leopold was not one that Europe was prepared to hear. That is why, on thinking about the lies that noble ideals such as civilization and humanitarianism conceal, I could not help but think about the story of Marlow in the last section of Joseph Conrad's *Heart of Darkness*.

Marlow, the captain of a ship belonging to "the Company," is sent to the Congo to find Kurtz, an ivory trader who had gone missing in the interior. The journey is arduous, but eventually when Marlow finds Kurtz he is able to witness the depth of horror and violence to which he has descended. After Kurtz gives Marlow the report to take back to the company, he also hands Marlow a packet of papers and a photograph of Kurtz's fiancée, in order to keep them out of the manager's hands. A few evenings later, Kurtz dies, with one phrase on his lips: "The horror! The horror!" Marlow returns to England, but the memory of Kurtz haunts him. He manages to find the woman from the picture, and he pays her a visit. She talks at length about his wonderful personal qualities and about how guilty she feels that she was not with him at the last. When the woman asks Marlow what Kurtz's last words were, Marlow lies and says that her name was the last word he spoke. "'But I couldn't,' reflected Marlow. 'I could not tell her. It would have been too dark — too dark altogether.'"[19]

The truth would be too dark to tell. That I think is exactly what prevented Europe from hearing the true story of the colonial project of civilization. *King Leopold's Ghost* reveals how ideals, especially noble ideals, while inspiring, can also stand in the way of our seeing what is really happening. With this realization, I began to see that ideals like "democracy," "development," "civilization," and "progress" have become such tantalizing but misleading notions, forming the basic imaginative canvas yet obscuring reality. They have become the lies that both African leaders and social ethicists desperately want to believe.

Thus, as I read Hochschild's account and was able to see the Congo as a good example of the politics of self-deception, I realized that the challenge of Christian social ethics in Africa is to question even the cherished notions of progress, development, and democracy — notions that form the imaginative framework of thinking about the future in Africa. I was beginning to see that only by avoiding assumptions about these concepts is

19. Joseph Conrad, *Heart of Darkness*, ed. Ross C. Murfin, 2nd ed. (New York: Bedford Books, 1996), 94.

it possible to get to the real story that drives modern Africa, and the kind of imagination that would make a new future in Africa possible.

3. The Politics of Greed and Plunder

Reading *King Leopold's Ghost* also led me to see that the real story that drives modern Africa is one of personal ambition and greed, which in the case of King Leopold expressed itself in the plunder of the Congo. It is the same story that drives the Congo today. Even before the death of King Leopold, the Belgian government had taken over the administration of the Congo Free State, renaming the territory the Belgian Congo. In 1960, the Congo became independent under Lumumba; it became Zaire in 1971 under Mobutu; and it has since been renamed (by the Kabilas) the Democratic Republic of the Congo (DRC).

Yet for all these differences in external formalities, the Congo still operates by the same law of plunder and greed. The actors change, but the script seems to be unchanged. The recent fighting in eastern Congo, which has left over 3.8 million dead and many more homeless, only indicates its escalation and democratization. Where once there was state-sponsored violence and plunder, there is now an array of private militias, some with the backing of neighboring countries like Uganda and Rwanda, each fighting for control of a portion of the mineral and natural resources of the Congo.

Moreover, the more I thought about these connections, the more the Congo's story became a lens through which I was beginning to understand other African countries. For whether it is Uganda, Zimbabwe, Liberia, or Sierra Leone (as the recent movie *Blood Diamond* so clearly depicts), one confronts the same story of the politics of greed, dispossession, and state brutality, with perhaps the only difference being the degree of sophistication. As Michela Wrong points out, the Congo is but "a paradigm of all that was wrong with post-colonial Africa."[20] For the Congo's combination of rich natural and human resources and economic and political collapse reflects tragic waste, selfish ambition, greed, and crippled potential that is the story of many African countries. What perhaps sets the Congo apart, according to Wrong, is the radicalization of a certain

20. Michela Wrong, *In the Footsteps of Mr. Kurtz* (New York: HarperCollins, 2001), 10.

kind of "negative excellence": "It is as if the Congo has embodied within its history the faults of any normal African state and pitched them one frequency higher."[21]

Accordingly, with *King Leopold's Ghost*, I was able to see more clearly not only how the colonial project's founding narrative was a story of power, greed, and plunder, but how such a story had come to be subsumed into the successor institution of the nation-state. It would be impossible to understand the current socio-political melodrama of the Congo, or any other African country for that matter, without drawing attention to this founding narrative. Similarly, any suggestions for a way forward that do not confront this founding narrative of modern Africa are misleading at best. It is the ghost in *King Leopold's Ghost*. For to the extent that this underlying story of politics in Africa has been left unquestioned, it has continued to haunt us, producing the distinctive expectations and character of African politics, thus ensuring a social history that in the end makes greed, plunder, and violence appear all too natural. Like a ghost, the story continues to hold Africa in its enchanted grip — a grip made more horrific and inescapable by its invisibility.

4. The Wanton Sacrificing of Africa

What also became clear to me in reading *King Leopold's Ghost* was the intimate connection between the story of greed and plunder on the one hand and the sacrifice of African lives on the other. It was not only the fact that Africans soon found themselves drafted into King Leopold's civilizing mission and its rubber economy; it was that African lives came to have meaning and value only in relation to this project. Accordingly, they were violently conscripted into Leopold's rubber regime, which made them disposable. Particularly chilling are the efficiency and casualness of the

---

21. Wrong, *In the Footsteps*, 10. Wrong herself notes that her "attempt to understand the puzzle" (that kept Mobutu in power for thirty-two years, endearing himself to both his Congolese citizens and Western props alike, while at the same time succeeding to reduce Congo to a state of near collapse) "kept returning me to [*Heart of Darkness*]. . . . No man is a caricature, no individual can alone bear responsibility for a nation's collapse. The disaster Zaire became, the dull political acquiescence of its people, had its roots in a history of extraordinary outside interference, as basic in its motivation as it was elevated in rhetoric." Wrong, *In the Footsteps*, 11-12.

ways African lives were wasted in *King Leopold's Ghost*. One already encounters this easy disposability of African lives in Conrad's *Heart of Darkness*, even though Kurtz was at least able to name it for the "horror" it was. For many others in King Leopold's Congo, however, the waste of African lives seemed to have reached a certain degree of acceptability as part of the official policy of Leopold's civilization.

But once this dispensability of African lives had been accepted and came to be expected as part of the official, normal way of nation-state politics, postcolonial successors to the colonial project have had no qualms perpetuating the same wanton sacrificing of lives in pursuit of their political ambitions and greed. Thus, we see the same wasting of lives in the fighting in eastern Congo as with the LRA in northern Uganda. Similarly, a Mobutu or a Mugabe will never voluntarily step down from office in the national interest. Instead, he will readily sacrifice, waste, starve, and kill "his people" for his own political ambition.

Moreover, reading *King Leopold's Ghost* allowed me to see the Rwandan genocide as a metaphor of African politics — an extreme example of the politics built on the assumed disposability of African lives as part of official state policy. While previously the state depended on a few of its functionaries (Fiévez, for instance), Rwanda reveals a radical democratization of this expectation, with the state attempting to recruit everyone (the Hutu masses) into the service of its violence. Moreover, if Rwanda revealed the readiness with which the Hutu masses had come to expect, anticipate, and participate in the wastage of Tutsi lives, it also reveals the readiness with which the West has come to expect and allow the wastage of African lives to go on. The portrayal of the wastage of lives in Africa as "tribal" violence seems to carry with it a certain degree of acceptability — and indeed expectation — in the West.

Even as I began to see these connections between African politics and the sacrificing of African lives, as well as the expectation and even anticipation of Africans' disposability, I was also beginning to see theologically that a new claim regarding African lives is being announced and enacted: namely, that these are not unique, precious, sacred lives; these are Africans, mere bodies to be used, mere masses to be exploited. That this *theological* claim has come to be widely assumed is obvious from the casualness with which the wastage of African lives is accepted.

For a new future to take shape in Africa, the wanton sacrificing of African lives would have to be confronted — no, interrupted — by a different

story and its accompanying practices in which the sacredness, the precious-
ness, the inviolability, and the dignity of African lives are foregrounded.

5. The Visible Invisibility of Christianity

Another striking observation from *King Leopold's Ghost* was the near invisibility of Christianity. I knew as a matter of historical fact that the time of
King Leopold's adventures in the Congo was also the time of great missionary work. Many missionaries came to the Congo during this time and
built churches, schools, and dispensaries. Yet, at least in Hochschild's account, the role of Christianity remained largely invisible. At first I was not
sure how to account for this silence or whether to read it as a shortcoming
in Hochschild's account. But the more I thought about it and discovered
clues in Hochschild's account, the more I realized that the reason for this
silence might have to do with the fact that even though extensive evangelization and conversion to Christianity happened around the same time
in the Congo, Christianity by and large remained in the background of
King Leopold's civilizing mission. In one telling observation, Hochschild
notes that missionaries often found themselves acting as mere observers
on the battlefield.[22]

Yet elsewhere Hochschild notes how, in the course of their brutal
raids throughout the territory, soldiers often collected orphaned children
and brought them to the Catholic missionaries, as the report below from
the mother superior in charge of a mission orphanage testifies:

> Thousands more children perished during the long journeys to get
> there. Of one column of 108 boys on a forced march to the state colony
> at Boma in 1892-1893, only sixty-two made it to their destination; eight
> of them died within the following few weeks. The mother superior of
> one Catholic colony for girls wrote to a high Congo state official in
> 1895, "Several of the little girls were so sickly on their arrival that . . .
> our good sisters couldn't save them, but all had the happiness of re-
> ceiving Holy Baptism; they are now little angels in Heaven who are
> praying for our great king."[23]

22. Hochschild, *King Leopold's Ghost*, 172.
23. Hochschild, *King Leopold's Ghost*, 135.

This report is at once telling and extremely disturbing, and confirms the extent to which the missionary sisters' efforts to care for orphaned children is located within the story of King Leopold's rubber terror. The mother superior does not question why "several of the little girls were sickly" or why they were orphaned in the first place. That just seems to be the way things are. And within that reality, there was just very little the sisters could do. "Our good sisters couldn't save them, but . . . they are now little angels in Heaven who are praying for our great king."

What the mother superior's words suggest is that, given the context, all Christianity could offer us was a limited form of salvation — prayer for the king and a heavenly reward for the little angels. No doubt this assumption itself was part of a typically Western view of Christianity as a religion whose proper area of competency was "pastoral" and "spiritual," that is, clearly distinct from the determination of material and bodily practices that properly belong to the field of politics. It was this version of Christianity that the missionaries accepted and worked out of, and into which they evangelized their African converts.

Clearly, this version of Christianity could only serve as a backdrop to the story of politics in Africa. It had very few resources to offer regarding the political, material, and social disruption of Leopold's rubber terror. If Christianity is to be about the business of shaping a new future in Africa, it was becoming clear to me, Christianity itself would have to find a way of overcoming this Western heritage, to move beyond the narrow spiritual and pastoral areas to which it is consigned and claim full competence in the social, material, and political realities of life in Africa.

"Can Christianity Save Us?"

To be sure, this latter version of Christianity was what the African converts were looking for in the Congo — one that offered a way out of — or at least a way to confront — the disruption and violence of Leopold's rubber economy. Thus, in one of the most revealing paragraphs of *King Leopold's Ghost*, Hochschild narrates how King Leopold's policies of plunder, torture, and violence raised all sorts of challenges for missionary work — none, however, as serious as the question raised by the Africans to a British missionary as to whether Christianity had any power to save them from the rubber economy:

The missionaries had come to the Congo eager to evangelize, to fight polygamy, and to impart to Africans a Victorian sense of sin. Before long, however, the rubber terror meant that missionaries had trouble finding bodies to clothe or souls to save. Frightened villagers would disappear into the jungle for weeks when they saw the smoke of an approaching steamboat on the horizon. One British missionary was asked repeatedly by Africans, "Has the Savior you tell us of any power to save us from rubber trouble?"[24]

It is this question, "Has the Savior you tell us of any power to save us from rubber trouble?" that finally laid out for me the task and challenge of Christian social ethics in Africa and the outline of this book. For it is exactly the same question that is at the heart of Christian social ethics in Africa today — the question that African Christians are putting before Christianity. As I have noted, even though a lot has changed in Africa, it is still trapped in the same triangle of modernity, violence, and plunder as the Congo was under King Leopold's civilizing mission. And, even though there has been much allusion to the growth of Christianity in Africa in the twenty-first century, both the validity and the future prospects of African Christianity will depend greatly on its ability to provide Christians with concrete resources with which to face Africa's social history.

Does Christianity have the power to save Africa? How? And what would that salvation look like? If *King Leopold's Ghost* is a story of ambition and greed, which mobilizes power as terror and leads to the sacrifice of lives, can there be another story — a story of self-sacrificing love that involves a different notion of power and thus gives rise to new patterns of life, engendering new forms of community, economics, and politics? What kind of stories would sustain such practices, and with what end in view? Where might one go or look to discover these forms of politics? These are the questions at the heart of this study.

The Central Argument of the Book

The central argument in this book is that at the heart of Africa's inception into modernity is a lie. Modernity claims to bring salvation to Africa, yet

---

24. Hochschild, *King Leopold's Ghost*, 172.

the founding story of the institutions of modern Africa rejects Africa itself. This story has shaped colonial Africa and continues to drive the successor institution, the nation-state. Historically, the story translated into myriad forms of use and abuse, sacrificing African lives and ultimately Africa itself. This is why a new future in Africa requires much more than strategies and skills to solve the problems of nation-state politics. It requires a different story that assumes the sacred value and dignity of Africa and Africans, and is thus able to shape practices and policies, or new forms of politics, that reflect this sacredness and dignity.

The argument is developed in three parts. Part I, "Sacrificing Africa," moves from a critical exploration of the current paradigms of Christian social ethics (which I refer to as "old formulas") to reveal the founding narrative of politics in Africa. In the first chapter, I examine the current paradigms of Christian social ethics in Africa in order to show the limitations of their shared assumptions. These approaches all take the institutions of church and state in their current formulations for granted and therefore neither fully engage the founding story of nation-state politics nor fully explore the range of imaginative possibilities of Christian social existence in Africa. This is what I call the "reticence of Christianity," which is based on envisioning Christianity as a "religion" whose competency lies in the spiritual and pastoral fields of life, and surrenders the determination of social-material processes to the realm of politics. The critical point I make in this chapter is that by operating out of this reticence, Christianity uncritically assumes the same foundational narrative that denies and sacrifices Africa, and in the end becomes indistinguishable from the social sphere characterized by desperation, violence, and corruption. In this way, Christianity not only lets down Africa; it also surrenders a key soteriological claim about Christ's power to save. That is why I argue in chapter two that social ethics in Africa need to focus more on stories than on skills. Such a focus not only offers tremendous opportunities for Christianity, but also provides a fresh appreciation of how all politics is grounded in stories, and it is on the level of stories that the most decisive work of political imagination needs to take place.

In fact, once the intricate relationship between politics and stories is established, one begins to question the assumption that sustains much of social ethics in Africa, namely, that nation-state politics are dysfunctional. This assumption is false. In chapter three, I show that chaos, corruption, violence, and poverty are not the outcome of a dysfunctional institution, but part of how modern Africa works *given* the imagination-set of its founding narratives. Using the work of Basil Davidson, I trace this performance back to the founding stories of Africa's emergence into modernity, more specifically to the story of "Africa without History." The effect of this chapter is not only to confirm a link between politics and stories, it is to show that all politics is theological, in that it involves claims about life, reality, and the ultimate meaning of life. The more specific effect of this central chapter of the book is to show that the denial and exploitation of Africa — in a word, the sacrificing of Africa — is hard-wired into the imaginative landscape of modern Africa.

Part II, "Daring to Invent the Future," explores attempts to move beyond this deeply entrenched imagination. My overall goal in this section is to develop a theoretical framework to confirm that the search for a new future in Africa is essentially an ecclesiological task by highlighting the essential theological elements integral to that task. The section begins with a discussion in chapter four about the life and revolutionary leadership of Thomas Sankara in Burkina Faso. What makes Sankara's story significant for our discussion is his clarity about the need for a new basis for politics in Africa, as well as his extraordinary accomplishment, within his short reign, in transforming Upper Volta from one of the poorest countries in Africa to one characterized by food security, a steady improvement in living conditions, and a newly discovered sense of pride and confidence by the Burkinabe people. Thus Sankara's life and leadership provides a map of the type of revolutionary thinking and praxis required to "invent" a new future in Africa. The fact, however, that Sankara's revolution could not be sustained beyond his untimely assassination points to a number of critical elements that are *essential* to the task of inventing the future in Africa yet missing in Sankara's revolution. In a critical assessment of Sankara's project, I show that his revolution lacked the elements of memory, community, and lament, practices that require a definite *telos* and narrative. The effect of this discussion is to confirm that Christianity is very well suited to engage the task of social imagination in Africa, given its founding narrative that is reenacted and remembered through the disciplines of community, memory, and lament.

I take up this conclusion in chapter five through a discussion of the life and work of the late Cameroonian theologian Jean-Marc Éla. In his critical and constructive essays, occasioned by and written during the years of his pastoral ministry in rural Cameroon, Jean-Marc Éla decries "the Babylonian captivity" in which Christianity in Africa shies away from the task of social imagination. He calls on the churches to be what they are called to be — the critical link between revelation and history, thus shaping a "different world right here." Éla's work confirms that the church is not only needed, it is essential to the task of shaping a new future in Africa. But Éla's work also shows that for the church in Africa to be up to the task, the African church itself must be "reinvented" in a manner that frees it from its shyness, or what Éla calls "the sociological burden of religion." Another highly significant conclusion that emerges out of a consideration of Éla's own life — from his pastoral life among the rural populations of northeastern Cameroon, to his exile in Canada, to his recent burial in his home village — is that for the church to be capable of inventing a new future in Africa, it has to be characterized by a practical theology of relocation and marginality.

Chapter six follows up this observation with a short exploration of the relationship between power, violence, and Christianity, using Chinua Achebe's *Things Fall Apart*. Both Okonkwo's Umuofia and the colonial regime that sought to "civilize" Umuofia were grounded in a particular story that involved a vision of power as invincibility. The effect of this vision of power, as is evident in *Things Fall Apart*, was to shape lives and practices characterized by fear and violence. The conclusion that emerges from this exploration is that when Christianity is firmly grounded in this vision of power, like the church at the center of the village square in Umuofia, it cannot but radiate and perpetuate the same formations of fear and violence. On the other hand, the church located on the outskirts of the village near the "evil" forest not only welcomed twins, slaves, and other outcasts; it encouraged gentleness, mercy, and care. The result of this particular reading of *Things Fall Apart* is to confirm "relocation" as an essential theological and ecclesiological requirement in the task of inventing the future in Africa.

The full effect of the discussion in this second section is to offer a theoretical framework for a new conversation of social ethics for a new future in Africa and to confirm that a life of revolutionary madness (à la Sankara), the church as a community that lives by a distinctive *telos* and narrative praxis (à la Jean-Marc Éla), and a practical theology of relocation (à la *Things Fall Apart*) are essential to this task. This is what makes the search for a new future in Africa essentially (although not exclusively) an ecclesiological task. Once this theoretical framework has been established, what remains is to show that this task is not merely theoretical by displaying concrete examples of how, what, who, and where this task is engaged.

This is what I do in Part III, entitled "The Sacrifice of Africa," through three representative stories. In chapter seven, I use the story of Bishop Paride Taban of the Sudan to highlight what a practical theology looks like. For over twenty years, as the bishop of Torit, he worked tirelessly in the context of war. Yet when the war was over, at the critical time of nation building when Taban could have become a key figure, he resigned his position as bishop and withdrew into the remote Eastern Equatorial region, where he set up a peace village in Kuron as an experiment to "fight tribalism in a small way." This chapter confirms that behind Taban's experiment is an ecclesiological vision, a model of the church that is essential to the theological reimagination of, and the search for, a new future in Africa.

The story of Angelina Atyam and the Concerned Parents Association in chapter eight illuminates a similar practical ecclesiology. After Angelina's daughter Charlotte was kidnapped by the Lord's Resistance Army from a girls' secondary school, Angelina's experience of pain, loss, and anger led her to discover the gift of forgiveness, and out of that journey she began a ministry of advocacy on behalf of all suffering children. Angelina's story, particularly her fierce advocacy of forgiveness, both resists and interrupts the madness of the Kony sovereignty of terror and its wanton sacrificing of the children of northern Uganda. Her life and work reveal not only the possibility and shape of a new future, but the radically different type of sacrifice that makes this new future possible.

Moreover, this new future is not simply a fantastic ideal. It is real. If both Taban's and Angelina's work have already confirmed that, I use the story of Maggy Barankitse in chapter nine to display its ambitious extravagance and concrete everydayness. In many ways, Maggy's Burundi and its violent history of ethnic hatred highlight various aspects of the performance of the founding story of Africa's modernity (narrated in chapter three): tribalism, violence, poverty, desperation, the lies of identity, and the wastage and sacrificing of Africa. In Burundi, Maggy's life is caught within this drama, but even within it, she is able to discover a different story of love, in which she discovers her identity as God's beloved. This story not only fills Maggy with the strength to resist hatred (and other lies), it shapes her call of "Yes" to love. Her ministry of Maison Shalom in Burundi, where Maggy brings together orphaned and abused children of all ethnicities (Hutu, Tusti, Twa, and Congolese) and raises them as one family demonstrates the new future made possible by the story of love.

Taken together, these last three chapters provide a compelling argument for, and display of, the type of future Christianity makes possible in Africa. That is why in narrating each person's story I locate it within a particular biblical narrative: Taban's story within the story of Zacchaeus, Angelina's story within the anointing at Bethany, and Maggy's story within the story of the five loaves and two fish. Through this kind of analysis, which could be referred to as Christian social hermeneutics, the biblical stories and the contemporary stories illuminate each other in a way that both reveals the limits of nation-state politics in Africa and provides an interruption and alternative to it.

This kind of analysis also confirms the assumption that sustains the argument of the book: that politics has to do, in great part, with stories, particularly with the founding narratives or stories of "in the beginning." Thus the stories of Taban, Angelina, and Maggy illumine different aspects of the Christian story of creation and the type of practices and communities this story makes possible. In the end, this story makes possible the practices and communities that in turn make possible a new sacrifice of Africa (in the sense of the Latin root of sacrifice, which is to "make sacred": *sacra* + *facere*), and is thus able to interrupt the wastage (sacrificing) of Africa assumed within the founding narratives and institutions of modern Africa. A fresh conversation of Christian social ethics in Africa is about the possibilities and reality of this new and redemptive sacrifice of Africa, or — which is the same thing — a new and redemptive politics within Africa.

PART I

Sacrificing Africa

CHAPTER 1

Saving Africa: The Reticence of Christianity

Indeed our ways of dying are our ways of living. Or should I say our ways of living are our ways of dying?

Zakes Mda, *Ways of Dying*

Of Churches and Coffins in Africa: A Christian Continent in Distress

Christian social reflection in Africa must begin with a rather disturbing observation: churches and coffins are perhaps the two most prevalent images associated with Africa today. That Africa is an overwhelmingly Christian continent requires no elaborate argument. If in 1900 just 25 percent of the Catholic population lived in the southern hemisphere, today that figure stands at 66 percent, or two-thirds of the world's 1.1 billion Catholics, and by mid-century that figure is projected to be 74 percent, with Africa — sub-Saharan Africa in particular — contributing the lion's share of that percentage. During the twentieth century, the Catholic population in sub-Saharan Africa exploded from 1.9 million to 130 million, an astonishing growth rate of 6708 percent. A similar shift is underway in other Christian affiliations. Moreover, the youthful energy and dynamism with which African Christians embrace and practice the faith has also increased, which is apparent not only in the lively prayer and worship services, but in the public display of Christian symbols, names, and images in marketplaces, banks, and hair salons. So, as the Christian center of gravity shifts to Africa, the lively expression of the faith here is giving rise to a growing confidence that Africa is a Christian continent.

But if Christianity is on the rise in Africa, so too are the realities of civil wars and social unrest. A new outbreak of fighting in eastern Congo, in a civil war that has lasted over ten years, has left more than 3.8 million people dead and many more homeless. This year marks the sixteenth anniversary of the genocide in Rwanda, which left close to a million people dead; the insurgency of Kony's Lord's Resistance Army (LRA), which has killed over 200,000 people in northern Uganda and abducted over 26,000 children, has now spread into the Sudan and northeastern Congo; the 2007 elections in Kenya erupted in violence; the collapse of Zimbabwe; the implosion of Liberia in the 1980s; the civil war in Sierra Leone; and many other examples confirm the same patterns of violence and economic failure in Africa. Out of 13 million deaths around the world between 1994 and 2003 attributed to armed conflicts, the United Nations estimates that more than 9 million occurred in sub-Saharan Africa.[1] On the United Nations' list of the world's fifteen most impoverished nations, nine are in Africa. In 2008, over 1.5 million Africans died of HIV/AIDS, and 22 million are infected. The poverty and poor health conditions in which the majority of Africans live make the situation worse.

No one has captured the ubiquitous reality of death in Africa better than the South African novelist Zakes Mda in his 1995 novel, *Ways of Dying*. As the title suggests, the novel is about death as embodied in the lives of a professional mourner (Toloki), a nurse whose duty is to narrate the last moments of a person's life and way of dying, and the coffin maker, Nefolovhodwe, who has recently become rich thanks to his new popular product, the collapsible coffin. The novel opens on Christmas with the funeral of Noria's son, a young boy killed by a rebel gang purportedly fighting for the liberation of the community. "There are many ways of dying," the nurse shouts. "This little brother was our own child, and his death is more painful because it is of our own creation. It is not the first time that we bury little children. We bury them every day. But they are killed by the enemy . . . those we are fighting against. This little brother was killed by those who are fighting to free us."[2]

1. John Allen, "Five Reasons the Papal Trip to Africa Is Important," *National Catholic Reporter*, http://www.ncronline.org/printpdf/12592 (accessed March 13, 2009).

2. Zakes Mda, *Ways of Dying* (Oxford: Oxford University Press, 1995), 7.

The way Mda tells the story, the people who reside in this squatter camp are so used to the reality of violence and death that the only thing surprising about the death of this young boy was the manner of his death. For the residents in this squatter camp, the issue is no longer whether to live or die, but how to die. As Toloki tells Noria, "Death lives with us every day. Indeed our ways of dying are our ways of living. Or should I say our ways of living are our ways of dying?"[3]

Toloki's observation, "Our ways of dying are our ways of living," is more than a figure of speech for many in Africa. If churches and coffins represent two dominant cultural realities in Africa, they also represent the predicament of a continent suspended between hope and despair. They capture the hope and pain, the beauty and tragedy, the dreams and frustrations of a continent that is at once overwhelmingly Christian and at the same time politically, economically, and socially distressed. It is misleading to suggest that Christianity (the churches) represents all that is hopeful about Africa, and the social, political, and economic systems represent all that is tragic (coffins) about the continent. The picture is far more complex. The fact that Mda's novel opens with a funeral *on* Christmas Day points to a far deeper complexity between Christianity and the social systems in Africa. At the same time, however, putting the matter this way points to the complex relationship between the world of churches and the world of coffins. Probing this relationship constitutes the first order of business for Christian social ethics in Africa.

During the late 1990s some African theologians moved in this direction, among them, the Kenyan Jesse Mugambi. In *From Liberation to Reconstruction*, his description of the plight of the African could just as well have been written today.[4] Africa, Mugambi noted, "is faced with a food deficit; it is the most hungry continent in the world. It is faced with debt crises . . . it is the most indebted continent; it has the highest level of illiteracy in the world, and half of the world's refugees are Africans."[5] Mugambi then raised questions about the fact that Africa is an overwhelmingly Christian continent. How can such a contradiction be explained, Mugambi wondered. Is this religiosity authentic and genuine, or is it superstition arising from de-

3. Mda, *Ways of Dying*, 89.

4. Jesse Mugambi, *From Liberation to Reconstruction: African Christian Theology after the Cold War* (Nairobi: East African Education Publishers, 1995).

5. Mugambi, *From Liberation to Reconstruction*, 160.

spair? How could it be that people who continue to call upon God most reverently are the ones God seems to neglect most vehemently? Could it be that "the Gospel has reached many people in Africa as very bad news"?[6]

Mugambi's probing questions promised a fresh start for Christian theological and social reflection in Africa. Unfortunately, this line of questioning was neither sustained nor pursued, even by Mugambi himself. Instead, after raising these questions, Mugambi himself moved too quickly into the default mode of offering suggestions of what the church should do to assist in reconstruction. The church, Mugambi suggested, should be the *catalyst* of the process of reconstruction and play a key role in preparing the people for this immense task and in rehabilitating those marginalized in the process.[7] In moving too quickly to the solutions of what the church's role should be, Mugambi capitulated to the temptation of "prescriptive haste" into which many others have fallen. Although there seems to be no more urgent task than offering ways in which Christianity can contribute to a new future in Africa, this approach becomes a temptation when, in the rush to come up with relevant recommendations, insufficient attention is paid to what is actually going on, particularly regarding the underlying stories that reproduce the realities of corruption, civil war, violence, and poverty throughout Africa's social history.

Moreover, this approach assumes that Christianity possesses a sort of ahistorical innocence in the social history of Africa; it assumes that Christianity stands outside the fray of social-political processes and is able to provide recommendations to a field outside herself. In this way, the recommendations do not engage the politics in Africa, which inform not only social patterns and individual lives but Christianity itself. For given Toloki's observation, even the most cherished beliefs and observances like Christmas and Easter have become "ways of dying." In fact, once this observation is acknowledged, then it becomes clear that Christianity's challenge is not simply to offer good recommendations, but to rethink its own role in a social history where churches and coffins are not mutually exclusive, but form each other's reality. This is the reality that Christian social ethics so often overlooks in its haste to prescribe solutions.

6. Mugambi, *From Liberation to Reconstruction*, 40, 140.

7. Mugambi, *From Liberation to Reconstruction*, xiv, 51, 176. For a full discussion of Mugambi's work see "A Different World Right Here: The Church within African Theological Imagination," in Katongole, *A Future for Africa: Critical Essays in Christian Social Imagination* (Scranton: University of Scranton Press, 2005), 153-84.

What Can the Church Do? The Social Relevance of Christianity

As the conversation about Christian social ethics in Africa has predictably followed the pattern of prescriptive haste, its recommendations tend to fall within three broad, although not mutually exclusive, paradigms: (1) spiritual formation (the spiritual), (2) social-material intervention (the pastoral), and (3) advocacy and mediation (the political).

(1) Deeper Evangelization: The Spiritual Paradigm

This approach, most often associated with evangelical Christians, tends to view Christianity's social impact in terms of spiritual influence and motivation. Christians who belong to this paradigm see a spiritual crisis at the heart of Africa's woes, and they view the primary goal of Christian mission to be the formation of a *spiritual* identity. When one accepts Christ, one becomes a new person and is "born again"; the rebirth is first and foremost a *spiritual* rebirth, which happens in the inner world of one's *religious* consciousness.

What this widespread view means is that the good news Christianity proclaims is not primarily about social, political, and material life, but rather the inner spiritual life of the individual. Nevertheless, the inner spiritual transformation of the individual does have far-reaching social consequences, as one's new spiritual identity as a Christian must bear fruit through the way one concretely lives in the world, relates to others, and interacts within the social sphere.

The late Ghanaian theologian Kwame Bediako, for example, suggested that the reception of the gospel in Africa has "imbued local cultures with eternal significance and endowed African languages with a transcendent range."[8] This effect can have significant consequences for politics in Africa where, according to Bediako, a key problem is the tendency to sacralize power and authority. The tendency, which so often translates into the dictatorial tendency of African leaders, Bediako argues, has its roots in African traditional politics, or more specifically in the religious world of ancestors that underpins political life. When one becomes a Christian,

---

8. Kwame Bediako, *Christianity in Africa: The Renewal of a Non-Christian Religion* (Maryknoll, N.Y.: Orbis, 1995), 120.

however, one accepts Jesus as the supreme ancestor and the Savior who desacralizes all earthly powers and politics, thereby checking their inherent tendency to absolutize themselves. Accordingly, "the recognition that power truly belongs to God, which is rooted in the Christian theology of power as non-dominating, liberates politicians and rulers to be humans among fellow-humans, and ennobles politics."[9] Thus the realization that all power belongs to God curbs the tendency towards dictatorship and abuse of power so prevalent in African politics. What is significant to note is that such a benefit is not an isolated skill that the Christian can pursue as part of "good governance"; it is a benefit that "flows over" from a new relationship with God, the result of having accepted Christ as "our supreme ancestor."[10] This is the fruit of one's having come to a new spiritual identity in Christ.

For Bediako then, and others who stand within this spiritual paradigm, the response to Africa's woes lies in a call for deeper evangelization and discipleship — in drawing people to Christ and grounding them more deeply in a new spiritual identity. The new spiritual identity not only affects the way the new Christian understands issues like power, leadership, and service; it also provides inspiration and the motivation to work toward a more peaceful social order — an order that more closely reflects God's Kingdom here on earth.[11] That is why, within this paradigm, an immediate way to influence politics and effect positive change in society is to ensure that Christians are elected into public office, and that once elected, it is hoped, they will use their influence to enact positive social policies and programs to create an equitable, just, and democratic country. According to this paradigm, this is how Christianity, which is at its heart a spiritual message, is able to impact material, social, and political processes.

A similar assumption operates in the dominant theological trend of *enculturation.* The main preoccupation of this trend has been to seek ways for the Christian message to find deep roots and genuine expression in African culture, with the hope that the fruits of a truly enculturated Christianity will impact the African Christian who has been, and still is, prey to

9. Bediako, *Christianity in Africa,* 247.

10. This may be something like a Weberian scenario, where ironically the less explicitly socially active forms of Christianity provide enduring social benefits (Max Weber, *The Protestant Ethic and the Spirit of Capitalism* [Los Angeles: Roxbury Publications, 1998]).

11. Bénézet Bujo, *African Theology in its Social Context* (Nairobi: Pauline Publications Africa, 1999), 9, 83, 89, 90.

injustice, disease, and other social ills. More specifically, the hope is that a genuine African Christianity should inspire the commitment of African Christians to work for a peaceful social order.[12] Here too the assumption is that the *spiritual* qualities and habits have far-reaching social implications. In this way, Christianity works more or less like a time capsule with "the latent capacity of cultural changes held in religious storage to emerge over time when circumstances are propitious."[13]

(2) Development and Relief: A Pastoral Paradigm

If words like "Christian identity," "influence," "motivation," and "implications" are at the heart of the spiritual paradigm, concepts like "intervention," "relief," and "development" characterize the responses of the pastoral paradigm. This approach is quite consistent with, although not limited to, the longstanding social involvement of the Catholic church and mainline Protestant churches. Within this paradigm, the church's social involvement is often portrayed as a kind of intervention — a response to the worsening social situations of suffering and instability in Africa that either directly result from government policies or are the cumulative effect of government neglect. A deep and practical humanitarian concern underpins this paradigm. Faced with a perceived social crisis in Africa, the church responds by providing relief and assistance, a response that is illustrated by the post-synodal exhortation *Ecclesia in Africa*.[14]

Coinciding with the 1994 genocide in Rwanda, the synodal meeting in Rome expressed great concern about this tragic event and about worsening conditions in Africa. The synodal bishops were convinced that the church could make a difference through pastoral and social agencies: "For many Synod Fathers contemporary Africa can be compared to the man who went down from Jerusalem to Jericho . . . Africa is a Continent where countless human beings . . . are lying, as it were, on the edge of the road,

12. Bujo, *African Theology in its Social Context*, 9, 83, 89, 90.

13. David Martin quoted in Paul Gifford, *African Christianity: Its Public Role* (Bloomington: Indiana University Press, 1998), 36.

14. John Paul II, *Post-Synodal Apostolic Exhortation* Ecclesia in Africa *of the Holy Father John Paul II to the Bishops, Priests and Deacons, Men and Women Religious and All the Lay Faithful on the Church in Africa and its Evangelizing Mission Towards the Year 2000* (Nairobi: Pauline Publications Africa, 1995).

sick, injured, disabled, marginalized and abandoned. They are in dire need of Good Samaritans who will come to their aid. For my part, I express the hope that the Church will continue patiently and tirelessly its work as a Good Samaritan."[15]

Even though *Ecclesia in Africa* does not spell out exactly what being a Good Samaritan entails, such a self-understanding is consistent with the church's historical role in the provision of education, healthcare, and social services. If a humanitarian concern inspires the church's work in these social services, it is sustained, as the story of the Good Samaritan shows, by a theological conviction that the gospel is and must be a liberating social force that can help Africans "rediscover their humanity" and "regain a sense of dignity."[16] "Integral human development," the pope notes, "is at the very heart of evangelization. Between evangelization and human advancement — development and liberation — there are in fact profound links. These include links of an anthropological order, because the man who is to be evangelized is not an abstract being but is subject to social and economic questions."[17]

Reflecting on Luke 4:18-19, the pope notes how the essential link between salvation and liberation is obvious in the life and ministry of Jesus, who came to relieve human misery and combat every kind of neglect. He came to *liberate* humanity; he came to take upon himself our infirmities and diseases. "The entire ministry of Jesus is marked by the concern he showed to all those around him who were affected by suffering: persons in mourning, paralytics, lepers, the blind, the deaf, the mute."[18]

In suggesting this link between the ministry of Jesus and service to the poor, the pope does not wish to suggest that the gospel is nothing more than a tool for human liberation. What makes Christ's mission unique is an essential religious dimension, which invites people to a new relationship with God. This relationship is not limited to the spiritual field but is inte-

15. John Paul II, *Ecclesia in Africa*, sec. 41.

16. Mugambi's suggestion for a theology of "reconstruction" also seems to boil down to this. The gospel, Mugambi notes, ought to be "Good News" that "rehabilitates individuals and groups that are marginalized by various natural and social circumstances. In contemporary Africa, the Good News understood in this way ought to rehabilitate the afflicted individuals in every region, country and locality. The Gospel ought to help Africans regain their confidence and hope." *From Liberation to Reconstruction*, 176.

17. John Paul II, *Ecclesia in Africa*, 68.

18. John Paul II, *Ecclesia in Africa*, 68.

gral to it, which is to say it encompasses all the dimensions of a person's life. "The liberation that evangelization proclaims cannot be contained in the simple and restricted dimension of economics, politics, social, or cultural life: it must envisage the whole man, in all his aspects, right up to and including his openness to the absolute, even the Divine Absolute."[19]

John Paul II's reflection in *Ecclesia in Africa* nicely illustrates the theological assumptions that underlie the church's social involvement in the pastoral paradigm. Yet even though I have used *Ecclesia in Africa* as a lens, this approach is not limited to the Catholic church. It is at home in many mainline denominations, a number of which have well-developed relief, development, social, or outreach ministries that are an integral part of their church's mission programs. Increasingly evangelical churches are awakening to this social dimension of Christian mission. As a result, a number of evangelical churches in the West, particularly in America, are responding to Africa's social crises with a slew of campaigns that address the end of poverty, the fight against AIDS, and provide basic necessities like food and water. Rick Warren's P.E.A.C.E. initiative in Rwanda is one of the better-known initiatives, representing a growing trend in the evangelical world.[20]

The result in Africa has been that almost every church, ministry, and Christian agency in Africa is involved in some kind of relief or development project, ranging from running an orphans' education fund to raising rabbits and pigs, to setting up bakeries, to establishing micro-credit institutions and services. The growing influence of this trend is evident in the case of the Soroti Catholic Diocese Integrated Development Organization (SOCADIDO), which is better known than the Diocese of Soroti itself. The case of SOCADIDO is not unique. In fact, the growth in Christian churches' social services ministries, combined with the failure of most governments in Africa, have made the sector of Christian social services the single biggest employer in many African countries, with organizations like World Vision International topping the list. Given the growing involvement of Christian agencies in this area, it is not surprising that many

19. John Paul II, *Ecclesia in Africa*, 68. See also Anastasia Lott, "The Relationship between Evangelization and Development," *AFER* 34, no. 2 (1992): 66-78.

20. For a full discussion of Rick Warren's P.E.A.C.E. initiative in Rwanda, see Katongole, "Violence and Christian Social Reconstruction in Africa: On the Resurrection of the Body (Politic)," *The Other Journal*, http://www.theotherjournal.com/article.php?id=115 (accessed January 2006).

churches in Africa now require a degree in development studies, project management, or some other such certification as a prerequisite for ordination or ministry.[21]

(3) Mediation, Advocacy, and Reconciliation: A Political Paradigm

Commitments to justice, democracy, and human rights characterize this paradigm. The increasing prominence of this paradigm in Africa can be gleaned from the statement by José Chipenda, general secretary of the All Africa Conferences of Churches (AACC) at the time of the 1994 genocide in Rwanda: "The concern for justice must permeate every action by churches; and justice involves looking at the murky political issues which cause massacres and refugee exoduses and denouncing injustice without taking partisan positions. It seems in the case of Rwanda that de-politicized emergency aid is easier than long-range initiatives for justice, peace and reconciliation."[22]

Historically, "long-range initiatives for justice, peace, and reconciliation" (as Chipenda calls them) have taken many forms. On numerous occasions, church leaders have spoken out courageously against government corruption, human rights violations, injustices, and other political abuses. Even though the response of the politicians has often been to accuse those who do so of "meddling in politics," this has not stopped church leaders from speaking out against injustice. In fact, some church leaders have paid with their lives for taking a stand. Church leaders have also issued pastoral letters on matters of national significance as a way of encouraging democratic participation and helping Christians form their consciences in the face of political decisions. The Catholic church in particular has taken this approach, which is an integral element within the Catholic social teaching tradition.

It must be noted though that in this paradigm the notions of justice, democracy, and human rights are invoked, since it is assumed that Chris-

21. See, e.g., Joseph Therese Agabasiere and Boniface Zabajungu, eds., *Church Contribution to Integral Development*, Spearhead Series 108-9 (Eldoret: AMECEA Gaba Publications, 1989). See also Isabel Apawo Phiri, Kenneth R. Ross, and James L. Fox, eds., *The Role of Christianity in Development, Peace and Reconstruction: Southern Perspectives* (Nairobi: All Africa Conference of Churches, 1996).

22. Hugh McCullum, *The Angels Have Left Us: The Rwanda Tragedy and the Churches*, Rise Book Series, vol. 66 (Geneva: WCC Publications, 1995), 44.

tian churches have a unique responsibility to ensure democracy, to become "midwives of a democratic transition and reconstruction," and to "provide education for human rights and democracy."[23] The more avid proponents of this paradigm even go so far as to identify the search for democracy as the essence of Christian mission. For example, in his *A Theology of Reconstruction,* Charles Villa-Vicencio has argued that the tasks of nation building, democracy, constitutionalism, and the defense of human rights converge with the task of Christian theology: all concern the "realization that all people are created in the image of God, enjoying equal human worth."[24] Coming from a slightly different angle but showing an even closer identification of democracy with Kingdom values, the Uganda Joint Christian Council (UJCC), an ecumenical association of the Catholic, Anglican, and Orthodox Churches, issued a statement in 1995 encouraging Christians to participate in the democratic process through the election of members to the Constitutive Assembly. By advancing the values of democracy, the statement argued, Christians advance the values of God's Kingdom:

> We appeal to you to show a similar commitment and participation in all the remaining stages of the democratization process. We urge Christians to fully recognize that many of the values of God's Kingdom which Jesus Christ preached and supported by his actions are at the same time the pillars on which genuine democracy must be founded. We have a duty to support these values and to see them serve as the basis of our new constitution and the new democratic governance. These values are justice, peace, equality, freedom, nation-building and leadership as service.[25]

---

23. Clement Majawa, "The Church's Role in Defining Genuine Democracy in Africa," in *African Theology Today,* ed. Emmanuel Katongole (Scranton: University of Scranton Press, 2002); and John W. De Gruchy, *Christianity and Democracy: A Theology for a Just World Order* (Cambridge: Cambridge University Press, 1995). The 1994 joint conference of AACC and the World Council of Churches (WCC) in Nairobi came to similar conclusions, as the various position papers and general discussions underscored the role and responsibility of the church to provide education for human rights and democracy and to become an agent of social integration and reconciliation. See J. N. K. Mugambi, ed., *Democracy and Development in Africa: The Role of Churches* (Nairobi: All Africa Conference of Churches, 1997).

24. Charles Villa-Vicencio, *A Theology of Reconstruction: Nation-building and Human Rights* (Cambridge: Cambridge University Press, 1992), 126.

25. Uganda Joint Christian Council, "Participation is the Sure Road to Democracy in Uganda," 16 March 1994.

In the face of ongoing conflicts and civil wars in Africa mediation and reconciliation are increasingly key notions in mobilizing the church's social and political role within this paradigm. The role played by Archbishop Desmond Tutu during the transition from apartheid to New South Africa, as well as in the Truth and Reconciliation Commission, has inspired calls for Truth and Reconciliation Commission-like processes in other countries like Rwanda, Uganda, and Sierra Leone. Similarly, the key role of Archbishop Odama and the ARLPI (Acholi Religious Leaders Peace Initiative) in advocating for an end to armed conflict in northern Uganda and in eventually bringing Joseph Kony, the leader of the LRA, and the Museveni government to the talks has been hailed as another example of how religious leaders can play a role in shaping political processes of their countries. Similarly, "conflict resolution," "conflict management," "mediation," "advocacy," and "peacebuilding" are becoming buzzwords within church circles, with institutions like the Hekima Jesuit Peace Institute in Nairobi, the Mindolo African Peacebuilding Institute in Zambia, and the West Africa Peacebuilding Institute — these latter two inspired by the Eastern Mennonite University program in peacebuilding — being examples of the multiplicity of peace studies programs in Africa. Operating from an ecumenical perspective, these institutes train students in strategies of conflict management, conflict resolution, and peacebuilding. Furthermore, the number of reconciliation ministries in Africa has risen; they include the Nairobi-based African Leadership and Reconciliation Ministries (ALARM); the Ministry of Peace and Reconciliation Under the Cross (MiPaREC), based in Giteega, Burundi; and many others.

What the different initiatives and programs confirm is that if conditions in Africa have been stressful, it is not because African Christians and the Christian churches have been callous to the plight of the continent. Yet despite the growth of Christianity and the social activism of the churches, Africans in general are 40 percent worse off than they were in the 1980s.[26] One then wonders: What accounts for the dismal social impact of Christianity in Africa? Why has Christianity, despite its overwhelming presence, failed to make a significant dent in the social history of the continent?

26. Gifford, *African Christianity*, 15.

The Burden of a Western Legacy: The Reticence of Christianity

One major reason why such a socially active Christianity has yet to make a dent in the social history of Africa is that all three paradigms are based on the premise that Christianity is a religion — and therefore distinct from the realm of politics. In other words, Christianity in Africa, in spite of its outward appearance to the contrary, still operates under the burden of a Western legacy, both in its social outlook and self-understanding. The broad outline of this specifically Western conception can be neatly summed up thus: Politics is the sphere of *temporal* power, presided over by a presumably "neutral" state, which determines the social frames of reference and commands obedience in *temporal* affairs, or what William Cavanaugh calls the discipline of *bodily* performances.[27] Christianity's competency, and thus the church's own competency, it is assumed, does not lie in this sphere of politics, but in her own sphere of religious competency, where she exercises moral and spiritual authority. Of course this does not mean the church can remain indifferent to what is happening in the temporal order. The church can still be active in the social order (pastoral paradigm). In fact, the church can even affect the social order — if not directly through pressure and advocacy (political paradigm), then *indirectly* through moral and spiritual influence (spiritual paradigm).

Thus, the more one attends to this conclusion, the more it becomes obvious that the different paradigms all share the same prescriptive haste. And whereas this prescriptive approach does at least on the outside bolster the social significance of Christianity in Africa, the burden of its Western legacy and the neat religious field within which Christianity is supposed to operate ends up rendering the church's own social nature questionable, increasingly marginal, and eventually obscure. In other words, the self-understanding of "religion" not only places Christianity, at least imaginatively, outside the boundaries of the historical, material, and political processes that shape the social history of Africa; it obscures the full import of the gospel as a social vision, meant to inspire and shape new visions, processes, and disciplines of bodily performances. In the end, the self-understanding of Christianity in the religious domain contributes to the gradual disappearance of Christianity as a social and polit-

---

27. Cavanaugh, *Torture and Eucharist: Theology, Politics and the Body of Christ*, Challenges in Contemporary Theology Series (Oxford: Blackwell, 1998), 181 et passim.

ical body. The disappearance takes many forms, ranging from reticence to frantic activism.

Reticence: Waiting for Politics to Show Up

Even though Christianity statistically has a powerful social presence in Africa, when it comes to facing the critical challenge of social imagination, it tends to remain shy and self-effacing. This reticence can be traced to all the three paradigms above, but is particularly evident in the spiritual paradigm. For as noted, in this paradigm, even when it is acknowledged that the church forms patterns of behavior, the assumption is that such formation does not constitute social formation, but rather is a process that impacts inner motivation through inspiration and lessons that must then be applied in the social realm "out there." For example, in the article "Proclaiming Peace and Love: A New Role for Churches in African Politics," Isaac Phiri notes that the key "power of the religion" lies in "its ability to transform and propel human behavior through its idealistic invocations and convictions."[28] Accordingly, if the church can teach Christians Christ's law of love, that ideal will not only inspire individuals with "possibilities for self-transcendence," but also infuse an ethical commitment to the selfless love of others, including one's political opponents — qualities that have far-reaching implications for peacemaking in Africa's fragile transition to pluralistic democracies.[29] Thus, even though Phiri acknowledges that the church has to do with the formation and transformation of Christians, this formation of a new identity is not a social formation. Rather, Phiri describes the formation as both an *individual* and an *internal* process, whose social effect is felt only later, to the extent that the personal and inner transformation is "applied" in the social world of Africa's politics.

Exactly the same assumption lies behind this statement by the editors of *Politics and Liturgy* in the *Concilium* series: "Since politics is the control of power in society, the ways in which liturgy uses symbols of power has much to say in forming images and concepts of power which

28. Isaac Phiri, "Proclaiming Peace and Love: A New Role for Churches in African Politics," *Journal of Church and State* 42, no. 4 (2000): 793-94.
29. Phiri, "Proclaiming Peace and Love," 795.

Christian peoples bring to bear on political questions."[30] What is helpful about this statement is the acknowledgment that liturgy not only forms Christian habit but also gives Christians new ways to imagine power. What is unfortunate, however, is the assumption that such imagination is not primarily a social imagination. It *can* become socially significant to the extent that it can be brought to "bear on political questions." In other words, in terms of social formation, the best liturgy can do is to *prepare* individuals for the challenges of the *real* world of politics.

The point we are making is not merely academic, as it reflects Christianity's ambiguous relationship within Africa's social history. First, it implies that by operating as "religion," Christianity is never fully at home within the social, material, and political complexities of African life. Rather, her presence in these realities is marked by a certain ambivalence and even shyness. She is involved, but she cannot be too involved, lest she be accused of "meddling" in the affairs of politics.

Second, to the extent that it feels it never fully owns these processes, since its competency lies in the religious domain, Christianity's social significance in Africa can never be proactive in imagining new frames of references (ideals, visions of human flourishing), but its social task is understood only in terms of "influence" — thus the preoccupation with motivation, relief, and advocacy.

The practical implication of this observation is that even though the church appears to be one of the most viable and active institutions, especially in the rural areas, where nation-state influence seems minimal, the churches live with a posture of uncertainty, as if waiting for the real power to show up to provide the determinative frame of references for social and material realities. Only after this other power has framed these realities with whatever ideology that is currently available — tribalism, poverty, industrialization — only then does the church feel that its presence can contribute to the process of social construction or respond to the crises of failure through its pastoral and outreach programs. Given this scenario, it is perhaps not surprising that many have referred to the church in Africa as a sleeping giant that is yet to wake up to the full potential of the gospel as a social vision of reimagination.

---

30. David Power and Herman Schmidt, "Editorial," in *Politics and Liturgy,* ed. Herman Schmidt and David Power, *Concilium: Religion in the Seventies,* vol. 92 (New York: Herder and Herder, 1974), 9, cited by Cavanaugh, *Torture and Eucharist,* 11.

Activism: The Church as an NGO

The flip side of reticence is frantic activism, which also reveals the impact of the Western legacy. Having surrendered the social sphere to the realm of politics, Christianity's role and usefulness within the social realm seems to be constantly in need of justification. The justification comes in the form of an unyielding temptation to be both practical and relevant to the task of social reconstruction, as determined by the field of politics. The irony is that the more desperately churches seek to be relevant to a process that has already been determined, the less clear it is that they have anything to offer. This observation is true not only in relation to development and relief work, but also within the political paradigm and in relation to the church's advocacy on behalf of justice, human rights, democracy, and reconciliation. Charles Villa-Vicencio's *A Theology of Reconstruction* particularly highlights this shortcoming.

Written shortly before the first democratic elections in South Africa, *A Theology of Reconstruction* seeks to make a timely theological contribution to South Africa's transition from apartheid to democracy by exploring the relationship between theology, on the one hand, and constitutional writing, law-making, human rights, and economic justice on the other. With the end of apartheid, South Africa is at a critical juncture with the immense task of political reconstruction, a task to which everyone must contribute. What is particularly significant for our purpose is the way in which this timely contribution portrays the churches and Christian theology as both indispensable to the process of social reconstruction and yet increasingly marginalized.

At the start, Villa-Vicencio affirms a very positive contribution to social reconstruction by theology — a contribution that is as dialectically important and indispensable as the political task of constitution-making. Citing the work of John Witte, he notes that the relationship between law and religion should never be reduced to either "dualistic antinomy nor monistic unity." "Law," he suggests, "helps to give society the structure, the order, the predictability it needs to survive. Religion helps to give society the faith, the vision, the *telos* it needs to move forward." "Without religion, [Witte argues,] law decays into empty formalism. Without law, religion decays into shallow spiritualism. Part of the crisis of our law today is that it has become formalistic, dispirited, undirected, lacking in vision. It has lost its religious dimension. Part of the crisis of our religion is that it has become spiritualistic, disorganized, diluted, lacking in discipline. It has lost its legal dimension."[31] The positive and indispensable role of theology affirmed here, however, is not carried throughout the book. Instead, throughout *A Theology of Reconstruction,* it is increasingly qualified by Villa-Vicencio until it is not clear what role if any is left for the churches and theology to play in the task of social reconstruction.

First, Villa-Vicencio notes that even though "contemporary quests for liberation and reconstruction" can be "interpreted in a variety of different ways and responded to in terms of language and behavior originating in different cultures and traditions," theology or religion cannot foster any specific "interpretation of that process. . . . Theologically it is not the primary task of the church to impose a theological interpretation on this process. Its task is rather to *assist* those who do interpret life theologically to understand current developments, while encouraging those who do not interpret life theologically to respond to the liberatory struggle in other ways."[32]

Second, in a further qualification, Villa-Vicencio suggests that it is not only the case that theology cannot provide a distinct reading of social construction; it also cannot bring any specifically theological or religious insights to the debate. Rather, any insights it might have must be insights that can "enable people (all kinds of different people) to find unity in action as they respond to the liberatory events of life by drawing on a variety of different cultures, speaking a variety of different languages, and by employing many different interpretative frameworks."[33] This means that, according to Villa-Vicencio, any theological insights that are socially significant must be translated into a language understandable to all. For "unless the Church's theological values make sense to those beyond its own membership, and are given expression through secular debate in a language understandable to a broad constituency of people . . . it may never be heard at all."[34]

In the end, it seems the only relevant contribution that theology can make is through insights, programs, and processes shared by all. This is the reason Villa-Vicencio insists that "In a radically pluralistic society the church . . . needs to learn with Bonhoeffer what it means to speak of its

31. Villa-Vicencio, *A Theology of Reconstruction,* 11-12.
32. Villa-Vicencio, *A Theology of Reconstruction,* 24, emphasis added.
33. Villa-Vicencio, *A Theology of Reconstruction,* 25.
34. Villa-Vicencio, *A Theology of Reconstruction,* 4.

most fundamental values in a religionless or secular way. This is perhaps the only way in which it will be heard. For this to be achieved the church is obliged to address human rights. Without this basic commitment it is likely to find itself marginalised from the political quest for reconstruction. It may have no other tangible social contribution to make to the creation of a new age."[35]

What becomes clear from these qualifications is the very narrow parameters in which Villa-Vicencio confines the church's social contribution if, by his requirements, the church is to remain relevant. In the end, it is clear that for Villa-Vicencio there can be no other way to talk about social construction responsibly than in terms of democracy and human rights, notions that are themselves grounded in "an understanding of what it means to be human."[36] Religion and theology can only be relevant if they facilitate, promote, or support these human aspirations. Thus his conclusion cited above: this is the only way the church can be heard. Either it affirms these human aspirations or it has no other tangible social contribution to make.

Again, this is not merely an academic point; it reflects the actual dilemma in which churches are caught. In terms of responding to the pressing needs, whether of reconstruction, development, or the search for democracy in Africa, the church is caught between a rock and a hard place. It must get involved lest it appear to be irrelevant. But for its contribution to be considered relevant, it must not require Christian convictions, stories, or beliefs. In other words, the more active and relevant the church might appear to be, the less distinctively Christian its contribution must be.

From a practical point of view, once the urgent task has already been defined as one of "development," or "democracy," or "poverty," then what counts as a relevant response significantly gets narrowed down to a question of skills and techniques, for example, to fight poverty or ensure democracy. And of course the more the challenge becomes one of skills and techniques, and the more the churches position themselves to respond relevantly through the skills and techniques of mediation, micro-finance, development studies, project management, human rights advocacy, or peace studies, the less clear it is that there is anything unique or distinctive about the Christian contribution. The church increasingly becomes just another NGO.

---

35. Villa-Vicencio, *A Theology of Reconstruction*, 116.
36. Villa-Vicencio, *A Theology of Reconstruction*, 130.

So it is not simply that the churches' responses are inadequate, but that the unyielding pressure for relevancy is a distraction to Christian social engagement. For the narrow limits of what constitutes relevancy within a social sphere that is already framed and very tightly controlled pushes the churches into a posture of activism, which at the same time obscures the most determinative contribution Christianity can offer, namely, that of imagining the social frames of reference in new and fresh ways grounded in her unique story and calling.

Cooption: On Reproducing Tribalism, Violence, and Corruption

The final effect is that by operating from within a "religious" domain, Christianity in Africa not only easily surrenders its own social vision but also uncritically assumes the same visions and patterns of life as those shaped through the determinative institution of nation-state politics. This is what makes the church's message and indeed her way of life indistinguishable from that of any other actor within that social history. This observation is particularly poignant when one realizes that the dominant patterns of social life within Africa's history have been shaped by negative ideologies of violence, war, tribalism, poverty, despair, and even genocide.

The case of Rwanda is very instructive. Christianity has played an active role throughout Rwanda's history, and before the genocide, close to 90 percent of Rwandans self-identified as Christians. Yet not only did many Christians, including church leaders, fail to offer any form of marked resistance to the call to eliminate the Tutsi in 1994, many killings took place within the churches, with Christians killing other Christians. The church had been so thoroughly socialized by the dominant vision of Rwanda as a society inherently marked by Hutu-Tutsi rivalry that the elimination of the Tutsi "cockroaches" was easily projected as a civic duty. The church was in fact incapable of questioning this structure of tribal conflict (grounded in the Hamitic story) or offering any credible alternative because it had never understood its mission in terms of political imagination, but only in terms of providing relevant contributions to the politics of the day. The church, the Catholic church in particular, not only became a dominant actor in Rwanda's social and political history; it also became the state's most reliable partner in elaborating, advancing, and defending the Hamitic story. Mahmood Mamdani notes, "When it came to breathe institutional

47

life into the Hamitic hypothesis, the colonial church acted as both the brains and hands of the colonial state. In this instance, at least the church did both the strategic thinking and the dirty work of the state."[37] Since the dominant discourse and practice of Christian social responsibility in Rwanda succeeded in securely locking the self-understanding and mission of the church within the dominant political vision of a tribalized society, when it came to the final showdown, the church simply performed the story so well that being a Christian made no visible difference.

Rwanda in 1994 may represent an extreme case, but it was not unique. One can cite many other cases in Africa where the churches, having taken the dominant story of tribalism for granted, have not only been unable to challenge it or provide credible alternatives, but themselves live out of the dominant story and thus reproduce it.

The same case we are making in relation to tribalism can be made in relation to the story of violence generally. One of the clearest examples of the socialization into violence as a means of social interaction is provided by the example of the leadership struggle involving the Anglican bishop of Busoga, Cyprian Bamwoze. For over eight years, factions within the diocese tried to unseat the bishop, whom they accused of nepotism, mismanagement, and embezzling diocesan funds. The conflict received enormous publicity and sucked in all relevant organs of church and state, including the high court. Given how dramatically this case shows how Christian churches can imagine themselves as mini-states and use violence as a means of resolving disputes or access to power, it is better to quote at length Gifford's description of one day's events within this power struggle:

> On 13 July the four bishops comprising the investigating committee published their report. In this they listed all the reasons advanced for or against removing the bishop, and tried to arrange them in some sort of order. This report seemed to support the bishop, but its recommendations seemed to acknowledge the basic justice in the rebels' cause. The first of these recommended that the diocese be split into three new dioceses; and the second that Bamwoze remain as a diocesan bishop if requested to do so by any of the three new dioceses, or take early retirement within one year of the acceptance of the report. This report, however, solved nothing, because when Archbishop Okoth on

---

37. See Katongole, *A Future in Africa*, 98, 105.

10 August visited the diocese to communicate the recommendations of the committee, the anti-Bamwoze faction refused to meet him in a hotel and assembled at the cathedral instead. The archbishop refused to speak to the crowd assembled inside on the technicality that he could not enter a cathedral in his province without the consent of the local bishop, and offered to address the crowd outside the cathedral. The "mammoth gathering which had now turned into a mob" insisted that he address them inside the cathedral, and began dragging him there. It was only with considerable difficulty that the archbishop reached his car, and managed to drive off, the "rear window smashed by stones thrown by the wild crowd." On 27 August [Bishop] Bamwoze himself was subjected to similar physical violence at Batambogwe.[38]

As in the case of Rwanda, the story of Bishop Bamwoze confirms that when the patterns of violence have become so naturalized as a way of social interaction and as a means of settling differences within a social history, Christians and Christian churches also end up getting fully drawn into that performance, such that being a Christian does not make any difference.

A similar cooption is reflected by what one might refer to as the Bonnke factor within African Christianity. Reinhard Bonnke, a charismatic preacher and founder of the Christ for all Nations Ministries, travels across Africa, where his crusades attract hundreds of thousands and in some places even millions of attendants.[39] The crusades, called "Holy Spirit Evangelism in Demonstration," are characterized by nightlong sessions of praise and healing, interspersed by Bonnke's charismatic preaching. In his preaching, Bonnke expounds a popular theme: "Africa Shall Be Saved," or "Africa Is Being Saved," and offers as a demonstration promises of deliverance, miracles, blessings, and prosperity. Bonnke's version of evangelical-Pentecostal-charismatic synthesis represents a brand of Christianity that is sharply on the rise in Africa. Its popular appeal has much to do with its relevancy to the social and economic needs of postcolonial Africa.

Yet, the more closely one examines this dominant trend within African Christianity, the more one realizes that it cannot provide a critical challenge to the political and economic illusions of a postcolonial Africa. Rather, it nicely locates itself within the dominant imagination of postcolonial politics and economics in Africa, and quite often reproduces

38. Gifford, *African Christianity*, 126-27.
39. See Christ for All Nations website, http://www.cfan.org/.

its patterns, its modernity, and its illusory promises of success and prosperity. This is what accounts for the prosperity-gospel preaching that characterizes many charismatic churches in Africa, and makes not only Bonnke but other preachers like Creflo Dollar popular evangelists in Africa. The miracle of instant prosperity that many of these preachers promise as part of being born again seems none too far from the shameless corruption that characterizes the politics and economics of Africa. From this point of view, prosperity gospel peddlers merely represent the religious version of the "politics of eating."

Conclusion

When operating exclusively from a religious sphere, the church's role in Africa's social history helplessly swings between the postures of reticence, frantic activism, and total cooption. What all these postures reflect, however, is the particularly Western concept that Christianity as a religion is not a social vision, but only becomes socially relevant when it contributes to the social and material processes that are determined and controlled by the sphere of politics. This assumption must be set aside if Christianity is to recover its essential social vision. But this recovery is impossible when Christian social reflection is preoccupied with the prescriptive agenda of generating recommendations, strategies, and skills to help politics work.

Therefore, Christian social ethics needs to resist the prescriptive temptation in order to recover the unique social contribution the church can make in the search for a new future in Africa. For the most determinative contribution Christianity can make in Africa is not in terms of advocacy for nation-state modalities, but instead fresh visions of what Africa is and can be. As we will see, other dominant approaches to social ethics in Africa have similarly overlooked this determinative nature of founding narratives.

CHAPTER 2

Reimagining Social Ethics in Africa:
From Skills to Stories

Whoever can give his people better stories than the ones they live by is like the priest in whose hands common bread and wine becomes capable of feeding the very soul, and he may think of forging in some invisible smithy the uncreated conscience of his race.

Hugh Kenner

Understanding how important stories are to Africa's future requires understanding how the larger conversation about social ethics has developed in Africa. Social ethics is a growing and popular discipline, with a proliferation of programs and courses on good governance, human rights, peace studies, ethics, and development at many universities and other institutions of higher learning in Africa. One common element within all these programs is the recognition that Africa's enduring social problems are somehow connected to the institution of the nation-state. Therefore, the conversations generated by these programs focus on ways to reform the functioning of the nation-state, with the assumption that once the nation-state in Africa becomes more "functional" and more democratic, peace and development will follow. Like Christian social ethics, social ethics in Africa is driven by a prescriptive agenda, often accompanied by packaged "solutions" from the West. A look at some of these recommendations and the assumptions that sustain them will help to illustrate this point.

Change in Leadership

One of the most popular recommendations for a way forward usually involves a call for a change in political leadership. The call takes many forms, from the need for a national conference or mediation to resolve the leadership struggle (as in Kenya recently), to a call for fresh elections — monitored by international observers.[1] There is something right about the call for new leadership in Africa; a number of social problems in Africa arise out of the crisis of leadership. Not only does poor leadership lead to mismanagement and lack of planning; dictatorship in Africa continues to stifle democratic expression and leads to insecurity and the abuse of human rights. A change of leadership in Zimbabwe, for example, with Mugabe off the scene, promises to usher in a new era of freedom. The problem with many of these recommendations, however, is the way in which the social problems in Africa are *individualized* — it is assumed that the underlying problem has to do with the individual leaders or with a particular regime, and therefore will be addressed with the election or coming to power of new leaders. This, of course, does not happen. Quite often, not very long after the change of leadership, the new regime and its leaders turn out to be just as dictatorial as the previous regime.

Constitution Mechanisms

Closely connected with calls for a change in leadership are calls for measures to ensure the mechanisms of good governance, like human rights commissions, codes of conduct, inspectorate of governments, and other mechanisms safeguarded by the constitution. In many instances, the recommendations involve drafting an altogether new constitution and thus we find more than a third of the African countries have revised or completely rewritten their constitutions in the last twenty-five years. The hope is that within the new constitutions, human rights charters will be protected and good governance ensured.

---

1. National conferences became popular in the 1990s, especially among Francophone countries, but a similar idea lies behind the call for "power-sharing" arrangements (Paul Gifford, *African Christianity: Its Public Role* [Bloomington: Indiana University Press, 1998], 21).

But just like the call for new leadership, these proposals invoke an optimism that is not borne out by experience. Quite often, not very long after a new constitution is in place, it is suspended or amended by the leaders — as Uganda's recently was — to allow the president recently to run for an endless number of terms.

Economic Reforms and Structural Adjustment

The most sustained efforts in nation-state building in Africa include the search for the right models to use to develop Africa. Discussions in social ethics center around development and economic reforms — economic liberalization and globalization are the buzzwords — and social-ethical discussions engage in weighing the merits of the Structural Adjustment Programs (SAPs) sponsored by the International Monetary Fund (IMF) and the World Bank. Among other things, the SAPs call for mechanisms to ensure accountability, transparency, economic reforms, liberalization, privatization, and a commitment to a steady repayment of Africa's debt. While some hail these reforms as the most effective way to ensure Africa's development, others persuasively argue that the requirements of the IMF and the World Bank are sinking the continent deeper into poverty and into debt with a number of pressure groups calling for the total cancellation of Africa's debt.

Whatever might be said about the merits or demerits of the economic reforms called for by the Bretton Woods Institutions of the IMF and World Bank, they are based on the realization that the problems of Africa have to do not with individual leaders, but with the structures of Africa's political and economic life. Unfortunately, however, the recommendations never advance beyond guidelines for structural adjustment. In fact, one has the feeling that the various structural adjustment programs are sustained by a conviction that the problems of institutions are primarily of a technical or ethical nature, and that what African bureaucrats lack is either the expertise or the commitment to reform. That is why the IMF and World Bank packages usually include a missionary group of experts and technical aides, offering all sorts of structural adjustment skills, development strategies, and ethical guidelines in management, good governance, and the like.

Geographical Adjustments

A similar optimism sustains recommendations that call for redrawing national boundaries of African countries, whether the calls come through political rhetoric or armed secession. These recommendations rightly recognize the artificial nature of many African nation-state boundaries. The call to redefine Africa's boundaries is also often an attempt to reduce tribal rivalries; calls often involve boundaries that coincide with tribal identities so as to create culturally homogeneous nations, with the hope that such arrangements will solve the problem of tribalism in Africa. What the recommendations do not take into account, however, is that the problem of "tribalism" in Africa is not simply a matter of cultural differences, or the natural effect of having diverse groups under one state arrangement. The issue is far more complex. That is why, for example, culturally homogeneous countries like Rwanda and Burundi have witnessed far more of the negative effects of "tribalism" than linguistically diverse nations.

Enlisting African Culture and Traditions

Now and again, social-ethical discussions in Africa turn to the role of culture in development. Here too the votes are divided: some view African culture as the obstacle that needs to be overcome for Africa to achieve peace and development. They point to Africa's bondage to its cultural past as the cause of its current poverty and various conflicts.[2] The dominant trend, however, is to seek ways to make the nation-state at home in African culture. This trend is evident already in the work of the African leaders of independence, who, even as they accepted the nation-state as the only path towards Africa's independence, desperately tried to provide for some kind of spiritual and ethical foundation for the nation-state in African culture. Leopold Senghor's philosophy of negritude models this attempt well. Although unsuccessful as a political leader, Senghor tried to make what he thought were the emotive traits of the African personality ("Emotion is

---

2. For a more detailed discussion of the relation between culture and development in Africa, see Emmanuel Katongole, "Ethics in the Workplace and the Power of Culture: Is Ubuntu a Blessing or a Curse?" *Praxis: Journal for Christian Business Management* 6, no. 3 (1998): 2-5.

black as reason is Greek") the foundation of a new African identity and a new African politics of independence.

Other independence leaders tried to imitate Senghor's example and searched for inspiration in the African past that would give the African nation-state some kind of African legitimacy, and in the process they came up with different versions of "African democracy." Whether the foundation of African democracy was grounded in the African value of solidarity (as in Kenyatta's *harambee*), in African communalism (as in Nyerere's *ujamaa*), or in a version of African socialism (as in Kaunda's humanism and Nkrumah's consciencism), the goal was the same: to rediscover enduring aspects of African culture and bring them to bear on the modern challenge of nation-state building.[3] Mobutu's *authenticité* ideology in the 1970s was itself nothing but an attempt to use African artistic and cultural expression (music, dance, dress) as a way to offer Zaireans a sense of national unity and pride. The current interest in *ubuntu* in South Africa[4] is yet another version of the same old search for values that legitimate nation-state politics from the African past.[5]

---

3. See, among others, Jomo Kenyatta, *Facing Mount Kenya* (1938); Julius Nyerere, *Ujamaa: Essays on Socialism* (1938); and Kwame Nkrumah, *Consciencism: Philosophy and Ideology for De-colonization* (1946).

4. There is an attempt to recover the ethics and spirit of "ubuntu" in all areas: philosophy, theology, politics, economics, and even management theory. For a sampling of titles see, among others, Jabu Sindane, *Ubuntu and Nation-Building* (Pretoria: Ubuntu School of Philosophy, 1994); Augustine Shute, *Ubuntu: A New Philosophy for Africa* (Rondebisch, South Africa: UCT Press, 1993); L. Mbigi and J. Maree, *Ubuntu: The Spirit of African Transformation Management* (Randburg: Knowledge Resources, 1995); and Johann Broodryk, *Ubuntu Management and Motivation* (Pretoria: Ubuntu School of Philosophy, 1997). For comprehensive treatment, see Joe Teffo, *The Concept of Ubuntu as a Cohesive Moral Value* (Pretoria: Ubuntu School of Philosophy, 1994).

5. The same can be said of Thabo Mbeki's call for an "African Renaissance," which, among other things, involves a "re-discovery of the African soul, pride, great accomplishments . . . captured and made permanently available in the great works of creativity represented by the pyramids and sphinxes of Egypt; the stone buildings of Axum and the ruins of Carthage and Zimbabwe; the rock paintings of the San, the Benin Bronzes and the African masks, the carvings of the Makonde and the stone sculptures of the Shona" (Thabo Mbeki, "The African Renaissance," August 13, 1998, 5). The rediscovery of African past genius is premised on the availability, sponsorship, and furtherance of the nation-state project, more specifically in the case of Mbeki of the New South Africa. For my critical views on the African Renaissance, see Emmanuel Katongole, "African Renaissance and Narrative Theology in Africa: Which Story, Whose Renaissance?" *Journal of Religion for Southern Africa* 102 (1998): 29-40.

The fact that Mobutu's regime, for example, with all its veneer of *authenticité,* turned out to be one of the most corrupt in Africa just confirms that this interest in African culture is exploitative, in that it involves no genuine interest in African culture as such but in finding some usable parts to advance the cause of self-serving leaders and their ideologies. When successful, such attempts involve unhitching an African virtue — *harambee, ujamaa,* or *ubuntu* — from its context and historical way of life, bounded by mutual obligations and fellow feeling, and deploying it in the service of the self-interested politics of the modern African nation-state. That is why interest in African culture is both entertaining (as when troupes of African cultural dancers welcome a visiting head of state at the airport) and distracting, masking the underlying story while providing the nation-state institution with a veneer of authentic African legitimacy.[6]

Popular Democracy and Mass Participation

Many also noted the profound disconnect between the institution of the nation-state in Africa and the concerns and aspirations of the majority of African peoples. In practical terms, the people's alienation from the state machinery not only means that many view the nation-state as foreign, but that the institution neither fosters nor encourages the people's ownership of the political and economic processes of their countries. No one has faced this problem of the alienation of the state from the masses more squarely than the Algerian doctor, psychiatrist, and freedom fighter Frantz Fanon. Working and writing against the background of French colonialism in Algeria, Fanon noted the extent to which the colonial system was built on psychological and physical violence.[7] Fanon also noticed that in those African countries where independence had just been declared, what was achieved was a mere cosmetic "change of guards" that happened only at the top, with African petty bourgeois nationalists replacing white colonialists. For the masses, Fanon noted, nothing really changed; the peasants

6. For extended reflections, see Katongole, "Ethics in the Workplace and the Power of Culture."

7. Frantz Fanon's *The Wretched of the Earth* (New York: Grove Press, 1963) provides a particularly chilling catalog of French atrocities in Algeria. See also his *Black Skins, White Masks,* trans. Charles Lam Markman (New York: Grove Press, 1967), which offers a gripping account of the deep wound of alienation at the heart of colonialism.

continued to experience the same alienation and violence. It was this observation that led Fanon to see the necessity of a war of liberation both as a means to overthrow the colonial regime and a means of social and moral regeneration. An armed struggle, Fanon argued, would not only bind the fighting masses under an enduring sense of "nationalism"; it would create strong links between the leaders and the masses. In this way, independence would not only be won, but the whole process leading up to it would be "owned" and institutionalized through the setting up of local administrative councils in the "liberated areas." Accordingly, national politics would be grounded in a bottom-up process of mass participation.

Amilcar Cabral has made a similar argument in his writings and revolutionary struggles in Guinea Bissau and, together with Frantz Fanon, continues to be a key inspiration for revolutionary struggles in Africa.[8] The problem they seek to address — the alienation of the state machinery from the needs and aspirations of the people in Africa — continues to be one of the enduring legacies of colonial and postcolonial politics in Africa. However, the problem with both Fanon's and Cabral's argument for mass participation is the assumption that only violence can provide the social glue for a new postcolonial society. Mass participation is, according to them, mass participation in warfare and the armed struggle. This suggestion raises a number of questions. Once violence has been accepted as the social glue for anti-colonial struggle, what happens after the revolutionary struggle? Does the culture of violence magically turn into peace? And when one thinks of Rwanda in 1994, when the perpetrators tried to use mass participation in genocide as a way to create a new Rwandan society (composed only of Hutus), then it becomes evident that by itself mass participation is not a sufficient goal for political mobilization. The argument for mass participation requires a justifying account of mass participation: how, into what, and for what end. At any rate, Fanon and Cabral have limitations, namely, the failure to imagine a form of politics that does not require violence as its grounding narrative and whose *telos* is not simply to secure national sovereignty. Because neither Fanon nor Cabral envision

---

8. Amilcar Cabral, *Unity and Struggle* (New York: Monthly Review Press, 1979). Fanon's influence on Museveni, even though unacknowledged, is clear from the latter's autobiography, *Sowing the Mustard Seed* (London: Macmillan, 1996). See also Yoweri Museveni, "Fanon's Theory of Violence: Its Verification in Liberated Mozambique," in Nathan Sahmuyarira, ed., *Essays on the Liberation of Southern Africa* (Dar-es-Salaam, Tanzania: Tanzania Publishing House, 1971), 1-24.

another form of politics whose frames of reference do not depend upon nation-state modalities, they take for granted that the nation-state is the only hope, which must be won or secured at all costs, even through armed struggle and violence.

Christian Social Responsibility

We need not repeat our conclusions at the end of the first chapter, except to emphasize that Christian social ethics has decisively located itself within this larger conversation that continues to offer prescriptive attempts to save nation-state politics in Africa. Whether Christian social responsibility is realized directly by influencing government policy (political paradigm), indirectly by motivating or infusing Christian action in the world through love (spiritual paradigm), or in partnership with the nation-state through relief services (the pastoral paradigm), all the recommendations assume that nation-state politics is the primary way to effect social change. The result has been that, on the whole, theological social-ethical contributions have been indistinguishable from the secular contributions. Thus, even without denying that there are personal, structural, ethical, and geographical factors that complicate the social-political situation in Africa, all the above recommendations fail to address the underlying problem of the institution of the nation-state itself. As a result, in spite of the numerous elections, in spite of the constant change of regimes, in spite of the various structural adjustment programs, in spite of the multitude of new constitutions, in spite of the many development theories and strategies — in spite of all these, there fails to be any lasting positive social improvement in the lives of the majority of African peoples. On the contrary, elected regimes seem to be no less brutal than military regimes, single-party regimes no less dictatorial than multi-party regimes, culturally homogeneous nations (Rwanda, for instance) no more stable than culturally diverse ones (like Uganda, with over thirty-three language groups).

It must be clear by now that even if these nation-states are different in their external formalities, they operate from the same imagination. And as long as this underlying imagination is not questioned, adjustments in this institution cannot ensure an alternate social history. In other words, the socio-political problems in Africa may require personnel, geographical, and structural adjustments, but the first and crucial adjustment is a mythological adjustment that addresses the underlying stories that shape the imagination.

The Failure of Imagination

In short, my frustration with social ethics in Africa is not about its failure to come up with practical recommendations for improving the nation-state institution and its politics; indeed, there are too many of those. My greater frustration is with its failure of imagination, with the assumption that the nation-state institution is the only possible structure for modern social existence in Africa. In the case of Christian social ethics, the failure to imagine other forms of social structure outside the nation-state is fundamentally self-defeating, because this failure undermines the central claim that Jesus is the Savior and Lord of history. To assume that the only way Africa can be saved is through nation-state modalities, and that the church can only contribute to this process by helping nation-state politics, is ridiculous, especially in Africa, where the church has far more credibility than the corrupt nation-state institution. Even more ridiculous is the idea that the church can only make claims about Jesus as Savior by qualifying that his salvation is only "spiritual." The salvation promised by God to God's people, to which the birth, life, death, and resurrection of Jesus is a witness, is not merely spiritual: it is a concrete social, material, political, and economic reality that is ushered into existence by God's revelation in history. The failure of Christian social imagination is a failure to imagine and live in this new reality, which in 2 Corinthians 5:17 St. Paul refers to as God's "new creation."

Realism and Its Shortcomings

There is another way in which the failure at imagination of social ethics in Africa becomes apparent: the various recommendations and theological contributions have been driven by a realistic agenda. By this I mean that they have not only taken the institution of the nation-state for granted, but they have taken realities like "poverty," "tribalism," "underdevelopment," "violence," or even "Africa" as neutral descriptions of reality. Thus the discussion focuses on mechanisms and strategies of "how to end poverty," "how to stop violence," and "how to develop Africa." What these recommendations fail to recognize is that notions like "poverty" and "tribalism" are not neutral descriptions of reality, but performances grounded within a particular story and within a particular social imagination.

Because this rather significant observation has been missed, social ethics in Africa — Christian social ethics included — finds itself caught in a constant mode of frantic firefighting, always devising strategies to save Africa. From this point of view, calls for Christian social responsibility appear as desperate emergency calls for Christians to get on board with the urgent task of firefighting, and thus for Christians to bring out their own special gear and water hoses. The failure of imagination is a failure to step back from the world of fires and raise critical questions about why these perpetual fires are happening. What is it about Africa that makes violence, war, corruption, and poverty enduring realities?

The more one raises these kinds of questions, the more one begins to question another key assumption that has sustained social ethics in Africa, namely that the realities of poverty, war, and violence are indicators of a dysfunctional political economy. But as scholars like Mamdani and Chabal have shown, realities like chaos, unrest, war, and corruption are not indications of a failed institution; they are part and parcel of the way nation-state politics in Africa work.[9]

An Odd Institution

If one takes this conclusion seriously, as I think we ought to, then one begins to realize that there is something odd about the nation-state institution in Africa. This is not only because African nation-states, entities like "Uganda" or "Zambia" or "Malawi," do not function with the same coherent and consistent sense of "nation" as European or Western nations, but seem to be "countries in a cartological sense only," with a name and "a dis-

9. See, for example, Patrick Chabal and Jean Pascal Daloz, *Africa Works: Disorder as Political Instrument* (Bloomington: Indiana University Press, 1999), which provides a very powerful and well-argued account of the political instrumentalization of disorder and economic failure. According to the authors, the resurgence of ethnicity, witchcraft, and other cultural traits in Africa is not an indication of the continent's move backward, but the evidence of a unique and multifaceted path to modernization — in other words, it is a unique form of modernization.

tinctive color on a map" and nothing more.[10] It is also because of the ironic contradictions out of which many African nation-states operate that, tragically, they are not able to provide clean water for the people, but they are capable of waging multi-billion-dollar wars — usually against their own people. Moreover, in spite of the constant rhetoric (and feigned programs) to fight poverty, populations live in squalid poverty, while the leaders stash away millions in foreign bank accounts. The same leaders readily starve, kill, and maim their own people to ensure their stay in office. These and so many other contradictions confirm that there is something terribly odd about the nation-state institution in Africa. This odd nature needs to be investigated and its foundational narratives described and displayed if a new future is to be imagined.

From Skills to Stories

To attend to this task, the focus of social ethics must shift from the external formalities of nation-state politics to its inner workings or logic, from skills and technical strategies to myths and visions, from a preoccupation with fixing a broken institution to imagining new experiments in social life in Africa. As John Donahue says, quoting the social critic Hugh Kenner in an unrelated context:

> People in sorrow or depression suffer an impoverishment of imagination. They simply cannot imagine a world different from one in which they are locked . . . "Whoever can give his people better stories than the ones they live by is like the priest in whose hands common bread and wine becomes capable of feeding the very soul, and he may think of forging in some invisible smithy the uncreated conscience of his race."[11]

This task of the imagination calls not so much for experts and technical aides, but for storytellers who are able "to offer people better stories than the ones they live by." What makes Christian social ethics uniquely suited for this task is that stories, myths, and the imagination are the stuff of Christianity. All the realities of the Christian tradition — the Scriptures,

10. Gifford, *African Christianity,* 9.
11. John R. Donahue, "Twenty-two Shopping Days Left," *America* 185, no. 17 (2001), 31.

prayer, doctrine, worship, Baptism, the Eucharist, the sacraments — point to and reenact a compelling story that should claim the whole of our lives.

This is also what makes Christianity deeply political — not simply in the sense of having significant political implications, but that these realities are *real*. They involve an investment of bodies and are thus a unique *political* imagination. For as William Cavanaugh notes (following Cornelius Castoriadis),

> the imagination of a society is the sense of what is real and what is not; it includes a memory of how the society got where it is, a sense of who it is, and hopes and projects for the future. The social imagination is not a mere representation of something which is real, as a flag represents a putatively "real" nation-state; the imagination of a society is involved when the flag becomes what one will kill and die for. In other words, the social imagination is not a mere image of something more real; it is not some ideological "superstructure" which reflects the material "base." There is no substantive distinction between material and cultural production. The imagination of a society is the condition of possibility for the organization and signification of bodies in a society. The imagination is the drama in which bodies are invested.[12]

Cavanaugh's observation advances our argument in a number of significant ways. First, it highlights how all politics is related to the imagination and that the most enduring work of politics takes place at the level of imagination. Second, once we accept this concept of politics as social imagination, then we begin to see how nation-state politics in Africa represents an odd social imagination, and equally important, how Christianity itself is

---

12. See Cavanaugh, *Torture and Eucharist: Theology, Politics and the Body of Christ* (Oxford: Blackwell, 1998), 57. Another source that I have found helpful in understanding the relation between politics and imagination is Benedict Anderson's *Imagined Communities: Reflections on the Origins and Spread of Nationalism* (New York: Courier Companies, 1991). Anderson notes that "all communities larger than the primordial villages of face to face contact (and perhaps even these) are imagined." Members never meet their fellow members, "yet in the mind of each lives the image of their communion." For Anderson, the most vivid example of such imagined communities is the nation, which is imagined as an inherently limited and sovereign political community in which, "regardless of the actual inequality and exploitation that may prevail in each [nation], there exists a deep comradeship. It is this fraternity which makes it possible . . . for so many people, not so much to kill, as to be willing to die for such limited imaginings" (pp. 6-7).

a unique social imagination, a unique "drama in which bodies are invested." This conclusion bears critically the relation between Christianity and nation-state politics in Africa and allows a new conversation on Christian social ethics to emerge, a conversation committed to engaging the unique politics that is Christianity.

Cavanaugh's remark also indicates that the social imagination that politics is, the particular investment of bodies, is but a product of the stories. For the most part these stories remain invisible — the bedrock that continues to sustain and shape our lives and the way we view and operate in the world. This is particularly true of those founding stories — those stories of "in the beginning" — which after a while become so naturalized that one does not even see them as stories but as facts — as just part of the way things are.[13] In order to discover the story embodied within the modern institution of the nation-state in Africa and the odd "investment of bodies" it produces, we need to discover the founding story of modern Africa, within which nation building and the nation-state project are inscribed. Only by attending to this story and displaying its performance can a new framework for doing Christian social ethics in Africa emerge.

13. Emmanuel Katongole, *Beyond Universal Reason: The Relation between Religion and Ethics in the Work of Stanley Hauerwas* (Notre Dame: University of Notre Dame Press, 2000), 214-42.

CHAPTER 3

Performing Africa: Stories, Politics, and the Social Imagination of Africa

The elites needed the masses, and took steps to recruit them.

Basil Davidson

The deflated constitute a race unto themselves. I don't mean the unemployed; a flatterer and a floater can both become unemployed. A deflated person is someone beyond good and evil, beyond feeling the blues of unemployment. He has reached a point where he says to himself, "they don't need me because I don't know how to do anything. They don't know me. They don't see me." African dictatorships are producing this kind of man everyday. He knows that no matter what he does, he will not get anywhere. The statistics are against him: he will die young. He sits down and looks to see if people see him. He sees from others' gazes that he is transparent. He does not know how to do anything, and he does not want to do anything.

Manthia Diawara

Basil Davidson and "The Black Man's Burden"

The central argument of Basil Davidson's *The Black Man's Burden: Africa and the Curse of the Nation-State* is that Africa's societal crises derive from many upsets and conflicts.[1] The root problem, however, has to do with "the social and political institutions within which decolonized Africans have lived and tried to survive. Primarily, this is a crisis of institutions" (10). Specifically, the crisis relates to the nation-state, "Europe's last gift to Africa," whose introduction to Africa was marked by a myriad ironic contradictions, none perhaps as frustrating to Africa's efforts towards peace and stability as "the victory of the 'national' [struggle] over the 'social' [struggle]. This was going to form the central problematic of Africa's new states after the 1950s" (188, 138-39).

One way Davidson develops this argument is by assembling, at various places in the book, stories that provide a comparison of the process of nation-state formation in Europe with the African version of the same. A clear difference between the two, for example, is the role that the local history of struggles and aspirations plays in each process. For example, Davidson recounts how the rise of nation-states in fifteenth- and sixteenth-century Europe emerged out of the competing struggle of interests and ambitions in the shared history of customs, loyalties, and traditions. The "middle strata," as Davidson calls them, played a key role in this process by aligning their interests with the needs of the "laboring poor" and the latter's hopes for a "better life," forging these into a sense of "nationalism" or "national consciousness" that would eventually find embodiment within the nation-state (135-38). As Davidson says,

> the rise of nationalism in its nineteenth-century context was the outcome of a combination of effort between the rising "middle classes" . . . and the multitudinous masses of the "lower orders". . . . Indispensable to nation-statist success in all the many upheavals of the nineteenth century . . . were the agitations and uprisings of peasants and urban workers. (134)

Davidson provides helpful asides on the complexity of the European context, where the role of the *social* struggle in nation-state formation is primary. This means that, among other things, the satisfaction of the real or perceived needs of the "laboring poor" or masses — particularly their hope for a better life — became an indispensable factor in the rise of these

---

1. Unless otherwise noted, all the page references in this chapter refer to Basil Davidson, *The Black Man's Burden: Africa and the Curse of the Nation-State* (New York: Three Rivers Press, 1992).

new political formations. The "middle strata" could only hope to become rulers by staking their legitimacy as rulers on this commitment. It also means that the nation-state institution would be perceived as some kind of "supreme problem-solving formula" in European social history, that is, in the history of a people "emerging from the dead hand of tyrannical and foreign rule, whether Austrian or Russian or Turkish or other" (137). In any event, European nation-states are inconceivable except in terms of a *process* of transformation in a local history, in which the social struggles were the crucial factor, exerting from below the force of nationalism that shaped and legitimated nation-state ideology.

It is precisely this bottom-up process — the valorization of local history and the social struggles it embodies — as a force for nation-state formation that is completely missing from the story of the nation-state in Africa. Where nation-state formation in Europe was a *process,* in Africa it became a *project,* which both the departing colonialists and their nationalist-bourgeois successors assumed to be inevitable for African modernization and independence. But what is even more noteworthy is the fact that "within this peculiar chemistry of nation-state formation," as Davidson calls it, "the dynamic element which [in the case of Europe] so decisively transformed the social struggle of the masses into the national struggle" was, in the case of Africa, systematically "smuggled out of hearing, or simply censored out of sight" (159). To be sure, the social struggle was not just smuggled out of hearing; it was from the very start intentionally trivialized and dismissed as both irrelevant and a nuisance.

In the Beginning

Davidson traces this politics of the suppression of local history to the colonial project whose moral justification was grounded in projecting Africa as a continent "without history" — that is, until the European presence in Africa. This not only meant that Africa's history began with the European "discovery" of various places, rivers, lakes, and peoples; it also assumed that Africans had no previous experience in social existence that could serve as a helpful starting point in what was seen as the civilizing project of colonialism.[2] For already under the colonial dispensation and within the

2. Much of Davidson's work is directed at showing what a lie this is. See Davidson,

social anthropology that sustained it, which has remained unchallenged until the present, all such local history was devalued as "folklore," "animism," "paganism," "barbarism," and a host of other "isms," all of which came to be seen as both distracting and hard to absorb into the colonial project. Africa's wealth of ethnic cultures, for instance, came to be branded "tribalism" and "as such retrogressive."[3] "This diversity, it seemed, had to be just another hangover from an unregenerate past," which would have to be superseded by the civilizing project of colonialism (99).

That is why it is important to distinguish this distinctively modern and pernicious sense of "tribalism" from a more general notion of tribalism. As Davidson notes,

> [i]n a large historical sense tribalism has been used to express the solidarity and common loyalties of people who share among themselves as a country and a culture. In this important sense, tribalism in Africa or anywhere else has "always" existed and has often been a force for good, a force creating a civil society dependent on laws and the rule of law. This meaning of "tribalism" is hard to distinguish in practice from the meaning of "nationalism." Before the period of modern imperialism Europeans visiting and reporting on Africa seldom drew any such distinction. (11)

Accordingly, the colonial and neocolonial preoccupation with "tribalism" reflects a specific attitude according to which Africa's social history, instead of being viewed as a resource providing the building blocks for any modernizing projects, has been viewed as the "problem" which needs to be overcome. "The problem," so it seemed, "was for Africans to overcome an atavistic tendency to live in 'tribes' and to begin living in 'nations'" (75). Such a premise, however, could not but render the colonial project in Africa as self-defeating as it was violent. For in the end, as Davidson argues,

> the whole great European project in Africa, stretching over more than a hundred years, can only seem a vast obstacle thrust across every rea-

---

Black Man's Burden, 52-98, and also Basil Davidson, *The Search for Africa: History, Culture, Politics* (London: James Currey, 1994).

3. Chapter four of *Black Man's Burden* is particularly telling on the invention of "tribalism" and the decisive role this notion played in the purported and highly misleading debate between the modernizers and the traditionalists, or "tribalists," as they came to be known by their detractors.

sonable avenue of African progress out of preliterate and prescientific societies into the "modern world." . . . It taught that nothing useful could develop without denying Africa's past, without a ruthless severing from Africa's roots and a slavish acceptance of models drawn from entirely different histories. (42)

As a result, Davidson refers to the African nation-state as the "successor institution" — successor, that is, to the colonial project. Despite promising independence, the nation-state just became a neocolonial offspring, locally manned, but embodying the same story of alienation from Africa's social history.

One may disagree with some of the assumptions that sustain Davidson's work. For instance, Davidson seems to minimize the role violence plays within the formation and operation of the nation-state in Europe.[4] Also, there seems to be a questionable positivism in Davidson's work, which allows him to assume that class structure, capitalism, and the nation-state are inevitable. That is why he implies that, left to their history, African forms of social existence would eventually have turned into nation-states similar to the ones in Europe, as in the case of Asante, "which was not an exception but an example of a general process," suggests (77).[5] It is not clear why Davidson assumes this, except perhaps that he works with modernist assumptions according to which the nation-state is the inevitable, and thus only, form of social existence that can be called real (rational) in the Hegelian sense.[6]

Overall, however, I find Davidson's work highly insightful in its analysis of the underlying story as well of the various factors that came into

---

4. See, e.g., Anthony Giddens, *A Contemporary Critique of Historical Materialism*, Vol. 2: *The Nation-State and Violence* (Berkeley: University of California Press, 1987).

5. Adrian Hastings assumes the same inevitability of the nation-state, even though for Hastings the transition to nation-statehood is not a modern impulse, but a development grounded in, or at least made possible by, the transition from oral to written vernaculars. Scriptural translation, Hastings argues, plays a key role in this transition from orality to literacy and thus becomes a key factor not only in fueling but also in stabilizing national consciousness. See Adrian Hastings, *The Construction of Nationhood: Ethnicity, Religion and Nationalism* (Cambridge: Cambridge University Press, 1977).

6. In the same way, Davidson projects Enlightenment sociological views of religion upon African pre-colonial history, thereby portraying religious formations in Africa as some kind of sacred canopy whose goal is to provide legitimacy to independently originating social norms (81ff).

play in nation-state formation in Africa. For instance, the fact that the "nationalists of the 1950s came to embrace nation-statism as the only available escape from colonial domination" (55) explains the superficial character of African nation-states. For not founded on any enduring sense of historical adjustments within local aspirations and struggles, nation-states, as well as other institutions of Africa's independence, evolved out of a void. Accordingly, they were bound to become "shell states," having juridical statehood but not empirical statehood (12).

The Performance

Significant as this fact is, it is not so much the fact of the nation-state's superficiality but the underlying story — of Africa without a history — that we should focus on, for it is crucial for understanding the way the nation-state operates in much of Africa. To this story one can trace the various contradictions as well as many of the problems that have become endemic to Africa's political imagination. Therefore we need to attend to the African nation-state's "in the beginning" story in order to display how it underwrites a peculiar chemistry of nation-state politics in Africa and how it continues to shape the same patterns of desperation and violence in Africa.

Alienation and Self-Hatred

Occasionally, a revolutionary African leader points out the ideological poverty at the heart of the postcolonial nation-state as a way to explain the lack of nationalist analysis and the shortage of long-term thinking in Africa.[7] Overall, however, the fact that the nation-state in Africa ignores the experience, needs, and interests of the citizens is never seriously questioned. With Davidson one is able to see why this is the case, since by accepting that Africa's own experience and achievement could teach nothing and by committing themselves to "modernization" and "civilization," African leaders themselves came to embody the alienation from Africa's history.

Thus, Davidson connects the ideological poverty to the story of "Af-

7. See, e.g., Amilcar Cabral, *Unity and Struggle* (New York: Monthly Review Press, 1979); see also Yoweri Museveni, *What is Africa's Problem?*, ed. Elizabeth Kanyogonya (Minneapolis: University of Minnesota Press, 2000).

rica without a history" and shows how it is through educational institutions that such a story has come to be assimilated and accepted by Africa's
elite. For as he notes, "the largest and most serious consequence of this
ideological poverty lay in the general acceptance by literate Africans, at
least down to the 1970s and perhaps beyond, of their necessary self-
alienation from Africa's roots" (50).

Davidson retraces the alienation from Africa's social history to the
"recaptives" — those who had been taken into slavery for shipment to the
Americas but were "recaptured" and set free by the crews of the naval
blockade. But where the recaptives' alienation from Africa's social history
was a matter of fact, for their descendants as well as their non-recaptive
colleagues it was a *learned* sentiment; in fact, it was the goal of education to
teach the story of Africa as a "dark continent" and one "without a history"
that became unquestionably valid.

Thus Davidson notes that it was enlightened Africans, especially
those who "were sent to graze in the learned pastures of London's law
schools and courts," who reflected the full force of the alienation. "The
same alienation," however,

> invaded all those . . . Africans who now began to receive the benefits of
> literate education in mission schools in several colonies. Above the en-
> trance to every school there was an invisible but always insistent direc-
> tive to those who passed within the magic gate to the "white man's
> world": ABANDON AFRICA, ALL YE WHO ENTER HERE. (42)

To the extent that this philosophical underpinning of colonial education has not been questioned, but instead continues to be assumed within
the postcolonial nation-state project, this education continues to perpetuate the same anthropological and cultural pauperization. Thus, far from
being a source of empowerment, literary education in Africa produces a
particular form of self-hatred for which an arrogant and excessive lifestyle
is only a mask. One gets a glimpse of this self-hatred in the character of
Ocol, the main character in Okot p'Bitek's *Song of Lawino*. The product of
modern education, Ocol has learned to despise everything African and
sees no value in the traditions of his people. When his illiterate wife,
Lawino, pleads with him to have more respect for the "ways of our people,"
showing him the futility of cutting oneself loose from the traditions of
one's ancestors, Ocol responds with ballistic arrogance.

Woman,
Shut up!
Pack your things
Go! . . .
What is Africa to me?
Blackness,
Deep, deep fathomless
Darkness; . . .
Mother, mother,
Why,
Why was I born
Black?[8]

But one can also catch a glimpse of the same self-hatred in the excesses reflected in the personal and social customs of the elite, including the wearing of wigs by judges at court sessions.[9] When one thinks about it, however, it is not clear whether such a practice is qualitatively different from the case of Bokassa sending the presidential jet to Paris to get dishes for his coronation, of Mobutu building his bush palace of Gbodalite with marble pillars imported from Italy, or of a village peasant willing to pay half of his per capita income to have a bottle of champagne, whose taste he finds disgusting, at his wedding. All the examples reflect varying degrees of "learning" that because Africa's own experience provides nothing of value, "to become civilized Africans they must cease to be Africans" by acquiring European habits and tastes (47). Edward Wilmot Blyden noted that since the educated African is taught that "all native institutions are, in their character, darkness and depravity, and in their effects only evil and evil continually," he comes to be marked by an "insatiable ambition for imitation of foreign ideas and foreign customs" (43). The irony, of course, is that since the educated African never becomes European, he is bound to wander in some kind of no man's land, neither comfortable with being African nor able to become European. Herein lies the cultural misery of the whole nationalist project.

8. Okot p'Bitek, *Song of Lawino and Song of Ocol* (London: Heinemann, 1994), 121, 125-26.

9. Peter Kanyandago, "The Role of Culture in Poverty Eradication," in *The Challenge of Eradicating Poverty in the World: An African Response*, ed. Deirdre Carabine and Martin O'Reilly, UMU Studies in Contemporary Africa, vol. 2 (Nkozi: Uganda Martyrs University, 1998), 119-52. See also Kanyandago, "The Church's Role," esp. 153.

Clientelism: On Recruiting "the Savage Backwoods"

The wider implications of the alienation from Africa's history and traditions are even more telling. For in terms of nation-state politics, it means that the "national" politics over which Africa's educated elite would come to preside will have to stand in a constant tension with the local history and social struggle of the masses, from which they had not only become alienated, but set out to overcome in the name of modernity and civilization.[10] The result has been that "as those years went by, the gap between the educated groups and the 'savage backwoods' grew ever wider, leaving the educated groups to insist vainly upon their relevance or founder in their futility" (48). In the end, "the competing interests of the 'elites,' as they began to be called by sociologists and others, took primacy over the combined interests of the 'masses'" (112). The national conflict, embodied in the rivalries for executive power between contending groups of elites, took primacy over the social conflict. To use an image that is almost literal: it was as if the aircraft of the state and its beneficiaries took off and flew high above the forests and savannahs, its passengers not even able to notice the roads below, or the goats, cabbages, and millet — the lifeline of the masses. Given this disconnect between the political and the social, it is perhaps not surprising that the nation-state has failed to achieve legitimacy in the eyes of the majority of African citizens, since it does not connect and has never connected to their aspirations and everyday struggles.

From another angle though, what Davidson helps us to see, and what will over time emerge as a distinctive feature of Africa's political history, is the new exploitative relationship that soon developed between the petty bourgeois nationalists on the one hand and the "savage backwoods" (or the masses) on the other. For as Davidson shows, lacking a footing within the social struggle, the nationalist ambitions of the educated elite, not surprisingly, began to sound vacuous and self-serving. Once the nationalists realized this, they "discovered" that they needed the masses and took steps to recruit them:

> Having formed their parties of national liberation, the educated elite
> had to chase their voters. And so they did, penetrating places never be-

10. See Okot p'Bitek's use of such metaphors as "smash," "uproot," "set ablaze," and "destroy" (p'Bitek, *Song of Lawino and Song of Ocol*, 126-29).

fore seen, crossing rivers never before encountered, confronting languages never before learned, and all this with the help of local enthusi-
asts *somehow recruited*. They thus made contact with these "masses"
quite often with only the assistance of aged Land Rovers able, with
their four-wheeled drive, to go where no other wheeled vehicles had
ever been, but only just able, and not seldom abandoned by the way.
(108, emphasis added.)

We need to dwell a little longer on the phrase "somehow recruited."
For African politics continues to reproduce this same phenomenon in
which the masses and their aspirations, instead of being a force that shapes
and determines the national debates, are only belatedly "discovered" and
only "somehow recruited" by the nationalist politics in an occasional, exploitative manner. Within this politics, the various local and particular social struggles — at once rejected and dismissed as "tribalism" or the "savage backwoods" — are now and again "discovered" to be political capital
and thus "somehow recruited" by the nationalists in their quest for political power. Yet except in those occasional meetings and "contact with the
masses" (in search of their votes), the elites never take seriously the aspirations of the masses. In fact, as Davidson notes in relation to the pre-
independence nationalists: "Having won their national struggle, they at
once lost all serious thought about the social struggle" (145).

Similarly today, during political campaigns, politicians "discover"
the masses and their needs. They accordingly return to the villages and
"recruit" the masses using all sorts of gifts and promises. But as soon as the
forced and often rigged election is over, the politicians return to their man-
sions in the city, where they soon forget the social struggle of the masses as
well as any promises they might have made during the campaigns. To repeat the metaphor above, the aircraft of the state and its beneficiaries
would continue to fly high above the forests and savannahs.

Thus Davidson is right: what develops out of this "recruitment" of the
masses is really "not the politics of tribalism, but something different and
more divisive. This [is] the politics of clientelism" (206).[11] For tribalism at
least supposes that each "tribe" recognize a common interest represented by

11. Paul Gifford, in *African Christianity: Its Public Role* (Bloomington: Indiana University Press, 1998), has also noted this aspect of Africa's politics (pp. 1-20) in reference to the
authoritative Jean-Francois Bayart, *The State in Africa: The Politics of the Belly* (New York:
Longman, 1993).

a common spokesman and that there is the possibility of tribal unity produced by the agreement between "tribal representatives." Clientelism, however, that "Tammany Hall approach," as Davidson calls it, makes such a unity impossible, since it advances not the interest of any particular group, community, or "tribe," but the selfish interests of a leader. In this way, clientelism is nothing but a "dogfight for the spoils of political power" in which "politicians at regional and national levels [gain] and [reproduce] the support of local leaders by allocating to them state resources over which [these politicians have] influence or control. Each attempt[s] to maximize this support and his access to resources in competition with rival politicians."[12] Thus, what is produced and reproduced is, to use the expression popularized by Jean-François Bayart, the "politics of the belly" (la politique du ventre) of the leaders — into which the masses are recruited.

That is why the politics of clientelism is in effect being recruited not only into a performance, but into a story and its underlying imagination. It is being recruited into a story of an Africa as a no-man's land that is just there waiting to be exploited; it is being recruited into the story of a nation as nothing more than a "national cake" waiting to be shared out; it is being recruited into a story of naked drive for each person's own selfish gain.

"Tribalism"

It is therefore against this background of a politics of elite power struggles, which only "somehow recruits" the involvement of the masses, that one begins to understand the true nature of "tribalism" and the ambiguous role "tribalism" plays within nation-state politics in Africa. For in spite of the rhetoric that the nation-state is the only hedge against "tribalism," it is, in fact, the nation-state that reproduces "tribalism" in order to provide its own self-justification as the pacifier of that space of civil society purportedly overrun by tribal conflicts. But this is where "tribalism" becomes a particular form of social imagination, in which the anti-tribalism rhetoric is just meant to stoke the fires of "tribalism." For by increasing the fear and subsequent specter of tribal rivalry and conflict, the nation-state presents itself as the only hope against the chaos. Thus, what Cavanaugh notes in

12. Chris Allen et al., Benin, the Congo, Burkina Faso (London: Pinter, 1989), 24, as quoted by Davidson, Black Man's Burden, 207.

relation to torture in Chile is true in great part of "tribalism" in Africa: "part of the fine art of social control, of generating states of normality, is creating the appearance of a prior chaos."[13] The goal is "to discipline an entire society into an aggregate of fearful and mutually distrustful individuals," or mutually distrustful "tribes" in this case, which can then be subjected to the state's discipline and written into its performance — thus "somehow recruited" into its politics.[14]

The point I am making can be made more explicit by drawing attention to Mahmood Mamdani's recent work on Rwanda, *When Victims Become Killers: Colonialism, Nativism, and the Genocide in Rwanda*.[15] In this work, Mamdani sheds light on the process through which "Tutsi" and "Hutu" became fixed as exclusive identities in Rwanda. These two identities, Mamdani argues, reflect differences that have been constructed or created through a political ideology over a people who "spoke the same language, lived on the same hills, and had more or less the same culture."[16] Standard scholarship on Rwanda is, in this aspect, misleading because is it tends to assume that "Tutsi" and "Hutu" are identities based on physical differences, and then proceeds to search for the origins of these differences. That is why, Mamdani argues, the two extreme tendencies within Rwandan historiography are equally misleading: The "no difference" point of view tries to explain the Hutu-Tutsi difference as the outcome of a social selection characteristic of privileged classes throughout history, while the "distinct difference" perspective stresses that the differences actually began with separate migrations into the African Great Lakes region. Both explanations, however, fail to focus on the role of political imagination, through which differences in Rwandan cultural and political history are constructed as particular political identities — first created within the Belgian colonial history and then reproduced through the post-independence nation-state.[17]

Mamdami is thus right to note that Hutu and Tutsi do not represent two "natural" identities, but two "political" identities[18] — and "two re-

13. Cavanaugh, *Torture and Eucharist: Theology, Politics and the Body of Christ* (Oxford: Blackwell, 1998), 55.

14. Cavanaugh, *Torture and Eucharist*, 15.

15. Mahmood Mamdani, *When Victims Become Killers: Colonialism, Nativism, and the Genocide in Rwanda* (Princeton: Princeton University Press, 2001).

16. Mamdani, *When Victims Become Killers*, 52.

17. Mamdani, *When Victims Become Killers*, 59.

18. Mamdani identifies three types of identities: economic identities (the conse-

cently constituted communities, one Hutu, the other Tutsi, united by their hatred and fear of each other and thirst for revenge. What is now going on is a civil war between elites, who are fighting for power."[19] That this is the case, Mamdani argues, is evident from the fact that there has not been one single and constant definition of "Hutu" and "Tutsi" throughout Rwandan history; rather, their meanings have shifted as a consequence of every major change in the institutional framework of the Rwandan state. In other words, different power players in Rwanda's postcolonial history have imagined Tutsi and Hutu differently.

Mamdani's argument is quite instructive in trying to understand the recent history not only of Rwanda, but also of much of Africa. For the constructions of "tribe" and "tribalism" throughout Africa have developed in the same way as the Rwandan labels of "Tutsi" and "Hutu" and have had the same disastrous effects of creating and maintaining a politics of mutual suspicion and violence. That there are, for example, cultural and linguistic differences between the Pokot in northeastern Uganda and the Baganda in the central region is not the crucial issue; what is crucial is that these differences have become political factors, determining inclusion or exclusion from the political process, and access or denial of political rights and privileges. The fact that these differences have become *political* differences is the work of political construction and the result of a particular social imagination. This, of course, is not to say that they become any less *real* because they are the work of political *imagination;* this would be to equate imagination with the fanciful. But, as I have noted elsewhere, imagination, at least the type we are talking about here, is not something we have in our minds, but a pattern of possibilities fostered within a community by the stories and correlative commitments that

---

quence of the history of development of the markets), cultural identities (the consequence of the history of development of communities that share a common language and meaning), and political identities. Whereas modern political theory views political identity as arising out of either culturally based or market-based identities, Mamdani argues, political identities need to be seen as identities that exist in their own right — the direct consequence of the history of state formation, and not of market or cultural formation. "If your inclusion or exclusion from a regime of rights or entitlements is based on your race or ethnicity, as defined by law, then this becomes a central defining fact for you the individual and your group. From this point of view, both race and ethnicity [and I should add 'tribe'] need to be understood as political — and not cultural, or even biological — identities" (Mamdani, *When Victims Become Killers*, 22).

19. Mamdani, *When Victims Become Killers*, 58-59.

make it what it is.[20] The imagination, as we noted in the previous chapter, is "the drama in which bodies are invested."

Accordingly, by understanding how cultural differences are imagined and thus become political differences and even identities, we can begin to appreciate the role "tribes" and "tribalism" play within nation-state politics in Africa. For to the extent that "tribes" are imagined as communities that are naturally pitted one against the other, they become an ever-effervescent political capital to be exploited by competing elite interests. To be sure, the imagination of African "tribes" and "tribalism" was itself part of the colonial politics of divide and rule. Within the colonial dispensation, fracturing natives into so many "tribes" was a strategy that helped to mitigate the tension between the colonizer and the natives. In this way, the colonial system was able to use the "more advanced" tribes as civilizing agents or colonial proxies (e.g., the Tutsi in Rwanda and the Baganda in Uganda). This situation made these more advanced tribes at once both the target of popular resistance in the cultural sphere and the source of popular resistance in the civic sphere; while the "more advanced" tribes would be the target of hatred by the "more backward" tribes, they were generally the ones who spearheaded the movement for independence, thus becoming the object of hatred and systematic marginalization by the colonial administration.

This is why I find Mamdani's work quite instructive: it confirms Davidson's observation that "tribalism" can only be understood within the peculiar chemistry of the African nation-state. It "'reflects, in significant part, pathological characteristics of the contemporary [African] state': of the postcolonial or, as some prefer to call it, the 'neocolonial' nation-state which came from decolonization" (12).

But Mamdani's work is also significant for my theological argument, which I can only outline here but will develop more fully later. To the extent that the church in Rwanda simply accepted the labels of "Hutu" and "Tutsi" as descriptions of stable identities, it also accepted without question the colonial and neocolonial imagination of "Rwanda." By not questioning this imagination, the church could not challenge "Tutsi" and "Hutu" as false identities, and accordingly could not initiate (or at least draw Rwandans into) an alternative imagination in which, given the regenerating power of the Resurrection, it makes no sense to claim one's pri-

---

20. See Katongole, "Mission and Social Formation," in *African Theology Today*, ed. Emmanuel Katongole (Scranton: University of Scranton Press, 2002), 141.

mary identity as Hutu or Tutsi. Failing to initiate any alternative imagination, the Christian churches in Rwanda reproduced the same tribalization and racialization of the Rwandan society as the colonial and neocolonial politics had. This is why, when it came to the final showdown of these politics, the fact that Rwanda was overwhelmingly Christian did not make any crucial difference — a fact confirmed by the church's overwhelming involvement in the genocide.[21]

Violence

Rwanda also helps to dispel a widespread misconception that the unrest and violence in Africa is a byproduct of "failed states." Rwanda represents the opposite: "a state — albeit criminal — that was all too successful in mobilizing along rigidly hierarchical lines from the top down, from the head of state and his ruling clique down to the last village major, making possible the slaughter, mostly with clubs and machetes, of hundreds of thousands in barely three months."[22]

It is therefore misleading to suggest that such civil strife is prevalent in Africa because African states are weak, lacking the means to contain the violence. For as Davidson notes, the violence "flourishe[s] less because the states [are] weak than because their organization into separatist nation-states [gives] full reign to elitist rivalries" (186). In other words, the form of "pathological violence" prevalent in Africa today is incomprehensible without the history of the nation-state we have outlined above. Any attempt to abstract it from this story projects the violence as a "tribal" or "ethnic" affair, some kind of bizarre cultural trait of Africans — just the

21. The chilling story of 16 year-old Josephine Uwamahoro (a name that literally means the "peaceful one") is as instructive as it is unnerving. Josephine lost all her family and all her friends in the massacre in the church at Nyamata, the same church in which she and her family had celebrated the Eucharist every Sunday with some of the would-be murderous militias. That she survived was a miracle. She was left for dead in a heap of festering bodies of her family and friends after her neck and legs were hacked. After the war was over, she tearfully whispered to a journalist: "We will never come back to this church . . . The angels have left us" (Hugh McCullum, *The Angels Have Left Us: The Rwanda Tragedy and the Churches* [Geneva: WCC Publications, 1995], xix).

22. Bill Berkeley, *The Graves Are Not Yet Full: Race, Tribe, and Power in the Heart of Africa* (New York: Basic Books, 2002), 15.

sort of thing Africans naturally do now and again. But this is misleading, for there are often no cultural, "ethnic," or "tribal" interests at stake. The phenomenon of widespread violence in postcolonial Africa — military coups, civil unrest, state repression, insecurity — must itself be placed in the narrative of the politics of competing elite interests and power struggles. The nation-state project in Africa has not questioned this story of colonial violence and dispossession, but has, in fact, neatly reproduced it, thereby becoming the modern embodiment of King Leopold's Ghost.

The Politics of "Mere Survival"

Another unfortunate effect of the story I have told, in addition to its culmination in an endless cycle of violence, has been the loss of myth in Africa. Modernity has given myth a negative association with superstition and fictitious legend — a way of knowing which is less than scientific and thus less true. Accordingly, the hope of the Enlightenment project and the culture of modernity was to rid the world of myth through scientific knowledge and rational justification. But this way of looking at myth is misleading, since myths are really not so much about "knowledge" as about "vision" — the vision of something larger than one's life. Myths therefore are stories of epic dimensions, stories that invite their hearers to participate and become part of a drama that extends beyond one's small world. So often social and religious ideals are, or at least involve, "myths" that invite us to imagine and draw us into adventures that are beyond our own interests, goals, or accomplishments. The Kingdom of God in Christianity, the *ummah* in Islam, and the common good in politics are such myths. Although these myths involve and often require personal commitment and sacrifice, they embody a *telos* that is more than the sum total of these individual contributions. Myths therefore are stories of transcendence and as such offer hope and purpose for one's life.

Perhaps this is the reason why myths are often accompanied by a libretto of rituals and symbols that concretely embody the hope of and mark one's initiation and participation into the transcendental reality of the myth. Thus, whether it is such sacred symbols as the Cross or the Ark of the Covenant, or more secular ones like the Asante golden stool, the English crown, or the American flag, these mythical symbols embody a transcendent power beyond their material existence. The difference between them, therefore, is not whether they stand for a spiritual power, but rather the *sort* of spiritual power they stand for and the type of adventure into which they draw their adherents. Different myths involve or constitute different types of politics. But this also means that politics — genuine politics — is grounded in and requires some transcendental vision or myth.

From this point of view, the African nation-state represents a very odd institution. Given the story I have told, nationalist politics in Africa does not promote the realization of any transcendental goal — a common good, for instance. The contrary is the case. Instead of being an adventure that requires the virtues of commitment, service, community building, and sacrifice in view of a transcendent goal, nation-state politics performs the same discouraging drumbeat that accentuates Africa's poverty, backwardness, and tribalism. This is not a transcendent vision that invests people in an adventure above and beyond themselves. Instead, it shrinks people's vision and expectations and encourages them to think small, to not expect success, to grab whatever they can and shut up. Our analysis has shown that this disparaging drumbeat is in fact connected to the story of denial — "nothing good out of Africa" — that grounds nation-state legitimacies. However, the expectations of failure and "nothing good" mean that life is only about "mere survival." It is within this context that one understands the sense of politics as "eating" into which now everyone is somehow recruited. "Corruption" is a misleading characterization of this widespread phenomenon in Africa, for such a term often reflects a mere failure to approximate the rational-legal model of authority — a shortcoming that might be addressed through the right ethical principles and legal safeguards.[23] What often passes as "corruption" in Africa, however,

---

23. This is, for example, the way Gifford reads the widespread phenomenon that is often characterized as "corruption." "Western societies," Gifford notes, "rest on what Weber described as 'rational-legal authority'; power has come to be exercised through legally defined structures, for a publicly acknowledged aim. Operating these structures are officials who in exercising the powers of office treat other individuals impersonally, according to criteria that the structures demand. . . . African states have failed even to approximate to this rational-legal mode of operation. They can best be described through another of Weber's authority types, that of patrimonialism. This, as the name implies, is based on the kind of authority a father has over his children. Here, those lower in the hierarchy are not subordinate officials with defined powers and functions of their own, but retainers whose position depends on a leader to whom they owe allegiance. The system is held together by loyalty or kinship ties rather than by a hierarchy of administrative grades and functions" (Gifford, *African Christianity: Its Public Role* [Bloomington: Indiana University Press, 1988], 5).

only makes sense within the peculiar history and chemistry of African modernity. For as our analysis here has shown, without legitimation by any transcendental dream or vision, nation-state politics soon turns into a dogfight of the ruling elite for the spoils of political power, or a means for "eating." Within this politics of the state as a "national cake" (to be shared), corruption is just another form of "eating." Even when, as happens every so often, the government answers to its own rhetoric of "anti-corruption" measures and sets up an anti-corruption unit, this too becomes simply another means of "eating." Those in charge of the "anti-corruption" committee are compensated with large stipends and allowances, simply to come up with a bogus report, which the government never does anything about. Thus the anti-corruption effort becomes just another vehicle of corruption.

The Sacrifice of Africa

This observation confirms that this politics of mere survival not only makes corruption a perpetual feature of African politics, but also underwrites despair and hopelessness for the majority of the population. Nobody has captured this sense of desperation in postcolonial Africa as well as Manthia Diawara in his autobiographical work, *In Search of Africa*.[24] In this work, Diawara, the distinguished professor of film and literature at New York University, returns to Guinea, which he left as a young boy and to which he has not returned in thirty-two years. In a conversation with the Guinean author William Sissane, Diawara suggests that the only way forward in Africa is to become modern and to develop a politics of interest that can harness technology for different purposes. "'That is why,' Diawara adds, 'we have to resume the independence and modernization project.'" "Cliches," Sissane responds. "So far in Guinea, Sékou Touré's revolution has created three types of mutants: the flatterers, the floaters, and the deflated."[25]

Sissane, I am afraid, is right. In fact, what he says of Guinea is true for much of Africa. In the terms of the above analysis, the flatterers are those who have access to the "national cake" — those who are currently eating.

24. Manthia Diawara, *In Search of Africa* (Cambridge: Harvard University Press, 1998).

25. Diawara, *In Search of Africa*, 50.

Accordingly, the "flatterers say anything the president wants to hear — that's why they become the ministers, general managers, and ambassadors in every regime."[26] The floaters, as the name suggests, are just hanging onto the hope that one day they will be able to make the right connection or contact. Thus they "barely survive between governments." Most probably they will fail and will therefore join the majority and ever-growing number of deflated Africans. Finally, the deflated

> constitute a race unto themselves. I don't mean the unemployed; a flatterer and a floater can both become unemployed. A deflated person is someone beyond good and evil, beyond feeling the blues of unemployment. He has reached a point where he says to himself, "they don't need me because I don't know how to do anything. They don't know me. They don't see me." African dictatorships are producing this kind of man everyday. He knows that no matter what he does, he will not get anywhere. The statistics are against him: he will die young. He sits down and looks to see if people see him. He sees from others' gazes that he is transparent. He does not know how to do anything, and he does not want to do anything.[27]

It is this widespread sense of desperation that is the final outworking of the story of the nation-state. Locating the nation-state "in the beginning" of Africa's inception into modernity confirms that politics is indeed about stories. But it also confirms that the assumption within this narrative of Africa as a dark continent inhabited by tribes that are always at war with each other *creates* the very reality of "tribalism" and constant warfare that it imagines. The assumption of Africa as a no-man's land whose resources are up for grabs creates politics in which plunder, corruption, exploitation — *la politique du ventre* — are characteristic. The story that "nothing good can come out of Africa" leads to the constant devaluation of African lives and disparagement of whatever is African.

And as Davidson notes, one of the effects of colonialism "was to destroy or downgrade Africa's own institutions and cultures, which had given Africa's peoples, or many of them, a confident sense of possessing *and exercising* real control over their own lives" (223). To the extent that this legacy of colonialism is embodied and perpetuated in the successor in-

26. Diawara, *In Search of Africa*, 50.
27. Diawara, *In Search of Africa*, 50-51.

stitution of the nation-state, "despair rots civil society, [and] the state becomes an enemy" and a very onerous burden — "the black man's burden," according to Davidson (9).

Given this narrative, it is misleading to characterize the African nation-state as dysfunctional, because it has been extraordinarily "successful" in the performance of its founding narrative into particular visions, patterns of life, expectations, and unique characters and political identities. Thus the most decisive critique of nation-state politics in Africa is not its failure to provide even basic services such as water, health care, infrastructure, and security — though this shortcoming is telling in itself. The real issue is not so much what the state has failed to do *for* African men and women, but what it is doing *to* them.

What it is doing to them is framing their lives within a *telos* of "nothing good here" (hopelessness) and thus shaping expectations of mere survival, while producing the very same hopelessness and desperation it assumes. This denial of any transcendental purpose desacralizes the lives of African men and women, making them cheap and easily disposable. Given the fight for political spoils that is the permanent feature of Africa's elite politics, it is not difficult to see how the masses become an easy prey for recruitment into whatever cause — tribalism, warfare, banditry — that advances the selfish interests of the elite. In the end, this widespread desperation underwritten by nation-state politics in Africa constitutes the ultimate wastage — indeed, the sacrifice of Africa.

How does one proceed, given this story of Africa's modernity? One conclusion is obvious. Since the realities of chaos, poverty, violence, and tribalism are wired within the very foundational imagination of modern Africa, a new future in Africa requires more than skills and technical adjustments to improve nation-state legitimacies and operations. It calls for new stories, a different foundational narrative or narratives that can give rise to new expectations and a new imaginative landscape within which a new future in Africa can take shape. This search for a new future in Africa, which is a search for a different starting point for politics in Africa, must become the subject of a fresh conversation in Christian social ethics. People like Thomas Sankara, the former revolutionary leader of Burkina Faso, and the late Cameroonian theologian Jean-Marc Éla are critical voices within this conversation, because their lives and work reflect the restless quest for a different starting point for politics in Africa that is able to generate a fresh investment (beyond "mere survival") of the dreams and bodies of African men and women. In Part II, by examining their lives and work, we will not only be able to depict the shape of the quest for new forms of politics in Africa; we will be able to explore *theoretically* the conditions of possibility for a new future in Africa, conditions that point to the church as a most uniquely suited community for the task of the social reimagination of Africa.

Daring to Invent the Future

CHAPTER 4

Daring to Invent the Future:
The Madness of Thomas Sankara

We must dare to invent the future.

Thomas Sankara, 1985

I will pour out my spirit on all the people. Your sons and daughters will prophesy; your old men will dream dreams. Your young men [and women] will see visions.

Joel 2:28

Thomas Sankara and the Burkina Faso Revolution

Thomas Isidore Sankara was born into a Catholic family in Yako in Upper Volta in 1949. After finishing his basic secondary school education in 1966, Sankara entered military school in Ouagadougou. He graduated and began his military career in 1969 at the age of nineteen. A year later, he was sent to Madagascar for officer training at Antsirabe, where he witnessed popular uprisings in 1971 and 1972. Returning to Upper Volta in 1972, he became commander of the Commando Training Center in Po. In September 1981, Sankara was appointed secretary of state for information in the military government but soon resigned in opposition to what he saw as the regime's "anti labor drift."

After Major Dr. Jean Baptist Ouedragogo, a member of Sankara's Communist Officer's Group, came to power through a coup, Sankara was named prime minister in January 1983, but was soon dismissed and placed under house arrest. His arrest sparked a popular uprising and military coup organized by Blaise Compaoré (another member of the Communist Officer's Group), who released Sankara and made him president on August 4, 1983, at the age of thirty-three.

A French colony until official independence in 1960, Upper Volta was (and still is) one of Africa's poorest countries. In 1981, the infant mortality rate was 208 for every 1,000 live births, the highest in the world; there was one doctor for every 50,000 people; 90 percent of Upper Volta's seven million people lived and toiled in the countryside, where drought and famine had plagued the country for many years. The average yearly income was $150.

In the next five years of his tenure, President Sankara carried out ambitious programs of land reform, anti-corruption measures, reforestation, education, and healthcare. The prices peasants received for basic food crops increased. The "head tax" was abolished, and compulsory labor performed for village chiefs was outlawed. The land was nationalized to guarantee peasants access to the soil and to the products of their labor. Basic health care services were made available to millions for the first time, and infant mortality fell dramatically, to 145 for every 1,000 live births by 1987.[1]

Other reforms in Sankara's revolution involved increased participation by the masses in political decision making as well as programs for women's empowerment. Sankara's government included a large number of women; they banned female genital mutilation, condemned polygamy, and promoted contraception. September 22 was declared a day of solidarity for men to do the chores traditionally reserved for women (go to the market, fetch water, prepare meals) in order to experience for themselves the conditions faced by women.

Even though some reforms were of a symbolic nature, they signaled a new direction for leadership in Africa. For example, when Sankara was appointed minister of state for education, he came to his first cabinet meeting on a bicycle. As president, he sold most of the government fleet of Mercedes-Benzes and made the Renault 5 (the cheapest car sold in Upper Volta at that time) the official service car of the ministers. As president he refused to use air-conditioning, because he said such a luxury was not

1. Thomas Sankara, *Thomas Sankara Speaks: The Burkina Faso Revolution*, trans. and ed. Samantha Anderson (New York: Pathfinder, 1988), iii.

available to anyone but a handful of his countrymen. When asked why he did not want his portrait hung in public places, as is the norm for other African leaders, Sankara said, "There are seven million Thomas Sankaras."

As Sankara's reforms became popular, especially among the youth and peasants, they alienated a small but powerful middle class of the local elite and foreign institutions like the IMF, the World Bank, and the French government, whose policies the revolution sought to reverse. Thus, on October 15, 1988, five years after he came to power, Blaise Campaoré, the man who helped Sankara come to power, assassinated him. Among the reasons he gave for the coup, Compaoré mentioned that Sankara jeopardized foreign relations with former colonial power France and with neighboring countries. Campaoré reversed nationalization and returned Upper Volta to the IMF fold.

Daring to Invent the Future: Vision, Revolutionary Madness, and Sacrifice

There are a number of elements that make Sankara's brief but impressive revolutionary leadership in Burkina Faso a good example of the type of social reimagination that is needed for a new future to take shape in Africa. Three stand out: intellectual clarity, revolutionary madness, and commitment and sacrifice.

Intellectual Clarity

Not unlike many African countries, Sankara's Upper Volta was built by a system of colonial and neocolonial exploitation. Sankara clearly understood this foundation of Upper Volta society, and was even able to trace the neocolonial exploitation to the story of plunder, which, we have noted, is hardwired into African modernity. It is this story of plunder at the heart of neocolonial politics, Sankara noted soon after coming to power, that made Upper Volta a "paradise for some and a hell for others":

> In essence, colonial society and neocolonial society differed not at all. The colonial administration was replaced by a neocolonial administration identical to it in every respect. The colonial army was replaced

by a neocolonial army with the same characteristics, the same functions, and the same role of safeguarding the interests of imperialism
and its national allies. The colonial school system was replaced by
neocolonial schools, which pursued the same goals of alienating our
children from our country and reproducing a society that would primarily serve the interests of imperialism and secondarily those of its
local lackeys and allies. . . . With the support and blessing of imperialism . . . [neocolonialists] set about organizing systematic *plunder* of
our country. . . . Driven solely by personal interest, they no longer hesitated at even the most dishonest means, engaging in massive corruption, embezzlement of public funds and properties, influence-
peddling and real estate speculation, and practicing favoritism and
nepotism.[2]

Moreover, Sankara was also aware that the confluence of colonial,
feudal, and neocolonial elite interests had particularly harsh effects for the
rural peasants and the youth, driven to a desperate existence of "mere survival." Talking about the wastage and desperation that characterized the
lives of the youth, he noted:

The peasant youth — who have the same attitudes as all youth, greater
sensitivity to social injustice, and great desire for progress, finally leave
the countryside in revolt, thus depriving it of its most dynamic elements. Their initial impulse drives these youth to the large urban centers . . . there they hope to find better paying jobs and to benefit from
the advantages of progress. The lack of jobs pushes them to idleness,
with all its characteristic vices. Finally, so as not to end up in prison,
they seek salvation by going abroad, where the most shameless humili-
ation and exploitation await them. But does Voltaic society leave them
any other choice?[3]

Sankara himself knew this life of desperation firsthand. A musician and
guitarist, he had tried, without much success, to make a living from his
skill as a guitarist playing in different bands in Ouagadougou.

If Sankara was clear about the underlying story that shaped modern
Upper Volta, he also clearly understood that reversing Upper Volta's social

2. Sankara, *Speaks*, 35, emphasis added.
3. Sankara, *Speaks*, 35.

history required not simply a few administrative adjustments, but a complete reversal, a "revolution" that would mobilize the liberation struggles of the peasants, women, youth, and masses to turn Upper Volta's systems upside down. During his years in military school, Sankara was introduced to the revolutionary ideals of the Cuban revolution. He became a great admirer of leaders like Castro and Che Guevara (Sankara would himself come to be referred to as the African Che), and he used their Marxist frame of social analysis to understand the inner workings and full effects of the neocolonial mechanisms of exploitation that shaped Upper Volta.[4]

Revolutionary Madness

Beyond serving as an interpretative lens, the revolutionary ideals of the Cuban revolution inspired the revolutionary praxis that characterized Sankara's leadership. Sankara understood the coup that brought him to power in 1983 as a "revolution," and as such to be about fundamental change (indeed, a "reversal") in Upper Volta's political, economic, and cultural systems. On a number of occasions, Sankara spoke about the courage that this task, which involved resisting the entrenched neocolonial structures, required. In a speech on the fourth anniversary of the revolution, he noted:

> You cannot carry out fundamental change without a certain amount of madness. In this case, it comes from non-conformity; the ability to turn your back on old formulas; the *courage* to invent the future. It took the madmen of yesterday for us to be able to act with extreme clarity today. I want to be one of those madmen. We must *dare* to invent the future.[5]

Indeed, for Sankara the whole project of seeking to "invent the future" was a form of madness. For instead of shaping the future according to predictable patterns of the past and realities of the present (the rational thing to do), inventing the future required reshaping the present according to a vision of a future yet to be born. Sankara, for example, rejected the no-

4. This is neither the time nor the opportunity to evaluate the implications of Sankara's Marxist legacy. We simply draw attention to the interpretative framework to highlight the conclusion that interpretative frameworks and clarity about both the challenge and task is essential for the search for a new future in Africa.

5. Sankara, *Speaks*, 144, emphasis added.

tion and inevitability of poverty and was one of the first proponents of the idea of "food security." In the five years of Sankara's leadership, through agricultural reforms and mobilization of the population, his country achieved food self-sufficiency, which shows that Sankara's "madness" was quite sane indeed. Inventing the future requires the audacity to live in the present with energy and visions drawn from the future.

This is what makes the task of inventing the future essentially one of imagination. As Sankara noted in an interview following his fourth-anniversary speech, "Yes, we must dare to reinvent the future . . . all that comes from man's imagination is realizable for man. I am convinced of that."[6] All Sankara's reforms must be placed in this project of social imagination, whose goal was to invent a free and prosperous Voltaic society.

What makes Sankara's revolutionary madness even more instructive for the argument of this book is that he understood that as necessary as the various structural and administrative reforms were, a far more determinative reform was needed: the rehabilitation of the self-image of the Upper Volta people from seeing themselves as subjugated and resigned to seeing themselves as capable of taking charge of their destiny. In a speech soon after he became president in 1983, Sankara noted, "I think the most important thing is to bring the people to a point where they have self-confidence, and understand that they can, at last . . . be the authors of their own well-being . . . And at the same time, have a sense of the price to be paid for that well-being."[7] To signal Upper Volta's new identity and new self-image, on the first anniversary of the revolution, he renamed the country Burkina Faso, "the land of the incorruptible."

Commitment and Sacrifice

Just as Sankara's revolution reveals the importance of courage and the role of the imagination in the task of inventing the future, the clarity, urgency, passion, and relentless commitment with which Sankara took on this challenge during the five years of his tenure as president offer us a clear glimpse of both the direction and exciting possibilities of this task.

The impact of Sankara's reforms was immediate and far-reaching.

6. Sankara, *Speaks*, 144.

7. As quoted by Demba Moussa Dembélé, "Sankara 20 Years Later: A Tribute to Integrity," http://www.pambazuka.org/en/category/features/51193.

His revolution proved to be an unprecedented experiment in indigenous economic, political, and social change, with the construction of infrastructure (dams, railways, schools, roads, etc.) through the intense mobilization of the masses powered by the principle of self-reliance. Millions of youth in Burkina Faso and elsewhere in Africa identified with Sankara's implacable opposition to both moral and political corruption and his willingness to speak out on behalf of the most oppressed people, as well as his revolutionary confidence. That is why the greatest impact of Sankara's revolution was the new sense of pride and confidence, and an emerging new identity that the Burkinabe people as well as others in Africa lived into during Sankara's time. This was recently confirmed by Basile L. Guissou, a former foreign minister in Sankara's government: "Back then we were afraid of nothing. Thomas was someone who believed strongly in what he said and was convinced of the value of his country. Even if we didn't have money or great mineral wealth, he believed that we could move our country forward."[8] Sankara's widow, Mariam Sankara, noted, "Thomas knew how to show his people that they could become dignified and proud through will power, courage, honesty and work. What remains above all of my husband is his integrity."[9]

These observations not only confirm the extent to which Sankara succeeded in his project of daring to invent the future; they confirm that the project of inventing the future in Africa is deeply connected to the specific gifts, charisma, and commitment of its leaders. Sankara not only totally identified with the revolutionary cause; he shaped it, directed it, and invited and mobilized others into its vision and possibilities. To this effect, Sankara was able to use not only his position as president, but his youthful charm, his gifts as an eloquent speaker, and his skills as a musician (he wrote the lyrics of the new national anthem himself) to advance the cause of his revolutionary madness. And he did so in a way that made it clear that the revolutionary cause was not about himself, but about the Burkinabe people, whose hopes and aspirations he sought to recast within a new identity and a vision of transformed society. For this cause, Sankara paid the ultimate price: his own life.

8. Howard French, "A Grisly Assassination That Will Not Stay Buried," *New York Times*, March 10, 1997.

9. Mathieu Bonkoungou, "Burkina Faso salutes 'Africa's Che' Thomas Sankara," October 17, 2007, http://uk.reuters.com/article/latestCrisis/idUKL1757771220071017.

That Sankara's revolutionary madness was able to accomplish so much within his brief tenure confirms that Africa needs revolutionaries like Thomas Sankara far more than technocrats. Africa needs leaders who are able to clearly understand its unique challenges as well as imagine new possibilities, who are mad enough to try to shape the present according to future possibilities, who have the courage to resist the pull of old formulas, who are selfless enough to mobilize and invite others into dreams beyond themselves, and who are willing to sacrifice for that revolutionary commitment. Such leaders stand in sharp contrast with the neocolonial elite of modern nation-state politics.

"He Expected Too Much": Sankara's Narrative Limitations

If Sankara's revolutionary madness exemplifies the possibilities of inventing the future in Africa and points to the type of leadership and gifts required for this task, it also raises questions. How are leaders like Sankara formed? What drives them? Where do they find their energy and focus? And how is the clarity of vision, courage, and madness essential to the task of inventing the future cultivated? How can such commitment and sacrifice be nurtured and sustained over time? One way to explore these questions is to examine some major *limitations* of Sankara's revolution, particularly the fact that most of Sankara's reforms have not been carried forth since his death.

The fact that Sankara's legacy has been almost totally forgotten may be due to the fact that Campaoré reversed most of Sankara's reforms soon after Sankara's assassination. I find the remarks of one Burkinabe peasant to the effect that Sankara "expected too much" as significant when exploring the limitations of Sankara's revolution. On learning of Sankara's death, the peasant noted:

> I wasn't surprised when he was killed — the Revolution took me by surprise but he didn't. He had bad men around him, people who just wanted to drive around in big cars. . . . [B]ecause of the revolution we know a little about the type of politicians we need. It taught us to work by ourselves and for ourselves. But Sankara wanted everything to happen too quickly — he expected too much.[10]

10. "Who Killed the Lion King?" *New Internationalist* 268 (June 1995), http://www
.newint.org/issue268/lionking.htm.

While such an observation may point to Sankara's impatience, it also points to the futility of trying to invent the future without the necessary elements of memory, community, and story.

Memory

Sankara had hoped that even after his death, the revolution would be carried forth by his supporters, especially the youth who were particularly inspired by his leadership. A week prior to his death, Sankara spoke to a gathering in Ougadougou commemorating the twentieth anniversary of the Cuban revolutionary Ernesto Che Guevara's assassination. He told his audience that while revolutionaries as individuals can be murdered, no one can kill ideas. Speaking specifically to the youth, he said:

> Fearless youth, thirst for your dignity; thirst for courage; thirst for ideas and the vitality that he symbolizes in Africa. . . . It is true you cannot kill ideas; ideas do not die. . . . If you kill Sankara, tomorrow there will be twenty more Sankaras.[11]

Initially Sankara's hope seemed to have been confirmed. The morning after his assassination, and for many days after, thousands of youth gathered at the site of his shallow grave in which his body and those of his murdered supporters had been hurriedly dumped. Many placed handwritten notes on Sankara's grave with messages such as, "We are all Sankara."[12] With time, however, the demonstrations died out.

As tragic as that may be, the fact that Sankara's memory could not be sustained — not even by the youth who had clearly caught Sankara's vision and revolutionary madness — shows that inventing the future requires more than catching the vision. It requires a sustained practice of memory that includes but is not limited to the telling of stories like Sankara's, a practice that itself requires a community committed to live by the same revolutionary madness.

For obvious reasons, Burkina Faso under Sankara's successor Campaoré, who did everything he could to erase Sankara's memory, could not be that community. Campaoré banned any gatherings and commemo-

11. Sankara, *Speaks*, 243.
12. Sankara, *Speaks*, v.

rations of Sankara's life, thereby leaving those who had caught Sankara's vision and madness without a possibility to become a community of memory, a community that would remember his story, and through such remembrance make present the spirit of Sankara's memory.

But the fact that Burkina Faso under Campaoré could not live with the memory of Sankara does in fact raise wider questions beyond Campaoré and Burkina Faso, such as whether the modern nation-state is able to live with the memory of a man like Sankara. Given the founding story of the African nation-state in the previous chapter, Sankara's memory is not only a challenge, but a threat. Since Sankara's story, particularly his assassination, shows his willingness to lay down his life for a new future, keeping his memory requires a community that knows something about self-sacrificing love. But the nation-state in Africa lives by the story of sacrificing the many — particularly the weak, the peasants, women, and the young — to advance the selfish interests of the elite few. One villager's assessment of Campaoré's regime confirms the story that drives nation-state politics:

> Politics here means who will give money. People who want to become ministers or deputies look to develop themselves first and the country after — they all know the Western way of life, they want everything easy. Politics is just a means of becoming rich and giving you a big car. And Blaise gives money to opposition groups so they will divide and, voilà, no opposition. Another Sankara simply couldn't arrive out of the current democratic landscape.[13]

Expecting this institution to honor the memory of someone like Sankara is clearly expecting too much.

Community

In many ways, Sankara's act of renaming Upper Volta Burkina Faso (the land of the upright) had deep symbolic and religious significance, particularly as it evoked the Old Testament and prophetic tradition of renaming as a mark of new identity and new story and relationship with God. It is not

---

13. "Who Killed the Lion King?"

clear that Sankara understood himself in this prophetic sense, although he did speak of the revolution in quasi-religious terms as the "total *reconversion* of the entire state machinery, with its laws, administration, courts, police, and army"[14] and as a "qualitative transformation of our minds."[15]

The tone and quasi-religious language through which Sankara came to characterize the goals of the revolution are quite telling. Sankara's parents had wanted him to become a Catholic priest; he ended up becoming a guitarist, military commander, and revolutionary leader. Nevertheless, that his vision and revolutionary madness came in the end to reflect prophetic and priestly undertones reveals the unique gifts a theological account and praxis can contribute to the search for a new future in Africa. In fact, behind Sankara's use of quasi-religious language and metaphors, one can detect a desperate search for a vision, a story, and language with which to shape and communicate his revolutionary ideals. He never fully found one.

Sankara, for instance, realized the need for communities that reflected the message of the revolution. To this end, he instituted nationwide committees for the defense of the revolution (CDRs). His hope was that these committees, operating at every level of society, would serve as the "yeast that must carry the revolution to all of our provinces and villages, into all public and private services, homes, and milieus."[16] In actual fact, however, the CDRs operated more as administrative tentacles and vigilante groups rather than incubators or exemplars of what a genuinely transformed new society might look like. In the absence of such exemplars, Sankara's message for "reconversion" and "transformation" was directed to the Burkinabe people at large — a community whose formative story was that of the nation-state. Expecting the nation-state to receive the call to "reconversion" and "transformation" was again expecting too much from an institution grounded in a story of selfish greed, power, and exploitation.

Story: Toward What?

If Sankara's dream was to build a new Burkinabe society, it was not exactly clear with what vision he hoped to build the new society. In many of his

14. Sankara, *Speaks*, 42.
15. Sankara, *Speaks*, 239.
16. Sankara, *Speaks*, 43.

speeches, Sankara seems to be desperately searching for a hook, a story around which to mobilize the revolution. In his famous Political Orientation Speech, two months after he came to power, Sankara spoke about the goal of the revolution in terms of happiness and self-determination: "its ultimate goal is to build a new Voltaic society, in which the Voltaic citizen, motivated by revolutionary consciousness, will be the architect of his own happiness."[17] In later speeches Sankara would return to this goal of self-determination, and in his speech on the fourth anniversary of the revolution he offered the emerging self-confidence of the Burkinabe people as both an embryo and sign of that self-determination: "We must have a new people," Sankara declared:

> a people that has its own identity, knows what it wants and how to assert itself, and what will be necessary to reach the goals it has set for itself. . . . Our people after four years of the revolution are the embryo of this new people. The unprecedented decline of passive resignation among our people is a tangible sign of this.[18]

On numerous occasions Sankara made it clear that the struggle for self-determination required deep conviction:

> We must assimilate the main lesson of this experience. . . . The democratic and popular revolution needs a convinced people, not a conquered people — a people that is truly convinced, not submissive and passively enduring its destiny.[19]

Sankara was, of course, right. The revolution, the madness, to invent the future in Africa requires convinced people. The crucial question, however, is, "convinced of what?" The critical point we are making here is that the goals of happiness, self-determination, and even a new identity are in and of themselves empty notions. They require a clear *telos* — what kind of identity? Self-determination towards what? — to make them an exciting and compelling alternative to the desperation and deflation of neocolonial society. In other words, to expect that notions of "conviction," "identity," and "self-determination" would in themselves be suffi-

17. Sankara, *Speaks,* 47.
18. Sankara, *Speaks,* v-vi.
19. Sankara, *Speaks,* vi.

cient to mobilize people for the challenging task of social reimagination is to expect too much.

In the end, it is the lack of a clear *telos* and a compelling story to name that *telos* that made it possible for Sankara's revolutionary madness and its astounding accomplishments to run out of momentum and fade out not long after his assassination. Moreover, politics has essentially to do with stories, especially those founding stories of "in the beginning." By not having an explicit account of "in the beginning," Sankara's revolution was not able to engage fully the realities of memory and community, which could have nurtured and sustained its revolutionary madness beyond Sankara's lifetime.

The foregoing analysis points to the necessary interconnections between the notions of memory, community, and story in the search for a new future in Africa. Because these are also deeply theological notions, they increasingly point to gifts that Christianity might offer in the quest for a new future. They point to the church in Africa as uniquely positioned to bear both the gift and the task of inventing a new future in Africa. To make a more direct argument regarding the church's unique role in this quest, we need to briefly draw attention, by way of conclusion, to another revolutionary madman who was engaged in a similar search for a new future for his people — the prophet Joel in the Old Testament.

Conclusion: The Prophet Joel: Memory, Community, Gift

Almost twenty-five hundred years separate Joel and Sankara. Nevertheless, they seem to share many of the same challenges. For unlike Sankara's Upper Volta, Joel's Israel is a community in total destruction. The prophet uses different images and metaphors to depict the plight of his community: "a nation has invaded my land" (1:16); "the fires have devoured the pastures of the wilderness, and flames have burned all the trees" (1:19); "the fields are devastated" (1:9) "by locust and plague" (1:4).

Faced with national tragedy and devastation, the prophet Joel calls for a period of mourning and fasting: "wake up, you drunkards, and weep" (1:5); "be dismayed, you farmers; wail, you vinedressers" (1:11); "put on sackcloth and lament, you priests; wail, you ministers of the altar" (1:13). If the call to lament sounds like a an inadequate response to the national disaster that Joel and the Israelites are facing, it nevertheless represents an acknowledgment that the problem is not simply a technical problem that can be fixed with the application of techniques and formulas. The practice of lament involves a recognition that the problem has to do with "our ways" which have turned away from God's plans. Lament points to the need to "turn back to me [Yahweh] with your whole heart" — the need, to use Sankara's words, for "reconversion."

Particularly significant is the fact that for Joel reconversion is not simply a call for individual readjustment; it is first and foremost the practice of calling together a community, of gathering an assembly (Hebrew *kahar*, Greek *ecclesia*). And so twice Joel invites the priests to "sanctify a fast, call a solemn assembly" (1:14), "to gather the people . . . assemble the aged . . . the children, even the infants at the breast" (2:16).

The more one examines Joel's response, the more one realizes that the point of gathering the community is to collectively remember God's story, particularly the story of creation and God's journey with Israel. The point of gathering a community is to "return" so as to stand again within that story. Thus Joel cries out, "return to me with all your heart, with fasting, with weeping, and with mourning" (2:12).

By reconnecting to that story and standing *within* that story, the promise of a new future is given as the gift of fresh visions and the promise of new dreams, to be received not by just a few, but the entire community: "Then I will pour out my spirit on all the people. Your sons and daughters will prophesy; your old men will dream dreams. Your young men [and women] will see visions" (2:28).

We might add that for Joel the "seeing of visions" and "dreaming of dreams" is not an indulgent fantasy. Joel's visions and dreams are real and concrete promises of fleshly abundance reminiscent of the story of creation: "I am sending you grain, wine and oil, and you will be satisfied; and I will no more make you a mockery among the nations" (2:19). Moreover, the visions are not limited to human beings but involve a comprehensive restoration of the entire creation, including the land ("O soil[,] be glad" [2:21]), animals ("do not fear, your animals of the field, for the pastures of the wilderness are green; the tree bears its fruit, the fig tree and vine give their full yield" [2:22]), and all humankind ("O children of Zion, be glad and rejoice . . . the threshing floors shall be full of grain, the vats shall overflow with wine and oil" [2:23-24]).

I draw attention to the prophet Joel because he represents both the challenge and task of social imagination, engaged from within a particular story of "in the beginning." In this case, Joel represents the type of framework that informs the church's commitment to a new future in Africa. The commitment is first and foremost about a "return" and "rediscovery" of the story of God's creation, and to stand within that story so as to "receive" the fresh gifts of visions and dreams of a new future: Africa. This is why the church's political existence begins with and is sustained through the discipline of lament. For lament is at once about memory and the formation of a community of memory, a community that constantly remembers God's story of creation and lives out in revolutionary anticipation the promise of God's new creation. This, from the Christian point of view, is what the social reimagination of Africa (inventing the future) is about.

Not only is the church well suited for this task; it is uniquely gifted for it and called to it. For the church's very mission and identity is to be a community of conversion, a community that is constantly gathered not only to lament the social, cultural, economic, and political disintegration of Africa, but to remember and celebrate the story of creation, God's constant journey with God's people, and God's self-giving through his Son, the revolutionary messiah who was killed but is now risen, who promises a new future through the sending of the Spirit as the first installment of that new creation. In the absence of such a community of memory, it is hard to see how the vision, madness, courage, and sacrifice necessary for inventing the future in Africa can be borne over the long haul.

CHAPTER 5

"A Different World Right Here": Jean-Marc Éla and Reimagining the Church in Africa

*Called to confess Jesus Christ in a continent which tends to be-
come a veritable empire of hunger, perhaps we should rethink the
whole question of understanding and experiencing faith. Our reflection must begin with the concrete practices and alternatives
wherein the memory and resistance of our people have been articulated.*

Jean-Marc Éla, *My Faith as an African*

J.-M. Éla and the Challenge of
Christian Social Imagination in Africa

Born in 1936 in Ebolowa, Cameroon, Jean-Marc Éla was ordained as a
priest in 1964. He subsequently earned doctorate degrees in theology from
the University of Strasbourg, France (1969), and in sociology from the
Sorbonne in Paris (1978). A prolific writer, Éla published dozens of books,
the most popular being *Ma foi d'Africain* (*My Faith as an African*) and *Le
cri de l'homme* (*African Cry*). For fourteen years after his return from
France, Éla worked as a priest in the mountain communities of the Kirdi
population in northwestern Cameroon. It was during this time as a missionary among the Kirdi that he developed and articulated most of the reflections in *African Cry* and *My Faith as an African*.[1] It is important to

---

1. See Jean-Marc Éla, *My Faith as an African*, trans. John Pairman Brown and Susan

highlight this social and pastoral context because it shaped not only Éla's methodology, but the content of his theological reflection. It is this pastoral context from which he has "not had the time to step back . . . in order to pursue systematic research on the questions that have arisen out of my work with the peasants" (MF, xviii). Accordingly, both *My Faith as an African* and *African Cry* are collections of essays whose unsystematic, rambling, repetitive style makes them at once provocative yet difficult to summarize. The essays constitute a unique genre of theological reflection, which Éla refers to as "shade-tree theology," a theology which, "far from the libraries and the offices, develops among brothers and sisters searching shoulder to shoulder with unlettered peasants for the sense of the word of God in situations in which this word touches them" (AC, vi).

If (or perhaps precisely because) Éla was not able to step back from the pastoral context of the rural communities, he was able to see clearly both the glaring contradictions of the dominant presence of (Catholic) Christianity and the abject misery and marginalization of the peasants at the hand of the dominant political, economic, and ecclesiastical institutions. These contradictions serve as the basis of his reflection. Unlike the usual approaches that begin with a description of the reality and then proceed to see what insights or recommendations theology can throw upon the situation, because the way he sees and understands the situation is grounded in his pastoral praxis, the description of the situation is itself the theological task. From this point of view, much of what Éla tries to do in *My Faith as an African* and *African Cry* is to redescribe theologically the reality of African communities in a way that displays possibilities and limitations, the gifts and challenges, of the church in Cameroon.

This is why it is misleading to refer to Éla's work as "liberation theology."[2] No doubt, much of Éla's writing suggests such a designation. Not only does he use the language of liberation quite a bit; he shares the uncompromising, totally committed, often indignant style of writing that has come to characterize liberation theology. One also finds the traditional

---

Perry (Maryknoll, N.Y.: Orbis Books, 1988), hereafter MF; *African Cry*, trans. Robert R. Barr (Maryknoll, N.Y.: Orbis Books, 1986), hereafter AC. Most of my reflections on J.-M. Éla's theology come from these two sources.

2. Éla is often classified together with Englebert Mveng, S.J., F. Eboussi Boulaga, L. Magesa, and J. M. Waliggo as liberation theologians in sub-Saharan Africa. See, e.g., Paul Gifford, *African Christianity: Its Public Role* (Bloomington: Indiana University Press, 1998), 269-70, 333.

themes associated with liberation, including the biblical Exodus motif, the materialistic Marxist reading of history, and the focus on economic exploitation. Even so, the label "liberation theology" is a misleading characterization of Éla's work.[3] For if he employs these liberation themes and metaphors, his goal is not to call the church to adopt more adequate strategies and priorities (for instance, an option for the poor) to galvanize the disenfranchised Africans towards their liberation. Éla employs all these liberation motifs with a view of a more demanding task, namely, *rethinking* the whole edifice of Christian faith in Africa. It is this task that drives Éla's "shade-tree theology." As he notes, "Called to confess Jesus Christ in a continent which tends to become a veritable empire of hunger, perhaps we should rethink the whole question of understanding and experiencing faith. Our reflection must begin with the concrete practices and alternatives wherein the memory and resistance of our people have been articulated" (MF, xvii).

Perhaps a better way to make obvious what Éla is doing through his reflection is to highlight four interrelated aspects in the call to "rethink the whole question of understanding and experiencing faith." Doing so will not only capture the provocative urgency of Éla's work, but also show that Éla's theological work, both in pastoral praxis and in writing, serves the critical and urgent task that Sankara clearly articulated: inventing the future. Éla's work provides a concrete direction the task can take; even more important, it confirms how and why the church in Africa is a gift suited to this task, not simply through pastoral intervention or advocacy outreach, but as the determinative community or *polis* in which the task of inventing the future takes place.

---

3. As Bujo notes, Jean Marc Éla's theology cannot be reduced to theology of liberation as opposed to the so-called theology of inculturation. According to Bujo, Fr. Éla called for "an African theology that incorporates oral culture, myths, symbols, etc. into its method and into the proclamation of the Gospel. For our theologian it is evident that his inculturating effort cannot be undertaken without taking into account liberation in a holistic sense, i.e., one that takes into account cultural identity and the political and socio-economic dimensions . . . For Jean-Marc Éla, liberation and inculturation do not oppose each other. They ought to be placed in a relation of 'perichoresis' for an African theology that takes into account each and every person." See Bujo and Muya, *African Theology in the Twenty-First Century* (Nairobi: Pauline Publications Africa, 2003), 212.

"A Continent Which Tends to Remain a Veritable Empire of Hunger"

First, for Éla the urgent need to rethink Christian faith in Africa arises not so much out of a critical reading of Marxist philosophy or Western theology, but from what he called the "shock of the gospel in Africa." The shock, which Éla was to experience through his pastoral experience, was the realization that even though Africa is a deeply and massively Christian continent, it "tends to remain a veritable empire of hunger" (MF, xvii). In his writing, Éla captures various angles of this "shock" as he describes the frustration, the apparently meaningless existence, the extreme and paralyzing poverty, the violation of basic rights, the colonial and neocolonial violence, the multinational exploitation, as well as hunger experienced by the people in northern Cameroon. It is this "rough ground" that, according to Éla, provides the unique context and challenge for Christianity in Africa today: "our practice of Christian faith faces a major challenge from African men and women who agonize over where their next meal is coming from" (MF, 87).

The problem, Éla notes, does not arise out of the lack of commitment by rural populations, which can be easily addressed through moral and spiritual motivation. Rather, the problem has to do with a social system "which has not been restructured from the bottom up to respond to the social needs of the majority" (MF, 71). Elsewhere he notes, "Food shortages result not so much from natural calamities as from the policies of an economic model that is [totally] oriented toward the outside world and abandons the most important part of the population" (MF, 70). Similarly, the health, medical, and educational systems are set up in such a way that only an elite minority benefit. As a result, a gulf grows between the living standard of the comfortable minority of the "haves" and that of the disinherited majority of the "have-nots." He notes,

> We must be aware of health problems in a context where African leaders dream of matching the pomp and luxury of the "Élysée" in France, while their people are sinking in the misery of huts and make-shift housing. On national holidays barrels of champagne are drunk in African capitals while millions of families lack safe drinking water and are condemned to live with parasitic diseases that weaken their constitution and slow down agricultural development. (MF, 71)

This is the context that frames the church's existence and work in northern Cameroon, a context that is not radically different from other places in Africa. Within this context, the challenge that Christianity faces is very concrete:

> How can the African human being attain a condition that will enable him and her to escape misery and inequality, silence and oppression? If Christianity seeks to be anything more than an effort to swindle a mass of mystified blacks, the churches of Africa must all join to come to terms with this question.[4]

Given this background, one might imagine that Éla's response would be to call upon the church to engage in more advocacy to help improve the economic and political institutions, which itself would be a bold suggestion. This, however, is not the direction in which Éla's theology moves. Instead, he is primarily concerned with the church's own existence and ministry among the people who have become the victims of such a history. In other words, Éla's theological reflection is not so much directed toward fixing the national political and economic systems as it is directed against the church itself, its own self-understanding, history, and mission. Éla invites the church to rethink its social mission so as to embody an alternative, more hopeful history than is proffered through the nation-state. The challenge of the gospel, Éla notes, is one of "rethinking the whole question of understanding and experiencing faith" (MF, xvii). If for Sankara this task requires the courage to turn on old formulas, for Jean-Marc Éla this task requires nothing less than an honest and critical look at the current models of church and Christian practice in Africa.

The Church in Africa: Under Babylonian Captivity

At various places in his writing, Éla offers a scathing critique of a "moribund Constantinian Christianity" whose "false universality" has reduced the churches in Africa to a mere institutional and canonical rubble (AC, 111). He also refers to the situation of the church in Africa as a kind of Babylonian captivity. "Christianity in Africa," he writes,

---

4. Quoted by Dibussi Tande, "In Memoriam," *Scribbles:* http://www.dibussi.com/2008/12/in-memoriam-jeanmarc-ela-cameroons-liberation-theologian-is-dead.html.

has been made captive by Roman structures that are weighed down by an ecclesiastical mentality; by the sociological burden of a religion of the "other world"; by forms of piety and devotion of Christianity in decay; by the disguised apolitical stance of Western missionaries; by the massive apathy, irresponsibility, and intolerable greed of certain members of the clergy; by the disembodied spirituality of some indigenous lay people; and by the lack of awareness or infantilism of African religious trained in a European fashion. (MF, 154)

As is clear from the above quote, the brunt of Éla's criticism (to which he returns) is directed toward the forms of disembodied spirituality that the Christian churches in Africa tend to promote by focusing their mission on the salvation of souls, a situation he compares to the distribution of "visas to eternity" (AC, 31, 7). In another place, Éla chides what he calls the "sacramental consumption" model of the church, whereby the church operates as a kind of supermarket for spiritual and sacramental goods — benefits regarded as necessary for the salvation and health of souls (MF, 122). It is not that Éla thinks that the church should not understand itself in sacramental and spiritual terms. The issue is that "in Africa where domination, hunger, exploitation . . . form an integral part of the collective memory, one cannot shut Christianity up within the limits of a religion of the beyond" (AC, 38). The root of the problem is that Christianity in Africa has failed to become a *way of life*, but has remained a *spiritual* affair.

Éla notes the Western legacy by which the church in Africa is reduced to a spiritual sphere in which its institutional existence and "security is promised by the powers that be on condition it accepts the privatization and marginalization of the Christian faith" (AC, 52). Such a history, however, only succeeds in rendering the church apolitical, thereby reducing Christianity "to a relationship with the supernatural," a relationship that "wafts above the everyday . . . [with] no impact on social, economic, political, and cultural realities" (AC, 48, 91).[5]

5. As noted in chapter 1, this Western legacy is at home in the secularized West. Accordingly, Albert Nolan is right when he notes "the only need for salvation that was experienced by European Christians who benefited from capitalism and colonialism was the need to have their feelings of guilt removed. . . . They felt no need, and could not imagine how anyone could feel any need, to be saved from oppression, from excess of suffering, from powers of evil, from the system. All such matters were conveniently excluded from the arena

Thus, to the extent that it fails to question and supplant this Western history, the African church, just like African politics and economics, reproduces the same alienating stagnation and paralyzing confusion as the other neocolonial institutions. That is the reason why, Éla notes, the churches in Africa tend to lack creativity and initiative and are instead characterized by mimicry and smug conformism, a situation that means that even the "so-called young churches are born with symptoms of early senility" (AC, 108).

The crucial challenge therefore, according to Éla, is for the African churches to face this Western heritage and thus reinvent new styles of presence and activity different from Western-inspired models of disguised apolitical and dematerialized spirituality. Unless such a challenge is faced, the danger is that the church itself as well as its practices (such as the celebration of the Eucharist) will become "the locus of our daily alienation" (AC, 4).

It should be clear that Éla is not simply calling for the enculturation or Africanization of the church. A mere adoption or introduction of a few African elements and practices within worship or other church practices is not enough to reverse this alienation of an institution grounded in neocolonial imagination. In fact, without rethinking the entire structure of church life from the perspective of African history, the quest for enculturation (or Africanization, or indigenization) will simply turn into "a vast entertainment project, whose purpose is to distract the exploited masses from the struggles of the present" (AC, 129).

---

of religion and salvation by the device of calling them material and worldly problems. The gospel is only concerned with 'spiritual' matters like the struggle with guilt and forgiveness that takes place in the individual souls." A. Nolan, *God in South Africa: The Challenge of the Gospel* (Cape Town: David Philip, 1998), 108, cited by Roy Musasiwa, "The Quest for Identity in African Theology as Mission of Empowerment" (Ph.D. diss., University of Natal Pietermaritzburg, 2002), 313. Even then, I suspect that Éla would find Nolan's attempt to reconnect the spiritual and material in Christian theology problematic. For what Nolan succeeds in doing is underwriting a Christianity that is "useful" to the extent it is able to provide motivation and legitimacy to the struggle for liberation, democracy, and justice within the liberal political framework. The full extent of Éla's critical and constructive proposals, however, is to see Christianity as a determinative form of political engagement within which notions like liberation and justice might be completely redefined.

Reimagining the Church, Rethinking "the Whole Question of Understanding and Experiencing Faith"

The challenge facing African Christianity is therefore not simply one of Africanization, or one requiring "deeper evangelization," or one of devising new doctrines or more adequate methodologies and strategies for intervention. It is the challenge of confronting the history in which Africa has been cast and the need to overcome this history with a different history. The mission of the church in Africa, Éla notes, must be placed in the context of the search for another history. For Éla, however, the search for another history is not a search for another grand narrative of Africa, but a concrete praxis that involves everyday realities like food, security, vegetables, drinking water, housing — all of which must be placed within the context of a struggle for

> another society, another humanity, another system of production, another style of living together, both within the family and society as a whole. We must struggle against alienating forces and, at the same time, give back to people their responsibility for themselves and their bodies, teaching them to challenge anything that smacks of chance and destiny. (MF, 84)

Particularly significant is the fact that such a search for an alternative history is neither initiated by, nor grounded in, the politics of the nation-state and its ideologies (globalization, new world order, etc.), to which the church can contribute its social pronouncements or spiritual inspiration. We have already noted how, for Éla, these are the very ideologies whose top-down structure perpetuates patterns of alienation and dependency. Thus the search for an alternative history takes place at the grassroots in communities of faith and in the ordinary realities of everyday life.

The challenge therefore is whether the church in Africa is part of this everydayness and part of the search for an alternative history, another society, another humanity, another system of production, and another style of living together. For this to happen, Éla suggests, the church in Africa would have to reinvent itself: "In the churches of Africa, as Baba Simon, the barefoot missioner from Cameroon put it: 'The time has come to reinvent Christianity, so as to live it with our African soul'" (AC, 120).

If Sankara helped us to see that the task of social imagination is the task of inventing the future, what Jean-Marc Éla now makes clear is that the task to invent the future in Africa requires the church in Africa to reinvent itself. No doubt such a task requires courage, since it calls for a thorough revision of church theology and practice. As Éla notes,

> The church in Africa is faced with a serious choice. Swept up in the mutations of African society, it finds itself before two inexorable alternatives: slip away into anachronism and become a stranger to the real questions of today's Africa or else become prophetic and daring, but at a price of a revision of *all* its language, *all* of its forms, and *all* of its institutions, in order to assume the *African* human face. (AC, 134, emphasis added)

In other places, in a manner that reminds one of the prophet Joel, Éla also talks about the reinvention in terms of a gift, which we must receive or "allow ourselves to hear," a gift that is able to "release" a new energy, a new power, and a new story that can shape the lives of African Christians in patterns of hopeful engagement:

> We must allow ourselves to hear the challenge of the originality of the gospel . . . the essential thing is to take up the gospel in everyday life . . . Only at this price will the Christian message, instead of being hammered out in paralyzing routines or shriveled up in little enclaves, be an energy *released* for the transformation of Africa. (AC, 119, emphasis added)

It would be a mistake to read the reference above in a foundational way, as if Éla imagines something like the gospel in its purest form that only later comes to be applied to a particular local history. For Éla, there is no pure, abstract gospel. There is no way to speak of the gospel without reference to the particular social history that is shaped by, and in turn shapes, the gospel. "Gospel" simply means, according to Éla, the good news of God's revelation within a particular social history. That is why the challenge facing the church in Africa is at the same time the task of rediscovering

> the gospel as a decisive force in history's march to the fore. . . . [T]he Kingdom of God [manifests itself] whenever the new universe is under construction — not a new world in the sense of a world-beyond,

but in the sense of a different world right here, a world being gestated in the deeds of the everyday. (AC, 53)

Éla's call to "re-think Christianity" is therefore an attempt to recover the deep and inseparable link between revelation and history. This link is particularly developed in the essay "An African Reading of the Exodus," in which Éla shows how the "the social and temporal reality is the locus of God's intervention and revelation" (AC, 28-38). In the exodus, not only does God reveal himself in the midst of Israel's history of slavery, his revelation (as the "I am") also discloses a new history or future for Israel. Thus, Éla argues, revelation is not so much a doctrine but a promise, which inevitably assumes a historical and social form: "Revelation stirs up a community in exodus, whose mission is not only to live in expectation of the fulfillment of the promise, but also to promote the historical transformation of the world and of life" (AC, 35). That is why, in the end, there is no way that the history and truth of God's revelation can be known, let alone vindicated, apart from the communities that such revelation forms. Those communities ultimately become, to use an expression Éla himself does not use, "demonstration plots" of that gift and promise. Not only is there a dynamic and internal link between revelation and history; the church in its social and historical concreteness *is* the link.

The Church as Social Imagination: The Kingdom of God "Gestated within the Deeds of the Everyday"

If the task of inventing the future is for Jean-Marc Éla a search for an alternative history of Africa, this search is at the same time a quest for a different experience of the church in Africa. It is a search for a church in and through which Africans can begin to experience a new world not "in the sense of a world-beyond, but in the sense of a different world right here, a world being gestated in the deeds of the everyday" (AC, 53). The church must recover its essential material and social nature. For this reason, the quest is not for churches that are spiritual enclaves or "mere administrative provinces of Rome, but *authentic* churches . . . adequate to engage *every* value of humanity" (AC, 111, emphasis added). Elsewhere he even notes that Christians of Africa are searching for a church that will rediscover its evangelical identity by seeking not just salvation within the spiritual realm but "the salvation and total liberation of the person, of society and of the material universe" (MF, 123).

It should perhaps be noted that when Éla refers to the "church," he has in mind not so much the institutional church, but the church in its local "shade-tree" geographical concreteness, the communities of the followers of Jesus in a particular place (this is perhaps the reason why Éla often uses the plural "churches"). It is within such local congregations, involved in the daily struggles for life and survival, that one is able to "deal with down-to-earth questions, and get back to ground level where the Kingdom of God is built day by day" (MF, 146). But also, it is here within the grassroots communities of faith that an alternative history for Africa can begin to take shape as "well-defined commitments" (MF, 146).

We should also note that Éla's focus on the church as a local community is not just a pastoral strategy for the building or formation of small Christian communities (Base Christian Communities), a priority already recognized by many Catholic dioceses in Africa. For unless the underlying ecclesiology is questioned, small Christian communities can easily turn into nothing more than administrative outposts of an outdated spiritual or "sacramental-consumption model" of church. What Éla is searching for instead is concrete communities and a theological practice that can resist and overcome what he calls the "sociological burden of religion" through a recovery of the deep material and social nature of the gospel. To put it more crassly, Éla's vision of church is one of concrete local communities in which everyday realities — drawing water, planting cabbages, digging pit latrines, rearing chickens, and receiving immunization against cholera — are as much matters of Christian salvation as the celebration of the Eucharist, baptism, and anointing the sick.

When one puts it in this manner, then it becomes clear that even though he does not use the exact terminology, Éla is calling for the church to be a distinct "social imagination." For as Stanley Hauerwas has argued, the social imagination is not a mental faculty, "something we have in the mind, but a pattern of possibilities fostered within a community by the stories and correlative commitments that make it what it is."[6] And as Bill Cavanaugh reminded us in an earlier quotation, the social imagination is a concrete politics, "the condition of possibility for the organization and sig-

6. Stanley Hauerwas, *Against the Nations* (Notre Dame: University of Notre Dame Press, 1992), 12, 51-60.

nification of bodies in a society. The imagination is the drama in which bodies are invested."[7]

That is what Éla is calling for — the church to be the community, the place and practice through which a compelling story (the "why" and toward what), as well as the very form through which the bodies of Africans can be more determinatively invested than in the current dramas of nationalist politics, which underwrites poverty, tribalism, violence, and the desperation of mere survival.

But the reference to Hauerwas and Cavanaugh also shows that the "reinventing" of Christianity that Éla was calling for in the early 1980s resonates with the recent direction of Christian social ethics in the West. Éla's call for the church to overcome the "sociological burden of religion" resonates with John Milbank's argument for theology as social theory, and Éla's constructive reference to the church as an alternative history resonates with Hauerwas's views regarding the church as a community with a unique story and distinctive politics. Given these similarities, it might be helpful to make a brief digression through the work of Milbank and Hauerwas respectively to highlight the similarities. Such a digression will also highlight some of the methodological and conceptual shifts that make Éla's theology both fresh and radical (exemplifying the type of madness that Sankara referred to) and his call for the church to shape "a different world right here" even more compelling.

Beyond the Sociological Burden of Religion: The Church as Polis

John Milbank on the Pathos of Modern Theology

At the beginning of *Theology and Social Theory,* John Milbank offers an unmitigated indictment of modern theology. "The pathos of modern theology," he writes, "is its false humility."[8] By this indictment, Milbank

---

7. See Cavanaugh, *Torture and Eucharist: Theology, Politics and the Body of Christ* (Oxford: Blackwell, 1998), 57. Another source that I have found helpful in understanding the relation between politics and imagination is Benedict Anderson, *Imagined Communities* (London: Verso, 1983), 6-7; see chap. 2, n. 12.

8. John Milbank, *Theology and Social Theory: Beyond Secular Reason* (London: Blackwell, 1990), 1. All page references in this section, unless otherwise noted, refer to Milbank, *Theology and Social Theory.*

means that Christian ethics have allowed theology's "social contribution" to be shaped by the secular disciplines of political science, economics, and sociology. That, according to Milbank, has been a fatal mistake, for

> once theology surrenders its claim to be a meta-discourse, it cannot any longer articulate the word of the creator God. . . . If theology no longer seeks to position, qualify or criticize other discourses, then it is inevitable that these discourses will position theology. (1)

Part of the problem, as Milbank sees it, has to do with the way modern theology has assumed that there is a social reality that exists independently of any particular, historical vision of human life. And since theology has assumed itself to represent but one such particular view of human life, it is thought unable to provide an objective account of social reality. Instead, it is assumed that theological discussions not only must be adjusted to this social reality, but also must give veridical priority to the disciplines of political theory, economics, and sociology — disciplines that provide a scientific and "dispassionate analysis" of this social reality. As a result of this assumption, Milbank notes, "[t]heology has frequently sought to borrow from elsewhere a fundamental account of society or history, and then to see what theological insights will cohere with it" (381). Theology then builds on, or, to quote Arne Rasmusson, "is then added on to sociological analysis."[9]

Milbank's intention in drawing attention to this assumption is critical, namely, to show that there is no such thing as a fundamental account in the sense of a neutral, rational, and universal account of social reality. We never perceive reality directly. What we see depends on the language we use, the stories we tell, the practices we live with. Accordingly, social reality itself is historically constructed, partly through the very disciplines that study it.[10] Therefore, Milbank is able to show that the secular sphere as a domain had to be instituted, or *imagined,* both in theory and practice.

9. Arne Rasmusson, "Historicizing the Historicist: Ernst Troeltsch and Recent Mennonite Theology," in *The Wisdom of the Cross: Essays in Honor of John Howard Yoder,* ed. Stanley Hauerwas, Chris K. Huebner, Harry J. Huebner, and Mark Thiessen Nation (Grand Rapids: Eerdmans, 1999), 233.

10. For a detailed discussion on this claim by Ludwig Wittgenstein, Alasdair MacIntyre, Thomas Kuhn, and others, see Emmanuel Katongole, *Beyond Universal Reason: The Relation between Religion and Ethics in the Work of Stanley Hauerwas* (Notre Dame: University of Notre Dame Press, 2000), esp. 104-40.

"Once there was no secular," Milbank notes, and then he goes on to show how the emergence of this secular domain is closely related to the rise of the absolutist state (which was the forerunner of the modern nation-state) and the new conception of the secular sphere as the sphere of pure power, pure instrumentality (9). His point is that it is precisely by *imagining* politics as a sphere of pure power that the new discipline of political science is given an object to study.

By doing similar analyses of the disciplines of economics and sociology, Milbank is able to show that these disciplines are not only empirical disciplines, but are also carriers of political, moral, and theological understandings of reality. They represent the self-description of modernity and its main actor, the nation-state.[11] Accordingly, these disciplines — just like any other disciplines — do not, and in fact cannot, depict reality in a neutral way; they do not offer a "dispassionate analysis," but a contingent reading of reality, based on a particular story. Different stories *(mythoi)* give rise to different social realities. Social reality, therefore, does not render itself into neat sociological analysis; it can only be narrated. This is what, according to Milbank, makes the modern Enlightenment tradition particularly misleading: by setting up these disciplines as "objective," "scientific," and "neutral" analyses of reality, it obscures its own particular narrative and thus the *mythoi* that are the basis of the politics of the liberal nation-state.[12]

And so, once these disciplines have been shown to be carriers of particular political, moral, and social imaginations grounded in the story of the liberal nation-state, then theology cannot accord to them the priority it has tended to reserve for them. In fact, for theology to fail to question these disciplines and simply build on them is to betray its "account of the final causes at work in human history, on the basis of its own particular and historically specific faith" (381). In this task, Milbank notes, "theology can of course learn a lot from sociology," but cannot give sociology, or any other

11. Rasmusson, "Historicizing the Historicist," 233.

12. Max Weber's sociology, for example, "both enshrines and conceals a particular history, namely the emergence of Protestantism, liberal Protestantism, and the Enlightenment, and together with these the rise of the bureaucratic state and capitalist economics" (76-77). For this reason, Margareta Bertilsaon refers to sociology as the "theology of the secularized state." Cited by Arne Rasmusson, *The Church as Polis: From Political Theology to Theological Politics as Exemplified by Jürgen Moltmann and Stanley Hauerwas* (Notre Dame: University of Notre Dame Press, 1995), 240.

social discipline, a privileged position. Instead, theology is itself shown to be a social science — and even the queen of the sciences, according to Milbank:

> Talk of a "Christian sociology" or of "theology as social science" is not, therefore, as silly as talk of "Christian mathematics" . . . precisely because there can be no sociology in the sense of a universal "rational" account of the "social" character of all societies. (380-81)

It is very important to grasp the full force of Milbank's claim. For it means that the goal of theology as a Christian sociology is to "to tell again the Christian *mythos,* pronounce again the Christian *logos,* and call again for Christian *praxis* in a manner that restores their freshness and originality" (381). Even though Milbank's own characterization of this Christian *mythos* remains philosophically complex, the task of Christian sociology, as Milbank conceives it, is a very concrete task.[13] The Christian *logos,* he notes, is not a "theory," but essentially the *praxis* of a particular community. "Christian sociology is distinctive simply because it explicates, and adopts the vantage point of, a distinct society, the Church" (380-81). For Milbank, therefore, there can be talk of theology as a social theory only because (or when) there is a distinctive form of Christian discourse and practice, itself grounded in the life of concrete communities called churches. Christian sociology is "not apologetic nor even an argument," but a narrative that requires, and is itself, the life of real historical churches:

> The theory, therefore, is first and foremost an *ecclesiology,* and only an account of other human societies to the extent that the Church defines itself in its practice, as in continuity and discontinuity with these societies. . . . But it should be noted that his possibility only becomes available if ecclesiology is rigorously concerned with the actual genesis of real historical churches, not simply with the imagination of an ecclesial ideal (380).

---

13. In a particularly interesting discussion, which is beyond the immediate scope of this section but which is related to the overall argument of our work, Milbank shows that what makes the Christian *mythos* compelling and thus capable of out-narrating the story of liberal competitiveness is the priority it gives to peace. For more on this, see Katongole, *Beyond Universal Reason,* 214-58.

If we are to characterize Christian sociology as a conversation, it is clear then that for Milbank the church's mythos offers a concrete "counter-history," "counter-ethics," and "counter-ontology" — counter, that is, to what Milbank describes as the nihilism and violence of modern liberal politics. For instance, "instead of a peace 'achieved' through the abandonment of the losers, the subordination of potential rivals and resistance to enemies, the church provides a genuine peace by its memory of all the victims, its equal concern for all its citizens and its self-exposed offering of reconciliation to enemies" (392).

Milbank's claim that Christian sociology "explicates and adopts the vantage point of a distinct society, the Church," does not entail an uncritical endorsement of church-as-is (381). Milbank is clear: a crucial and important part of the task of recovering theology as social theory, he notes, involves an "aspect of ecclesial self-critique" (381).[14]

Milbank's argument in *Theology and Social Theory* provides the type of theoretical framework that explains Éla's critical and often harsh revolt against the Babylonian captivity of the church. The church is held captive by its poverty of imagination, relegating it to the "spiritual realm," to a relationship with the supernatural that "wafts above the everyday." This, according to Éla, is the "sociological burden" which must be laid aside.

What makes Éla's call for laying aside this "sociological burden" of religion even more compelling is that he himself was a sociologist, and was able to see clearly the limitations of disciplines like sociology, politics, and economics. He was also a theologian, and he came to see what he was doing as a theologian as providing a more compelling and truthful description of society than he could through any other discipline. Moreover, as important as his advanced theological education was, only when he started to work among the Kirdis did he fully subsume both the sociological and theological disciplines to the service of what was now the more determinative pastoral work. His work as a priest became the most determinative form of sociology for him.

---

14. For Milbank, for example, "theology cannot shun the task of reflecting on 'the fate of the counter-kingdom' or on how, for the most part, the Church failed to bring about salvation, but instead ushered in the modern secular — at first liberal, and finally nihilistic — world" (381-82).

Stanley Hauerwas and the Politics of a Community called "Church"

If Milbank's work provides the sort of theoretical and methodological framework assumed by Jean-Marc Éla's critique of African Christianity, his constructive attempt to reinvent the church as concrete social imagination has many similarities with Hauerwas's vision of the church as a distinctive *polis*. Unlike Milbank, Hauerwas does not develop one overarching systematic argument to overcome the false humility of the church. Instead, Hauerwas's collections of essays deal with specific issues of a practical or theoretical nature.[15] The essays cover a wide range of topics, from handicapped children to sex, homosexuality, war, death in a family, and friendship. In this way, Hauerwas's theological reflection is very similar to Éla's shade-tree theology. In the cases of both Hauerwas and Éla, if the wide-ranging and practical orientation of their essays makes their work difficult to "systematize," it renders it interesting and even entertaining.[16]

There is also something therapeutic about Hauerwas's model of theological reflection that confirms that Christian ethical reflection need not proceed by way of a grand theory (say, of the state or politics), but in a practical, ad-hoc manner through narratives that help Christians locate their lives in the story of God's creation and redemption. For Hauerwas, Christian beliefs and convictions are so embedded in concrete practices and institutions that outside those practices they are meaningless. Accordingly, the only way to get to the truth of Christian convictions is through stories about the lives shaped by these convictions.

Behind this methodological commitment to narrative, the central conviction that drives Hauerwas's work is that Christian salvation is a very concrete and embodied experience. The gospel is the proclamation of God's saving truth. That truth is not merely spiritual; it is a story that

15. This is already a key difference that emerges between Hauerwas and Milbank, even as the substantive issues at the basis of their work converge. Thus, as he remains in fundamental agreement with Milbank's work, Hauerwas nevertheless expresses concerns about Milbank's style, particularly whether in his attempt to supply a counternarrative to that of liberalism Milbank does not reproduce exactly the violence of liberalism by trying to write such a grand narrative. Stanley Hauerwas, *Wilderness Wanderings: Probing Twentieth-Century Theology and Philosophy* (Boulder: Westview Press, 1997), 198.

16. For a helpful readers' guide, see Michael G. Cartwright, "Afterword: Stanley Hauerwas's Essays in Theological Ethics: A Reader's Guide," in *The Hauerwas Reader*, ed. John Berkman and Michael G. Cartwright (Durham: Duke University Press, 2001), 623-71.

shapes the material and social world in which Christians live. As Hauerwas puts it: "Any God who won't tell you what to do with your pots and pans and genitals isn't worth worshiping."[17] This is what makes Christian salvation a discipline of bodily practices and, by extension, politics. Salvation, he notes, is a matter of politics — "politics as defined by the gospel. The call to be part of the gospel is a joyful call to be adopted by an alien people, to join a countercultural phenomenon, a new *polis* called the church."[18]

This is how the church is central to Hauerwas's reflection. For it is the reality of the church as the community shaped by the story of God revealed in Scripture that reveals and confirms the truth of the Christian story, and also provides Christians with a way to interpret and engage the politics of any place in which they find themselves: "The gospel is a political gospel. Christians are engaged in politics, but it is a politics of the kingdom that reveals the insufficiency of all politics based on coercion and falsehood and finds the true source of power in servanthood rather than dominion."[19]

For Hauerwas the task of Christian social ethics is not one of simply providing theological recommendations in light of the given political or economic interpretation of reality. Rather, it is to uncover the political interpretation of the church in general and Christian convictions in particular. But as Rasmusson warns us, we should not imagine such Christian interpretation as though it were an interpretation "superimposed on 'bare reality' all can agree on."[20] All reality is "socially and historically constituted," dependent in great part on "the sort of community it is, the stories it tells . . . and the social practices it [concretely] lives."[21] The church in its concrete existence is *the* interpretation, which explains Hauerwas's often-cited but often-misunderstood claim: "The church does not have a social ethic. The church *is* a social ethic."[22]

---

17. Stanley Hauerwas, *The Truth About God: The Ten Commandments in Christian Life* (Nashville: Abingdon Press, 1999), 20.

18. Stanley Hauerwas, *Resident Aliens: Life in the Christian Colony* (Nashville: Abingdon Press, 1989), 30.

19. Stanley Hauerwas, *The Peaceable Kingdom* (Notre Dame: University of Notre Dame Press, 1983), 102.

20. Rasmusson, *Church as* Polis, 212.

21. Rasmusson, *Church as* Polis, 212-13.

22. Hauerwas, *Resident Aliens*, 43; *A Community of Character: Toward a Constructive Christian Social Ethic* (Notre Dame: University of Notre Dame Press, 1981), 40; and *Peaceable Kingdom*, 99.

This claim has a number of far-reaching implications. One immediate and relevant implication is methodological. Since Christian convictions cannot be isolated from their social context, but are themselves a socio-political vision, the task of Christian social ethics becomes essentially one of description — a way to display the reality of the church in its essentially social and historical existence. Hauerwas notes that "if theologians are going to contribute to reflection on the moral life in our particular situation, they will do so exactly to the extent they can capture the significance of the church for determining the nature and content of Christian ethical reflection."[23]

Another key implication connected to Hauerwas's claim for the church as a polis involves an attempt not only to recover the social-material vision of Christianity, but to redefine the meaning of politics itself. In this revision, politics is not simply about the struggle for power and the management of society, but also about the everyday and ordinary practices of life — potluck dinners, babies, sex, and caring for the sick, aged, or handicapped. The Kingdom of God, Hauerwas notes, is primarily present in such ordinary practices, which constitute the politics of the church. That is why the task of Christian ethics is to help Christians "see the significance of the everyday and the sacredness of the ordinary . . . those ordinary tasks are the most determinative *political* challenge to our culture."[24]

This shift in the understanding of politics from bureaucratic forms of management to concrete social engagements, from an exclusive focus on power and management to everyday practices, also involves a shift in the site of where the most interesting forms of politics happens, from power centers — New York, Yaounde, Kampala — to villages, grassroots communities, and congregations — in a word, to local places where Christians and others face the challenges of everyday life. That is why, Hauerwas notes,

> it is the task of those committed to the theological enterprise to develop the linguistic skills that can help congregations understand better the common but no less theologically significant activities which constitute their lives . . . e.g., pray, baptize, eat meals, rejoice at

23. Hauerwas, "Keeping Theological Ethics," 71.
24. Hauerwas, *Resident Aliens,* 424, as cited by Rasmusson, *Church as* Polis, 220.

the birth of a child, grieve at illness and death, re-roof church buildings, and so on.[25]

That is why the overall effect of Hauerwas's constructive proposals is to recast the church in its essentially local, social, and historical context and re-
position it as a unique politics.

There are a number of issues raised by Hauerwas's social ethics,
which we need not examine here. One immediate conclusion we do need
to highlight, however, is that the claim of church as a politics reframes the
discussion of Christian social responsibility in fresh ways. For once the
church has been shown to be a socio-political vision, then its relation to
nation-state politics cannot be simply one of affirmation or assistance. De-
pending on local historical circumstances, the relationship might be one of
affirmation, interruption, resistance, and even subversion. At any rate, one
should not read Hauerwas's claim that the church is "a community that
provides Christians with the 'space and time' necessary for developing
skills and habits with which to live their ordinary lives in a way that reflects
the story of God in Jesus Christ" in a way that suggests a replacement of
nation-state sovereignty with rule by the church. The "space" in question
may not even be a geographical space or territory, but a form of social existence (as in communities of "resident aliens") whose way of life opens up
and interrupts the hegemonic practices of the nation-state. Examples include gestures of peace interrupting constant arming and anticipation of
war, servanthood interrupting power and lordship, and charity and self-
sacrifice interrupting the politics of control and selfish ambition.

> Thus, within a world of violence and injustice Christians can take the
> risk of being forgiven and forgiving. They are able to break the circle of
> violence as they refuse to become part of those institutions of fear that
> promise safety by the destruction of others. As a result, some space,
> both psychological and physical, is created where we can be at rest
> from a world that knows not who is its king.[26]

This is precisely the "opening up" that Jean-Marc Éla has in mind when he
calls on the church to be the link between revelation and history in a way

25. Stanley Hauerwas, *Christian Existence Today: Essays on Church, World, and Living
In Between* (Durham: Duke University Press, 1994).

26. Hauerwas, *Against the Nations*, 117.

that opens within the space dominated by nation-state politics "a different world right here."

Our intention in drawing attention to the works of Milbank and Hauerwas has been to show the type of theoretical framework that Éla's theology assumes both in its critical and constructive dimensions. What this excursus has confirmed, moreover, is Éla's conviction not only that the church is in the position to undertake the task of inventing the future in Africa, but that it has both a mission and duty to do so. Specifically, for the church in Africa to undertake this task, it must reinvent itself beyond the false humility of reticence that locates its identity in the "spiritual" domain to become the dynamic link between history and revelation. For the church to invent the future in Africa, it must lay aside the "sociological burden of religion" in order to rediscover its fleshed-out, historical, and social embodiment, and its identity as a form of politics within the realities of everyday life.

This conclusion raises a number of questions. How exactly is the church in Africa able to reinvent itself in order to proclaim and become a demonstration plot of a "different world right here"? What does such a church look like? What are its essential characteristics and marks? With what stories does it live? What examples? What stories, skills, posture, gestures, and tactics does such a church need to engage other powers (e.g., nation-state politics and economics) that claim absolute sovereignty and control? These very significant and practical questions need more practical displays than theoretical arguments, which is the task of part III of this book. Before we move on this task, however, and by way of transition, we need to address some remaining theoretical questions about Jean-Marc Éla's "different world right here." In particular, we need to ask: right where? Where exactly is the location from which a new future in Africa is imagined and invented?

Two related facts from Éla's own biography may help answer these crucial questions. First, the son of a middle-class family in southern Cameroon, Éla claims that he first began to think of theology as a discipline that should be concerned with the local needs of believers while he was studying philosophy and theology in France at the University of Strasbourg in the 1960s. However, it was during his fourteen-year experience as a missionary working among the Kirdi of northwestern Cameroon that he developed and articulated most of the arguments in *African Cry* and *My Faith as an African*. This is a very significant observation. For if his status as the son of a middle-class family in southern Cameroon and as a priest and a scholar with Ph.D.s from two of the leading institutions in Europe prepared Éla for upward mobility, his relocation to rural northwestern Cameroon brought him face to face with what he calls the "shock" of the gospel in Africa, and renewed his appreciation for the opportunities of the church in Africa. In other words, it was his relocation to the rural margins that allowed him to see the urgency of the task of inventing the future, which cannot necessarily occur from so-called power centers.

This is related to another significant observation from Éla's own life. A vocal critic of both ecclesiastical and political institutions, Éla was despised by the government and marginalized by his own Catholic Church. He went into voluntary exile in Canada after the assassination of fellow Cameroonian priest and social critic Englebert Mveng in 1995. Éla stayed in exile, teaching at the University of Laval in Montreal until his death on December 26, 2008.

However, even before he went into voluntary exile, while still in Cameroon, Éla taught at the University of Yaounde and at the Faculté Protestante, but not at Yaounde's Catholic University. He was in Rome at the time of the 1994 Synod of Bishops for Africa, not as part of the official Cameroon delegation, but invited by an alternative group. When a reporter inquired why he was so marginalized, one church official suggested that Éla was just writing for the West, and that what he wrote had no bearing on the life of people in the villages. Another official suggested that Éla was a sociologist and not a theologian! But if Éla was marginalized by the powerful institutions of church and state, as these indications show, the "small people of God" in Cameroon (as one reporter called them) regarded him as both a prophet and hero, and it was they who received his body back from Canada and attended his funeral in Abang, near his native village, where he was declared an "ancestor," a title reserved for the most influential and highly respected leaders of the clan.

To the extent that Jean-Marc Éla's life illuminates the challenge and possibilities of inventing the future in Africa, it also confirms that for the church in Africa to engage this critical task, it has to be willing to live and minister out of a practical theology of relocation and marginality. The search for a "different world right here" involves a physical and existential relocation to marginalized and overlooked places and communities. The search for "a different world right here" is the search for a new, dynamic presence and experience of church, particularly in the marginalized places in Africa. But marginality does not simply refer to physical geography; it also includes leaving behind the dominant story of power and violence that has shaped African social history. As we have seen, this story easily sacrifices the lives of the "small people of God" in the name of the big stories of modernity, progress, civilization, and African identity.

Marginality, therefore, is about imaginatively relocating away from such a story and its dominant performance in order to stand within a different foundational narrative — the story of God's own relocation (as Word Made Flesh) — and from within that story rediscover the small, often discarded gifts, tactics, and signs of a different order. These are the gifts of a "different world" — a world shaped by a different story and performance, a world which, rather than sacrificing the small people, offers them a new reason to live, and thus invests their bodies differently in the world, thereby transforming their daily world of cabbages, goats, simsim, music, love, pain, suffering, and death into a sacred reality and the holy ground of God's saving work. Such a world does not have to exist as its own self-sufficient empire or on its own territory; it may open up in the "wild spaces," that is, in the cracks of the dominant performance of nation-state politics.[27]

This is the world revealed by the lives of people like Bishop Paride Taban in the Sudan, Angelina Atyam in northern Uganda, and Maggy Barankitse in Burundi. Before we tell their stories in Part III, it may be helpful to take a brief intermission with Chinua Achebe's classic novel *Things Fall Apart*. This literary masterpiece not only nicely brings together the themes of story, imagination, violence, and politics that are at the heart of this study; it concludes Part II of our argument by highlighting the elements of story, church, and a practical theology of relocation, which are essential to the task of shaping a new future in Africa.

27. For more on my use of "wild spaces," which I borrow from Sallie McFague, see Katongole, *A Future for Africa: Critical Essays in Christian Social Imagination* (Scranton: University of Scranton Press, 2005), 109-14.

CHAPTER 6

Things Fall Apart:
Christianity, Power, Violence, and Marginality

He was short and slight of build, and always seemed to be in great haste. His feet were short and broad, and when he stood or walked his heels came together and his feet opened outwards as if they had quarreled and meant to go in different directions. Such was the excessive energy bottled up in Enoch's small body that it was always erupting in quarrels and fights.

Chinua Achebe, Things Fall Apart

The story of Chinua Achebe's *Things Fall Apart* is familiar to many. Set in Umuofia, a collection of nine villages on the lower Niger, the plot of *Things Fall Apart* revolves around a man named Okonkwo. Although Okonkwo's father had earned no titles in the tribe, Okonkwo has risen to a highly regarded position in his society, showing himself to be skilled in battle and earning several titles. He is also a champion wrestler. He has taken three wives, has several children, and has built substantial wealth through his farming of yams, the staple crop of his village. He is a very successful man. Because of his great esteem in the village, Okonkwo is selected by the elders to be the guardian of Ikemefuna, a boy taken prisoner by the tribe as a peace settlement between two villages. Ikemefuna is to stay with Okonkwo until the oracle instructs the elders on what to do with the boy. And so, for three years, as the boy lives with Okonkwo's family, they grow fond of him; he even considers Okonkwo his father. Then the oracle decrees the boy must be killed. The oldest man in the village warns Okonkwo to have nothing to do with the murder because it would be like killing his own child. However, fearful of being perceived as softhearted and weak, Okonkwo participates in the killing of the boy despite the warning from the elder.

Shortly after Ikemefuna's death, things begin to go wrong for Okonkwo. When he accidentally kills someone at a funeral ceremony, he and his family are sent into exile for seven years. While Okonkwo is away in exile, white men begin coming to Umuofia. They introduce Christianity and a new government. Okonkwo returns to his village after his exile to find it a changed place because of the presence of white men. He and other tribal leaders try to reclaim their hold on their native land by destroying a local Christian church. In return, the leader of the white government takes them prisoner and holds them for ransom for a short while, further humiliating and insulting the native leaders. The people of Umuofia finally gather for what could be a great uprising, and when some messengers of the white government try to stop their meeting, Okonkwo kills one of them. He realizes with despair that the people of Umuofia are not going to fight to protect themselves because they let the other messengers escape. All is lost for the Ibo tribe. Okonkwo returns home and hangs himself.

What stood out to me most when I first read *Things Fall Apart* in high school in 1976 was the theme of colonial disruption, which had led to the disintegration and eventual collapse of the traditions and way of life of Umuofia. As I read the book now, even though the theme of colonial disruption is still prominent, the theme that more clearly stands out is the power and violence that shape both the traditional life of Okonkwo's Umuofia as well as the colonial regime that seeks to "civilize" Umuofia.

Read through this lens, *Things Fall Apart* serves as an incisive social commentary, with Umuofia and Okonkwo as characters that depict the society formed by a definition of power as domination and invincibility. It becomes clear that a society (Umuofia) built on this definition of power and strength cannot but be drawn into an ongoing drama of violence in which not only the weak are sacrificed, but the "strong" themselves get consumed by their own violence. It is ironic that Okonkwo, who had always lived under a dominating vision of strength and power, ends his life by committing suicide, which in Umuofia is considered a sign of weakness — the very reality that Okonkwo hated and feared. But given the role of story in shaping assumptions, Okonkwo's suicide comes as no surprise.

That Okonkwo's life is shaped by a vision of power requires no elaborate argument. From the start of the book, Okonkwo is portrayed as the "greatest wrestler," and throughout the story his ambition is to be the greatest warrior. He has no use for those he considers weak. He despises his father Unoka, who had won no titles but was just a "lazy" flute player skilled in the art of conversation. No doubt, part of Okonkwo's ambition for power derives from the stories of his upbringing. The stories told in Okonkwo's Umuofia are stories of ancestors when "men were real men." It is a culture that exalts warrior virtues and fears the show of affection, for affection is a sign of weakness — a weakness that children and women display, but not men. The ideal in Umuofia is to be a "real man."

From this angle, the stories told in Umuofia are not unique, in that stories of the quest for domination and invincibility are "masculine" stories of invasion and conquest, war and bloodshed. That is why patriarchy and the vision of power as domination go hand-in-hand, since at its core patriarchy reflects an inability to be at home with virtues like affection, gentleness, receptivity, conversation, hospitality, and rest, which are considered feminine.

Okonkwo embodies this unease to its extreme. He has three wives, but does not have anything that can be called a relationship with any of his wives. He rules over his family with an iron hand and an overbearing disposition. He constantly wishes Enzima were a boy and fails to love and accept her for the beautiful girl she is. When Okonkwo and his family are exiled in Okonkwo's mother's home village, in spite of the warm hospitality he is given, Okonkwo inwardly rejects the hospitality and does not feel at home.

Ironically, fear dominates the life of this man who is "the greatest warrior." This observation is telling, for like Okonkwo, those who live under the constant pressure to be "the most powerful," or "the strongest" (nation, society, church), live in constant fear of failure and of weakness. So, in Umuofia, both the weak and the strong lived in constant fear. Okwonkwo participates in the killing of the boy Ikemefuna precisely because of his fear of being considered weak. Okonkwo's fellow warriors also live in constant fear, even though they have learned to mask their fear in a show of manliness and they find ways to drown the fear through endless entertainments like wrestling, drinking palm wine, and sniffing tobacco. Okonkwo is also an exceedingly lonely man. Even though he has three wives, he sleeps alone. He, in fact, is unable to sleep most of the time — a prisoner in his own world of imagined power and invincibility.

And like any society built on this vision of power, in Umuofia the weak and innocent are readily sacrificed. Okonkwo himself kills Ikemefuna. Even though it is an offense to kill a kinsman in Umuofia, women and children are constantly beaten and abused; twins are abandoned — all in the name of seemingly high ideals such as "honoring the ancestors" and the "protection of the law of the land." But violence consumes not only the weak; in the end, violence destroys those who wield it. Okonkwo's violence increasingly turns inward, from the killing of Ikemefuna to the accidental killing of Ezedu's sixteen-year-old son when Okonkwo's gun inadvertently goes off during Ezedu's funeral, to Okonkwo's taking of his own life.

In fact, the more violence is associated with this story of power as domination and invincibility, the more one is able to see that *Things Fall Apart* is not merely nostalgic musings about the violent (colonial) disruption of a peaceful order (traditional society). The new order established by colonialism is no more or less violent than the traditional order it came to "civilize." In fact, the new order is nothing more than the old order turned upside down. That colonialism lives in a similar imagination as Umuofia is clear from the District Commissioner's constant reference to the queen as "the most powerful ruler in the world" (194), but also by the regime of violence he represents — depicted by the D.C.'s assistants' indiscriminate use of violence on the tribal chiefs. True, the new colonial order attempts to hide its violence from itself and justify it by ascribing to the new order such honorific titles as "civilization," "progress," or "democracy." But the irony of its violence is reflected in the title of the book the D.C. is thinking about writing: "The Pacification of the Primitive Tribes of the Lower Niger."

In the end, what Achebe depicts in *Things Fall Apart* is not one regime of violence replacing a peaceful tradition, or one peaceful colonial dispensation pacifying a violent primitive past, but a complex new form of violence emerging at the intersection of two forms of politics, each seeking to dominate the other. The imprisonment of the tribal chiefs, their violent abuse at the hands of the colonial agents, the decapitation of the head messenger by Okonkwo, and his subsequent suicide signal the meeting of these two stories of violence. To see the full extent of its performance as it works itself out in the social, cultural, political, and economic spheres of life in postcolonial Africa, one has to follow its progression through Achebe's *No Longer at Ease* and *A Man of the People,* the sequels to *Things Fall Apart.*[1]

In view of the above observations, *Things Fall Apart* raises two critical issues for social ethics in Africa. The first is about the imagination that drives modern nations. Achebe's depiction of Umuofia helps to extend our analysis in chapter three. For it seems to confirm that modern nation-states — not only superpowers like the United States, but all nations — are built on a vision of power as domination and invincibility. It seems that the desire of all nations is to be "the greatest," "the most successful," or "the most advanced" nation, which means that even small nations like Uganda are born with the soul of an empire. If this is the case, then the challenge for Africa is not simply to achieve sovereignty in order to determine its own destiny, but rather to interrupt this vision of power as domination with a different account of power and thus a different vision of society and politics.

The second critical issue, then, is whether this interruption is even possible. Can Christianity interrupt such violence? If so, how? *In Things Fall Apart,* the answer to this question is ambiguous. On the one hand, missionary Christianity could not interrupt the violence in Umuofia, as the church lived out of the same vision of power and became an extension of the colonial establishment. Missionary and colonialist arrived at the same time in Umuofia, and in many ways served the same goals, or at least supported each other's work. It was not easy to distinguish the District Commissioner from the missionary, as "the missionary often went to see his brother white man. There was nothing strange in that" (193). Moreover, if Umuofia had its Okonkwo, the new church had its own version of Okonkwo in the madly violent character of Enoch. In fact, the way Achebe describes Enoch is telling, and serves as a metaphor for the Christianity

---

1. *No Longer at Ease* is the story of Obi Okonkwo, Okonkwo's grandson who became a Christian and was sent by the missionaries abroad for studies. On returning to Umuofia, he discovers that everything in the village has changed; he neither can fit back into village life nor into the Western world of his education. In Obi, one can see the fate of many African Christians (noted in chapter 3) and those educated by the Western system; they must live in these two worlds with an acute sense of being "no longer at ease" and yet trying to make sense of these worlds by constantly shifting in between them. *A Man of the People* continues with the story of Obi's grandson who, as the product of missionary/colonial education, now enters the world of independence and post-independence politics characterized by tribalism, corruption, the abuse of power, and a looming civil war.

built on a vision of salvation as conquest and domination. Like Enoch, this version of Christianity is always erupting in quarrels:

> He was short and slight of build, and always seemed to be in great haste. His feet were short and broad, and when he stood or walked his heels came together and his feet opened outwards as if they had quarreled and meant to go in different directions. Such was the excessive energy bottled up in Enoch's small body that it was always erupting in quarrels and fights. (185-86)

Enoch's character is not only the mirror image of Okonkwo's; it also resembles that of Rev. Smith, the missionary "filled with wrath" who "danced a furious step" (185), and arrived in Umuofia prepared for war against pagan customs and ways of clan life. Fortunately, this is not the only type of Christianity that Umuofia experiences. For before Rev. Smith, they had Mr. Brown — the benign missionary who visits the people in the village and establishes friendships with some of the great men in the clan (179) whereby he learns a great deal about the customs and beliefs of the clan. He gradually wins the trust and the respect of some of the clan members and is presented with a gift of a carved elephant. He builds a school and a little hospital in Umuofia.

There is also Mr. Kiaga's church in Mbata that welcomes slaves and other social outcasts in their midst and rescues twins from the Evil Forest. All in all, Mr. Kiaga's church lives by and encourages gentleness, hospitality, affection, service, and even humility — the very same qualities Umuofia dismisses as women's characteristics or signs of weakness. But what is even more telling is the location of Mr. Kiaga's church — a location that seemed to have allowed it to cherish these qualities. Unlike Mr. Smith's church, Mr. Kiaga's church establishes its shrine at the margins of the village on a piece of land on the edge of the Evil Forest. Here on the outskirts of the fierce competition for domination and invincibility, Mr. Kiaga's church is able to nurture and sustain those values and qualities that Mr. Smith's church could not. In the end, the virtues of hospitality, care, and gentleness reflect a different form of politics, and thus offer an alternative to the competition for domination at the center of Umuofia's village life.

Located at the center of the village, both literally and imaginatively, Mr. Smith's church, on the other hand, is wedded to the vision of power that rules Umuofia, whether under the old regime of clan leadership or the new regime of Western colonialism, and it becomes another actor in the triangle of violence. Thus, it seeks to create its own territory through dogmatic self-assurance and its own power, thus in the end simply succeeding in forming its own patterns of fear and violence, as well as its own loneliness.

The implications for Christian social ethics in Africa are clear. To the extent that the church in Africa is grounded in a vision of power as domination and invincibility, it can only make the reality of violence and alienation in postcolonial Africa more intractable, and far more difficult to discern, let alone interrupt. For such a church cannot but view the sacrificing of the weak and innocent as sad but nevertheless inevitable collateral damage in the pursuit of so-called godly ideals like civilization, progress, nation-building, democracy, and even holiness. A church capable of inventing the future in Africa would not only have to draw from a different vision and story of power; its location, both imaginatively and concretely, would (like Mr. Kiaga's church) have to reflect this completely different account of power. It is this different account of power and politics that the Christian doctrine of incarnation names through the story of God who "dwelt among us" — thus providing a distinctive possibility and *telos* of what a new future in Africa might look like.

The discussion in this second part of the book highlights the need for a fresh start for politics in Africa. It points to the need for a grounding story to sustain the revolutionary madness that the invention of a new future in Africa calls for, and points to the church as a community that is uniquely called and gifted for this task. This last chapter confirms that these unique gifts of the church become visible and potent through relocation as an essential and primary ecclesiological posture. It is in fact through this mode of existence that the church in Africa is able to provide a compelling counter-narrative and interruption to the forms of modernity that readily sacrifice Africa. But this conclusion is still highly theoretical and speculative. That's why we need to turn, in the next part of the book, to some examples that display the practical and concrete possibilities of this new future that Christianity makes possible in Africa. We will do so using the stories of Bishop Paride Taban of the Sudan, Angelina Atyam of Uganda, and Maggy Barankitse of Burundi.

PART III

The Sacrifice of Africa

CHAPTER 7

Fighting Tribalism "in a Small Way":
Bishop Paride Taban and the Kuron Peace Village

He came to Jericho and intended to pass through the town. Now a man there named Zacchaeus, who was a chief tax collector and also a wealthy man, was seeking to see who Jesus was; but he could not see him because of the crowd, for he was short in stature. So he ran ahead and climbed a sycamore tree in order to see Jesus, who was about to pass that way. When he reached the place, Jesus looked up and said to him, "Zacchaeus, come down quickly, for today I must stay at your house."

Luke 19:1-5

We want to stop tribalism, but in a small way. You cannot do it all at once.

Paride Taban

The gospel story of Zacchaeus has many theological and practical implications for Christian social ethics in Africa. For even though Zacchaeus was a small man, everything around him happened in a big way. Zacchaeus lived in the big city of Jericho; he had a big government job as a tax collector. Needless to say, he was a wealthy man. Jesus, who was a big name in town, one day happened to come down to Jerusalem, the capital city, intending to pass through Jericho. A big crowd followed him, which prevented Zacchaeus from having a good view. But Zacchaeus, who was apparently a very smart

135

man, got this big and brilliant idea — he ran ahead of the big crowd and climbed a big sycamore tree. That way, he could have an unobstructed view of Jesus. Jesus was not impressed. When he came to the spot, he invited Zacchaeus to come down from the big tree, and invited himself to Zacchaeus's home. Zacchaeus hurriedly came down and took Jesus to his home.

There are many ways to read this story. One can read it as another example of how Jesus reached out to everyone, including sinners and tax collectors like Zacchaeus. But I also read this as a story of loss. In heeding Jesus' invitation to come down the sycamore tree, Zacchaeus had a lot to lose. He had to sacrifice the clear vision that being up on a tree provided and the "power" that that vantage point accorded him: the power of clear sight, the power of seeing without being seen — a panopticon — which is the real meaning of power, of touching without being touched. He now had to come down and join the messy, disorderly crowds and be seen and touched by them.

If Zacchaeus had to sacrifice a sense of power and distance, he also had a lot to gain: intimacy with Jesus and with the crowds, a new sense of community, a new sense of justice, a new sense of mission, and a new form of salvation as a concrete experience: "today salvation has come to this house" — not only to Zacchaeus's house, but to his entire town, for Zacchaeus declared: "half of my possessions I give to the poor."

The story of Zacchaeus has deep and far-reaching implications for the task of inventing the future in Africa because it is a story of relocation. As we noted at the end of the last chapter, daring to invent the future in Africa requires a church that is able to live out of a practical theology of relocation. This relocation is from the top to the bottom, from the city to the villages, from the universal to the local, from the center to the margins. This practical theology of relocation flies in the face of conventional wisdom, which assumes that the way to effect social change in Africa is from locations of power like the IMF, the World Bank, London, New York, Rome, Canterbury, Kampala. We tend to think that these places of power provide not only the right reading of what the problems of Africa are but also the right theories of economics or politics, and the right prognosis of what Africa needs in order to "end poverty," "eradicate tribalism," or "fight corruption."[1] And so

---

1. For a more detailed discussion of these theories see Katongole, "African Renaissance and Narrative Theology in Africa," *Journal of Theology for Southern Africa* 102 (1998): 29-40.

we are treated to one grand theory after another — incredible and magnificent promises of salvation for Africa through civilization, modernization, nation-building, globalization, privatization, a new world order, and the like. Relocation, on the other hand, points to forms of Christian social engagement that, having learned to suspect these old formulas, ground their praxis in the local, concrete, and particular communities of neglected villages. This is the story of Bishop Paride Taban and the Holy Trinity Peace Village of Kuron in southern Sudan.

Paride Taban

Taban was born in 1936 in Upari near Nimule in the Eastern Equatorial Province of Sudan, which was then still an Anglo-Egyptian colony.[2] When he was six, his family was moved to Katire. In this beautiful, mountainous, and thickly forested area of the Sudan, thirty-six miles from Torit, the British had established a timber industry with a sawmill. Taban's father was one of the workers at the sawmill, whose family, together with other families from other parts of the Sudan, was moved to Katire. That is where Taban grew up, in this small sawmill town, with families from different parts of the Sudan. Even though families spoke their tribal languages at home, the common language of the town was a vernacularized version of Arabic (pidgin Arabic or Juba Arabic). Taban's parents were not Christians. His father had a Muslim name, but he was not a practicing Muslim. Taban's mother was a traditionalist. The primary school in Katire went up to third grade, and so when Taban completed third grade, he was sent to another school — a mission school in Torit. It is here that he was taught the catechism and baptized into the Catholic faith.

Taban's decision to become a Catholic priest happened sort of backwards, when he was already in the seminary. At the end of fourth grade, when Taban was fourteen, he had to choose a school for his vocational training. But Taban did not know of any vocational schools or what career he wanted. However, two Catholic seminarians who were studying at

2. Unless otherwise stated, my reconstruction of Taban's story and work, including the direct quotations reproduced here, is based on personal interviews carried out during the Duke Center for Reconciliation Gatherings on the Great Lakes Initiative in Kampala (January 22-25, 2008) and in Bujumbura (January 12-16, 2009), hereafter Kampala 2008 and Bujumbura 2009 respectively.

Akoro Seminary had visited Taban's school and had left an impression on the young Taban, primarily because of their white cassocks and nice shoes. Taban had made a point of asking them where they went to school. They had mentioned Akoro seminary. He did not know that this was a school that trained priests, but had decided that he would go to Akoro seminary, because he liked the uniform. So, when at the end of the examination period the priest superior asked Taban about his career choice, whether he wanted to be a teacher or go to an agricultural school, Taban simply answered, "No, I would like to go to Akoro Seminary." Fortunately, after he joined the seminary and learned more about the church and the priesthood, he discovered that he actually wanted to become a priest. He went through the seminary program and was ordained a priest for the diocese of Torit in 1964. He was appointed auxiliary bishop of the archdiocese of Juba in 1980, and in 1983, he was appointed the bishop of the newly established diocese of Torit, a position he held until 2004.

Taban's ministry as a priest and a bishop were defined by war in Southern Sudan. In 1955, when Taban was nineteen years old, in the year Sudan gained independence from England and Egypt, civil war broke out between the north and south. The southerners, predominantly traditionalists and Christians, feared that the new nation would be dominated by the Islamic north. The southern army mutinied, and the resulting conflict, known as the First Sudanese Civil War, lasted for seventeen years until 1972, when a cessation of the north-south conflict was agreed upon under the terms of the Addis Ababa Agreement, following talks which were sponsored by the World Council of Churches. This led to a ten-year hiatus in the national conflict.

But in 1983, the year Taban was appointed bishop of Torit, civil war broke out again, following President Gaafar Nimeiry's decision to circumvent the Addis Ababa Agreement by creating a federated Sudan, including the south under a new Islamic Sharia law. Southern troops, led by the Sudan People's Liberation Army (SPLA), rebelled against the northern political offensive, and launched attacks in June 1983.

The war went on for more than twenty years, and devastated the entire social and political infrastructure of Southern Sudan. The bombings during the war displaced an estimated four million people (out of a total estimated population of thirty-two million), and killed an estimated two million people. It damaged the agricultural livelihood of the population, leading to food shortages, which resulted in starvation and malnutrition.

During this time of war, devastation, famine, and displacement,

Bishop Taban proved himself as a pastor to the people in Southern Sudan. Having been displaced by the fighting from his own diocese, he found himself homeless among other homeless people, feeding the hungry, healing the sick, comforting the dying, and giving courage to those frightened and fleeing from the war. Twice he was imprisoned, once for organizing food convoys to feed the hungry populations, in defiance of the rebel policy of using hunger and starvation as a way to force a town to surrender.

During this time he also traveled to many countries in the world, including the United States, Europe, and Australia, lobbying for peace for Southern Sudan. As part of this advocacy campaign, he co-founded the New Sudan Council of Churches (NSCC), an umbrella organization for Christian churches in Southern Sudan, which facilitated talks between the Southern rebels and the Khartoum government and helped negotiate the Comprehensive Peace Agreement (CPA), which was signed on January 9, 2005. The CPA granted Southern Sudan autonomy for six years, to be followed by a referendum in 2011 about independence.

While Taban's leadership and pastoral ministry during the war was impressive, what is even more impressive is that, just when the peace agreement he worked so hard to bring about was about to be signed, and with the prospects of a major role within the new government of Southern Sudan, Taban resigned his prestigious position as bishop of Torit and "retired" to one of the most remote parts of the Sudan to set up the Kuron Holy Trinity Peace Village.

Kuron Holy Trinity Peace Village

This is where Taban lives: not in a mansion but in a tent, not in a city but in the wilderness at the border of Ethiopia, among the most marginalized groups, where there is neither road nor school nor clinic, where there are no government services, or any other social services for that matter. It is here in Kapoeta East County in Eastern Equatoria, on a ten-square-kilometer piece of land, that Taban (the "mad and stubborn bishop," as President Omar al-Bashir once called him) started a Peace Village as a way to overcome tribalism.

"In my work as a priest," Taban notes, "I found that tribalism was very high. People live in their own groups, often devaluing and discriminating against people from other communities" (Bujumbura 2009). Taban experienced this tribalism for the first time when he moved from Katire to Torit, where his own people did not accept him because he did not speak the local language properly.

Even SPLA, which was fighting for the liberation and creation of a unified Southern Sudan, was not able to overcome tribalism. In fact, Taban notes, tribal factions and acrimony often pitted one group against another. The fact, for example, that the Dinka dominated the ranks of SPLA fighters was often the cause of internal friction and tribal divisions, which led to an attempted coup by a faction led by a Nuer commander. A number of people lost their lives in this power struggle.

The inspiration for the Kuron Peace Village came from Taban's experience of growing up in the sawmill town of Katire: "In the town, we knew no tribalism. We looked at each other, the families who were there, like one community, one family, and the common language was Arabic" (Bujumbura, 2009). The sense of harmonious existence and mutual respect was so much a part of the village life that even religious differences did not undermine this communion:

> As young children, sometimes a Catholic priest would come to the chapel, because there was no parish there — there was a chapel. Occasionally the priest would come to pray, and we joined the Catholic community to pray with them. And sometimes a Protestant pastor would come also to pray with the community of Protestants there. We joined them. And the time of the Muslims, when the Muslims had their occasions, we children would all go there and join them. In some ways, that is where a communism started. When we say communism it is Christians, but here also the Muslims who were really all united. That's an area where now, when we were having these workshops, I lived a life that is different from other parts of Africa (Bujumbura 2009).

Taban wanted to reproduce this kind of experience at Kuron. Another key inspiration behind Taban's Kuron Village was Neve Shalom (in Hebrew) or Wahat al-Salam ("oasis of peace" in Arabic), a cooperative village outside Jerusalem, where Israeli and Palestinian Jews, Christians, and Muslims live together in harmony. When Taban visited the Holy Land on a pilgrimage in 1993, he stayed for a day at Neve Shalom, which confirmed his determination to found a similar experiment in the Sudan as an alternative to war and tribalism.

Even as these experiments — Katire and Neve Shalom — offered concrete practical models, for Taban the key inspiration behind Kuron Peace Village is theological. It is the story of the Trinity: three persons in one God — Father, Son, and Holy Spirit — each unique, yet existing as one Godhead, as one indivisible union of harmonious differences. Thus he named the village The Holy Trinity Peace Village, whose logo of flame issuing from three logs represents not only the symbol of an African cooking fire, but the reality of the harmonious love of the three persons of the Trinity. Through the Holy Trinity Peace Village, Taban's hope is for Kuron to become an "oasis of peace," with people from different tribes and different religions — Muslims, Christians, and traditionalists — living together in harmony, "exploring their full potential to transform their lives and villages."[3]

A Flame

Like the image of the small flame in the middle of a big map of the Sudan, Taban's Holy Trinity Peace Village is a small yet radically ambitious project. That is the only way, Taban admits, to stop tribalism. "We want to stop tribalism, but in a small way. You cannot do it all at once." Taban's statement provides a counter-witness to the story of Thomas Sankara. For as we noted earlier, one of the shortcomings of Sankara's revolution was that he "wanted everything to happen at once." Like Sankara, who sought to invent the future in a way that involved a total transformation of the social, political, and economic institutions of life in Burkina Faso, Taban too hopes for nothing less than a total end to war and tribalism in the Sudan. However, unlike Sankara, Taban is content with small steps and a gradual journey towards this end. The difference between Sankara and Taban is not merely a difference in strategy; it is theological. Because the story of the Trinity informs Taban's vision, he knows that tribalism has in fact already been overcome by the love that is symbolized in the life of the Trinity. Accordingly, he is willing to live with the small signs and gradual journey into that which Christians believe is already realized. Where Taban's theological vision is able to shape his patience and hope in the journey, Sankara did not have this theological background to draw from, and so

3. The vision of Holy Trinity Peace Village states, "We aspire to build Oasis of Peace where communities live in full harmony exploring their full potential to transform their lives/their villages" (http://www.kuronvillage.net/vision.htm).

nothing short of an immediate victory could sustain his confidence in the cause of his struggle. Taban, however, can draw patience from how God deals with God's people throughout history, of which the reality of the incarnation is a decisive example. Accordingly, he has hope that through such experiments as Holy Trinity Peace Village, the flame of peaceful existence will be able to spread throughout Sudan and beyond.

But Taban also has the wisdom of his pastoral experience to draw from, which the young Sankara did not have, and speaks of other similar small flames that he has helped to ignite but which have now spread. For instance, as a young priest, he introduced the ox plough in his parish. People were not used to ox-plough technology; they cultivated with a simple hoe. When he started to use ox-plough technology, many objected that he was misusing the animals. But now, Taban notes, people who have seen the advantages of using the ox plough come to the parish from all over Southern Sudan to learn the technology.

Taban also opened the St. Bakhita Girls' School during the war in 1994 at Narus, near the border with Kenya. Today the school has an enrollment of over 1000 girls, and following this example, other schools for girls have since opened in the area. The peace village, Taban notes, "is like that. It will one day spread all over. Fire is started in a very small place, and it will burn and go different places. That is the meaning of this peace village" (Bujumbura 2009).

A Demonstration Plot

Hunger and famine have been very consistent problems in the Sudan, no doubt exacerbated by the civil war. This has not only resulted in starvation and malnutrition, but in a culture of begging for food. To overcome this, Taban has established a demonstration farm at the peace village to help people stabilize their food situation. From the farm, garden, and orchard at Kuron, people learn new farming methods that increase food production; they also cultivate new crops, which improve their daily diet. By adopting new crops and new farming methods like the ox plough, the communities not only have food surplus, but are less likely to engage in cattle rustling. This in turn reduces the conflicts in the communities as well as the frequency of famine and the begging for food.

Holy Trinity Peace Village also has a school and other educational programs that offer formal education for girls and boys and programs where adults learn how to read and write. It also has a clinic that runs a number of health care programs and training in sanitation and other basic health care skills. These and similar programs at Kuron confirm Holy Trinity Village's comprehensive vision of life that includes food security, education, health, and peaceful coexistence between people of different ethnic and religious backgrounds.

It has been five years since Taban founded the peace village at Kuron, so its full impact has yet to be realized. But, according to Taban's own assessment, Holy Trinity Village has already fulfilled one major objective: making the story of the incarnation real for the people of Kuron. That a bishop would come to live and work with a community of people at the extreme margins of society, a people that were completely abandoned by the official establishment, has given them a new sense of themselves. Today they say, "at least we know we are human beings" (Bujumbura 2009).

Thus the demonstration in Kuron is not simply a demonstration of peaceful coexistence, or of new farming skills and educational possibilities. It is the demonstration of a concrete, historical, and local salvation; it is the demonstration of the gospel (good news) that the story of Zacchaeus points to: "Today salvation has come to this house." This good news is the true meaning of the incarnation: "He dwelt among us." It is the very heart of Jesus' (and the church's) mission: "I have come that they may have life, and have it to the full" (John 10:10).

Relocation: An Ecclesiological Outline

That is why what Taban is doing in Kuron is not "development" or social work. What Taban is driving at — or better, what is driving Taban — is ecclesiology, a vision of what the church is called to be. That is why relocation is not simply about a change in geography or location but a theological category, an essential ecclesiological mark — indeed, the very mission of the church. The church exists for mission, to be a sign of God's saving presence among God's people. This presence is not abstract but is always concrete in a particular locality.

If relocation is the hallmark of the church everywhere, it is particularly significant for Africa. Relocation repositions the church within a different story and a different imagination of Africa. For if, as we saw in chapter 3, the underlying story that informs nation-state modalities in Africa is one that despises, rejects, and devalues Africa ("a continent without history"; "does anything good come out of Africa?"), this story consistently dismisses the villages as "backward," "primitive," "mere village life." A church that is grounded and lives out of the story of the incarnation presses into these very same discarded villages and backwaters in a way that redeems them and makes them sacred. This is the politics of the incarnation, the story of God who "dwells among us" and who invests local existence with an eternal significance.

Accordingly, if relocation names a commitment to the local, and especially the abandoned places, it names a unique type of "incarnational evangelism" characterized by the posture of self-emptying *(kenosis)* service out of which the church lives. This is the story and posture of God made concrete through the incarnation. It is this self-emptying attitude that Paul speaks about in the letter to Philippians:

> Your attitude must be the same as Christ's.
> Though he was in the form of God,
> he did not regard equality with God something to be grasped.
> Rather, he emptied himself
> taking the form of a slave, and taking on human appearance,
> he humbled himself, becoming obedient to death, death on a cross.
> (Phil. 2:5-8)

For the African church to live into this kind of self-emptying *kenosis* that Paul talks about, it has to sacrifice the elegance and magisterial authority that comes with distance. It has to come down within the confused mess of everydayness and risk becoming less and less churchly, so as to nurture and gestate, to use Éla's expression, "a different world right here," which is what the new future in Africa must be about.

Before he became a priest, Taban spent some time as a mechanic and a driver. When he was asked to become bishop, he is said to have noted the risk the pope was taking: "What will become of the church if they appoint a truck driver rather than a theologian as bishop?"[4] In view of his extraordinary story, it is now clear that the risk was worth taking. Taban's life exemplifies a vision of a church that loses itself in selfless service to God's

---

4. Mathew Haumann, *The Long Road to Peace* (Leominster, England: Gracewing, 2000), 31.

people. As a bishop, Taban admits, his calling is to serve not primarily the church, but God's people. In fact, when asked about what keeps him going in his day-to-day pastoral ministry, he responds, "As long as I keep my eyes fixed on God's people, and God's promises to the people, I can endure many hardships" (Kampala 2008). Pressed about what promises of God he has in mind, he cites the text of Jeremiah 29:11: "I know the plans I have for you, says the Lord, plans for your welfare, not for woe; plans to give you a future full of hope."

This promise of a new future is the end, or what theologians call the *telos* — the promise that drove Taban from his cathedral headquarters in Torit to live in a tent in the rural wilderness of Kuron. Taban knows that setting up or growing the church is not the goal of his ministry. The goal is to proclaim and work toward the realization of God's promise for a new future to the people within a particular location. Taban also knows that the new future that the prophet Jeremiah talks about is not a "spiritual" future, but a holistic future of food security where a past of hunger and starvation prevailed, and a future of peaceful coexistence where mutual suspicion and cattle raiding prevailed. Thus in the Trinity Peace Village, the Jie, Nyangaton, Kachipo, Toposa, Nuer, Dinka, and people from other tribes, along with Christians, Muslims and traditionalists, live and work together in cooperative harmony. What makes Kuron particularly provocative is that it is not a Catholic or Christian community, but a broader kind of "demonstration plot" of the new future made possible by the story of God of the incarnation. In other words, Holy Trinity Village confirms that the church is not the demonstration plot; the church's mission is rather to proclaim the good news of God's new future, to sow and nurture the seeds of the new creation, and to point to its signs. In doing so, the church somehow loses itself — that is, points less and less at itself, so that the full reality of God's new creation, which exists beyond the church, might blossom.

This is perhaps why Taban's own life and ministry reflects the same revolutionary madness as that of John the Baptist. In the wilderness of Kuron, Taban lives a simple lifestyle: he sleeps in a tent, lives on a vegetarian diet of fruits and vegetables, and drinks no caffeine — only water. He wakes up at 5:00 AM and after a round of physical exercises, he says morning prayer and Mass. After breakfast, he spends a few hours in the office organizing different activities before he goes out to spend the rest of the day in the village, either in the school teaching children and adults about topics that range from Bible stories to nutrition and sanitation, or in the farm working with oxen ploughs, or in the health clinic helping nurses in immunization of children, often interrupted by a call on his satellite phone. If Taban often feels overwhelmed by these everyday demands on his life and time, his clear sense that he is just a prophet of a reality bigger than himself keeps him grounded. Many times, he says, "I feel like a blind man, being guided by God" (Bujumbura 2009).

There is also something about Taban's former life as a truck driver that not only prepared him well but reveals an unconventional yet dynamic vision of the church that he represents. Taban still loves to drive and to talk about his adventures as a driver. And as Mathew Haumann notes, "He has got something of a rascal about him when he talks about his driving adventures."[5] This rascality points to a certain rebelliousness, which might remind us of what Thomas Sankara said: "You cannot carry out fundamental change without a certain amount of madness," which "comes from nonconformity, the ability to turn your back on old formulas, and the courage to invent the future."

But the adventures of Taban's driving also reveal the need for improvisation. Most of the places that Taban drives have no roads in the conventional sense of the word. His Land Cruiser wades through marshes and rivers and creates new paths through the bushes; a number of times Taban finds that a road or bridge has been washed away, or that a big tree has fallen in the middle of a path. He has to find a new path or improvise ways of crossing the river.

If Taban's life and work reveal something of his vision of church, then adventurous innovation and improvisation are at the heart of a church committed to a new future in Africa. These two characteristics are so much at the heart of Taban's Kuron peace village experiment that when asked for a vision of how he does it, he admits that he has no strategic plan, but only an invitation: "Come and see."

Conclusion

In many ways, Taban's life, practical theology of relocation, and leadership are reminiscent of the life and work of John Perkins of Mississippi, whose pioneering work in church-based Christian community development has

5. Haumann, *The Long Road to Peace*, 31.

spanned over four decades. In 1947, John Perkins moved from his home state of Mississippi following the fatal shooting of his brother by a white police officer. He settled in southern California, vowing never to return to Mississippi. However, after converting to Christianity in 1960, he, his wife Vera Mae, and their five children moved back to Mendenhall, Mississippi, where they established a community development ministry that included an interracial congregation (Voice of Calvary), a day-care center, youth programs, housing, a health center, and an adult education program. Whereas for John Perkins all these programs were part of his civil rights activism, the driving force behind all these programs was an ecclesiological vision, a vision of the church as an incarnational presence in broken neighborhoods. John Perkins articulates this practical ecclesiology around three Rs: Relocation, Reconciliation, and Redistribution (just distribution of economic opportunities).[6] John Perkins's work and theological vision of the three Rs has inspired a movement — the Christian Community Development Association (CCDA), which brings together various Christian ministries and associations committed to incarnational (and thus holistic) ministry within abandoned communities, particularly in America's inner cities.

I doubt Taban knows John Perkins. Neither does Taban articulate his vision around an explicit theology of relocation, but as our analysis has shown, Holy Trinity Peace Village is as much about incarnational evangelism as John Perkins's three Rs. One hopes that, like Perkins's work in Mississippi, Taban's Kuron experiment will be able to inspire a similar movement through Africa. For the Holy Trinity Peace Village embodies a Christian social ethics far more radical than any efforts at evangelization, relief and development, mediation, or advocacy could ever provide. Holy Trinity reveals the "different world right here" that Jean-Marc Éla desperately sought. If Éla was confident that the church was critical to this task of gestating a new future in Africa, Taban reveals the kind of church and practices through which this happens.

But Taban and the Kuron Holy Trinity Peace Village also confirm that for Christians, the story that informs, nurtures, and sustains the revolutionary madness that this task requires is not new at all. It is the familiar story of a God who became flesh and "dwelt among us."

---

6. For the story of John Perkins and the development of the three Rs see John Perkins, *Let Justice Roll Down* (Ventura, Calif.: Regal Books, 2006) and *With Justice for All* (Ventura, Calif.: Regal Books, 2007).

CHAPTER 8

The Sacrifice of Africa:
Angelina Atyam and the Politics of Forgiveness

One of the Pharisees asked Jesus to eat with him, and he went into the Pharisee's house and took his place at the table. And a woman in the city, who was a sinner, having learnt that he was eating in the Pharisee's house, brought an alabaster jar of ointment. She stood behind him at his feet, weeping, and began to bathe his feet with her tears and to dry them with her hair. Then she continued kissing his feet and anointing them with the ointment. Now when the Pharisee who had invited him saw it, he said to himself, "If this man were a prophet, he would have known who and what kind of woman this is who is touching him — that she is a sinner." Jesus said to him in reply, "Simon, I have something to say to you." "Tell me, teacher," he said. "A man had two debtors, one owed five hundred denarii, and the other fifty. When they could not pay, he canceled their debts for each of them. Now, which of them will love him more?" Simon said in reply, "The one, I suppose, whose larger debt was forgiven." "You have answered rightly," he said to him. "Do you see this woman? . . . Therefore, I tell you, her sins, her many sins, have been forgiven."

Luke 7:36-50

Every child is my child.

Concerned Parents Association motto

The Interruption at Bethany

The story of the anointing of Jesus' feet is a well-known story in the Gospels. All the Gospel writers tell the story, albeit with varying details. The story takes place at Bethany, a village outside Jerusalem. According to John, the event takes place at the home of Lazarus (John 12:1-8), Mark and Matthew place the event at the house of Simon the leper (Mark 14:3-9 and Matt. 26:6-13), while Luke identifies the host as Simon the Pharisee (Luke 7:36-50). According to John, it is Mary (presumably Martha's sister) who does the anointing, while Luke, Mark, and Matthew all refer to her simply as "a woman."

I find it particularly significant that all the Synoptic Gospels leave the woman nameless. Doing so heightens the sense of interruption resulting from the woman's presence and actions. She shows up uninvited at Jesus' dinner with his close friends. She obviously is not part of the group (Luke mentions that she was from the city — apparently a euphemism for the brothel). But her actions too are completely out of place, not the kind of actions one would expect at the dinner table: weeping and bathing Jesus' feet with her tears, wiping them with her hair, kissing them, anointing them. Everyone is uncomfortable except the one person who should know better, Jesus, who simply encourages them to "leave her alone."

In order to get a full sense of the impact of the interruption of the woman's actions at this dinner table, one must place it within a wider context. Whereas Luke does not specify the time when this event takes place, all the other evangelists note that it was right before the Passover (six days before the Passover, according to John; two days, according to Mark and Matthew). It is this timing of the woman's interruption and her anointing of Jesus' feet that make this a significant event for Christian social ethics in Africa. For with the Passover, Jesus' body is handed over to be tortured and eventually crucified.

Placed within this context just before the Passover, the anointing at Bethany represents a symbolic action that at once anticipates, and interrupts even before it happens, the abuse, battering, and sacrificing of Jesus' body. The anointing thus represents a different way of treating Jesus' body: it is a way of declaring Jesus' body sacred. That is why the anointing at Bethany represents a unique sacrifice (*sacer* [sacred] + *facere* [to make]). Accordingly, in the anointing at Bethany, the sacrificing (in the sense of wastage, abuse, battery) of Jesus' body is hereby anticipated, and interrupted, with a different sacrifice of anointing.

What makes this new sacrifice possible, and indeed accounts for its urgency as well as scandalous wastefulness, is the story of forgiveness and love. Thus, in response to the indignation of his host and others at the table, Jesus says: "Simon, I have something to tell you. You see this woman . . . her sins, her many sins, have been forgiven." John's version of the story makes a point of mentioning the fact that "the house was filled with the scent of the ointment" (John 12:3). The story of love and forgiveness now fills Simon's house with the fresh fragrance of extravagant intimacy, love, and service.

This story of love and forgiveness is also the story of Angelina Atyam, the co-founder of Concerned Parents Association, whose life and work has similarly interrupted the madness of war and suffering in northern Uganda.

Sacrificing Northern Uganda: Joseph Kony and LRA's Sovereignty of Terror

The situation in northern Uganda has been described by the United Nations as one of the worst and most neglected humanitarian crises.[1] For over twenty-two years, Joseph Kony and his guerilla fighters of "The Lord's Resistance Army (LRA) have been torturing, raping, murdering, and terrorizing the population in Northern Uganda. During this time, over 300,000 people have been killed, millions have been displaced from their homes, and over 26,000 children abducted and forced to serve as sex slaves and child soldiers. The abducted children are initiated into the LRA through forms of torture and abuse as a way to turn them into sadistic killers, but also to make it difficult for them to escape. They are raped; many are forced to kill their parents, family members, or their own friends who try to escape. Many children do not survive these atrocities. Those who survive are permanently scarred both physically and psychologically."[2] At

---

1. UN undersecretary for humanitarian affairs Jan Egeland, April 14, 2006, http://www.undispatch.com/archives/2006/04/humanitarian_cr.php.

2. Human Rights Watch, "The Scars of Death: Children Abducted by the LRA in Uganda" (New York, September 1997).

the height of the insurgency, to avoid being abducted, children became "night commuters." They trekked from their homes in the villages every evening and slept out in the open in Gulu and other towns, seeking refuge on verandas, at bus stations, and on church grounds before returning home again each morning.

A Sovereignty of Terror

The sheer brutality of the war in northern Uganda defies comprehension. The rebels burn villages, cut off lips and limbs, rape, and kill. A ruthless leader and self-proclaimed messenger of God, Kony claims he is fighting to liberate northern Uganda and to replace Museveni's government in Kampala with a government based on the Ten Commandments. Judged from this stated goal, Kony's rebellion is a tragic failure. The fighting in northern Uganda poses no serious threat to the government in Kampala, and Kony has turned against the very people he claims he is fighting to liberate.

That is why one needs to understand Kony's rebellion, and particularly Kony's use of terror, as a distinct form of social imagination and a bizarre form of politics. From this point of view, Kony has been, unfortunately, a great success: through a lethal mix of religious beliefs and quasi-military brutality, he has succeeded in establishing a unique form of political economy through new systems of coercion and exploitation. He has succeeded in establishing a sovereignty of terror, whereby control of the population, rather than territory, is the objective. As John Kiess notes:

> While a group such as the LRA would gladly take control of the state apparatus if given the chance, their form of sovereignty does not require it. *They* are able to control the local population through *their* own practices; *they* prevent people from moving at certain times of the day, *their* patterns of attacks send children night-commuting to regional centers, *their* actions exercise dominion over people's memory, *their* atrocities deeply control the dominant images of life that circulate in the north. For the LRA, the practice of the occult is not preparation for a future form or rule, it is a form of political rule now; a direct negotiation of authority and submission requiring no further translation into a more conventional political mode. . . . The LRA's actions

display not only a different imagination of sovereignty, but its material reality. Their kingdom has already come.[3]

Kiess's analysis of Kony's sovereignty of terror is exactly right. That is why in order to understand the rise and transformation of the LRA and Kony's kingdom of terror, one must place it within the wider story in which the people of northern Uganda, and the Acholi in particular, were drafted into the project of modern Uganda. Placed within this context, Kony's sovereignty of terror is revealed as a radical manifestation of the story of "fighting" that has shaped the way the north and the Acholi have been imagined (and in turn have imagined themselves) within the politics of Uganda.

The Story of "Fighting"

This story has its roots in the colonial anthropology and the British system of divide and rule, which viewed the north as more backward than the south and its people as fierce warriors. Thus, while the British colonial system developed agriculture and industry in the south, it neglected the north and viewed it primarily as a reserve for recruitment into the military. That meant that at the time of independence, even though it was the south that was more developed, the north had control over the armed forces, enabling Milton Obote to seize power in 1966. This northern dominance over the political and military future of Uganda lasted until 1986, when Museveni's National Resistance government came to power. This fact, plus the fact that Uganda's postcolonial experiment in nation-building has been based on the army as an instrument of domestic politics, means that the north has not been as marginalized from Uganda's political life as often tends to be assumed. Thus it is misleading to view the conflict in northern Uganda primarily along the faultlines of south/north social marginalization.

A far more accurate lens through which to understand the current melodrama of Kony is the political imagination through which northern Uganda has been framed, even by politicians from the region. And so, whether it was Obote, Idi Amin, or the Okellos in the 1980s, none of these

---

3. John Kiess, "Competing Forms of Sovereignty in the Great Lakes Region of Africa: An Exploration in Political Theology," unpublished term paper, 30.

politicians from northern Uganda challenged the founding story that cast the population of the north, the Acholi in particular, as "fighters" and "natural born warriors." Instead, they used this myth to bolster their own political power while at the same time continuing the colonial neglect of the region in terms of economic and social development, viewing it only as a vast reserve for military recruitment.

When Museveni, a southerner, eventually took power in 1986 after a long civil war, this not only shattered the myth of the Acholi as invincible warriors; it brought to an end the military career of most of the defeated former Uganda National Liberation Front (UNLF) soldiers, who were mostly from Acholi. They did not surrender, but quietly withdrew back home. Many still had their guns, and having no other skills or means of livelihood to depend on, they began to loot, steal, and create havoc in their villages, a development that made the ex-combatants internal enemies in Acholi society.

It is to this situation of social turmoil and lawlessness that the self-styled prophetess Alice Lakwena responded, at first creatively through a mix of traditional and Christian beliefs that involved rites of cleansing (many of the former combatants had committed atrocities against the civilian population in the south Luwero Triangle as they fought against Museveni's rebel National Resistance Army [NRA]), a new mythology of the Acholi as God's "chosen people," and a life of discipline.[4] Lakwena's vision was that of a radically transformed Acholi society, beginning with the ex-combatants but moving beyond them to others. However, having no credible alternative of how this might be achieved, Lakwena fell back onto the default story of "fighting," and thus remobilized and rehabilitated the "internal enemies" into fierce warriors of this new cause. She formed them into regiments of what she called "Holy Spirit Mobile Forces" (HSMF), who began waging war against government troops. Because they were disciplined, they recorded a number of victories against the NRA; this emboldened them, so they tried to march to Kampala to take power. They were, however, definitively defeated by the NRA near Jinja. The self-styled prophetess Lakwena ran into exile in Kenya, where she later died.

In the meantime, Joseph Kony, Alice Lakwena's cousin, attempted to keep the remnants of the HSMF alive. Through his own blend of spiritual-

4. For a good background account, see Heike Behrend, *Alice Lakwena and the Holy Spirits: War in Northern Uganda 1986-1997* (Athens: Ohio University Press, 1999).

ism, religious beliefs, and military tactics, Kony built up his own army of fighters, whom he later called The Lord's Resistance Army, with whom he continued to wage a war of resistance against the government forces. When the local population, who were already fed up with war and fighting, did not support him, he turned against them, kidnapping, maiming, terrorizing, and abducting children as the only way to fill the ranks of his rebel fighters.

The Sacrifice of Northern Uganda

Our aim in this brief sketch is not to provide a history of the LRA, a project that requires more time and space that we have here.[5] It is to account for the story of "fighting" that drives the LRA by locating it within the social history in which northern Uganda has been viewed as merely a reserve for recruitment into soldiering. Neither independence nor any of the successive regimes in Uganda have been able to offer an alternative imagination for the Acholi. On the contrary, with each successive regime, the Acholi and the people of northern Uganda have been drafted further and further into this story and its economy of warfare. Joseph Kony has pitched this story to unfathomable heights and driven its contradictions and horrific lies and practices to a hitherto unprecedented madness.

But Joseph Kony's regime of terror also reveals the extent to which this story of warfare, through which the north has been imagined as part of modern Uganda, has led to not only the region's economic marginalization, but the abuse, wastage, and wanton sacrificing of the innocent populations of northern Uganda, particularly the Acholi.

This is why northern Uganda desperately needs not only a cessation of fighting, but a story that can radically interrupt the story of warfare, with a vision of a new future that is grounded in a totally different idea of the Acholi and of society. This is what the story of Angelina Atyam represents — an interruption of a different social imagination grounded in a story of forgiveness and self-sacrificing service. A tragic interruption of her own life led Angelina to discover the gift of this new story.

5. For a good introductory treatment of the complex history of the LRA, see Frank Van Acker, "Uganda and the Lord's Resistance Army: The New Order No One Ordered," *African Affairs* 103/412 (July 2004): 335-57.

The Interruption of Angelina Atyam

Born in 1946 in Bobi, south of Gulu in northern Uganda, Angelina was trained as a nurse and midwife. Her husband George ran a Coca Cola distribution depot in Lira. Life was good, Angelina recalls. "I enjoyed my job, working with women and babies who are special in my life. I was married and my husband was a businessman. Our six children went to school. Life was good in Lira. Everybody was busy with daily routine."[6]

But that soon came to an end. On October 10, 1996, Angelina was alerted by a neighbor pounding on her door at 6:00 AM with the news that the LRA soldiers had carried out a raid at the St. Mary's Catholic boarding school ten miles away. That was where her fourteen-year-old daughter, Charlotte, attended school.

"I remember screaming and falling down. I could see fear in my husband's eyes. Our five other children were stricken with fear for their sister and for their own lives. A neighbor led us to pray and we managed to calm our souls. We then went to the school. It seemed like a graveyard. Parents were wailing. The children were all gone."[7] In all, the rebels had abducted 139 girls from the school. Following the attack, the deputy headmistress of St. Mary's, Sr. Rachele Fassera, followed the rebels into the bush and managed to secure the release of 109 girls. The rebels kept thirty girls, including Charlotte, whom they marched off with further into the bush.[8] Angelina and other parents were devastated when they realized that their daughters were not among those who had been released. They wanted to follow the rebels into the bush, but could not. All they could do was pray and wait for any news of the release of their daughters.

---

6. Unless otherwise stated, the source for Angelina's story, including some of the direct quotations reproduced here, is based on personal interviews carried out during the Duke Center for Reconciliation Gatherings of the Great Lakes Initiative in Kampala (January 22-25, 2008) and in Bujumbura (January 12-16, 2009), hereafter Kampala 2008 and Bujumbura 2009 respectively.

7. Angelina at the UN, 2005: http://ochaonline.un.org/cap2005/webpage.asp?Page =1180.

8. For the story of the Aboke Girls, as they came to be known, and their abduction and ordeal in the bush, see Els De Temmerman, *The Aboke Girls: Children Abducted in Northern Uganda* (Kampala: Fountain Publishing, 1995).

"Forgive Us our Sins": The Gift of Forgiveness

Every Saturday, the parents would meet at the Catholic cathedral in Lira for a day of fasting and prayer for their daughters. "One day," Angelina recalls, "as we were fasting and praying one of us got up and led us in the Lord's Prayer. When we came to the words, 'Forgive us our sins as we . . .' we found we could not go on. We all kept quiet. For we were all convicted about the bitterness and anger that was still in our hearts. We were angry with God, with the rebels, and even jealous of the parents whose daughters had returned home."[9]

That bitterness and anger, Angelina says, was a stumbling block that separated them from God. "So it was like our prayers were just hitting against a wall. We were wasting time."[10] For their answers to be heard, the parents realized they first had to put things right, which would mean forgiving their neighbors, forgiving family members, forgiving people out there in the communities, and even forgiving the rebels. "I was convicted of the need to first deal with our feelings of hatred and to pray for forgiveness toward the rebels — we had put a curse on them. Praying for those who had wronged us became our sacrifice," she said. This realization became the critical turning point for Angelina and the parents. After this, she recalls, "we began to experience a lifting of our burdens. God was at work among us."[11]

Then the group of Aboke parents, who up until then were only a support group for and among themselves, started sharing with the community about the strange gift of forgiveness they had received, a gift they now wanted other parents to experience. And so they organized events and meetings to share their story of forgiveness with parents in Gulu whose children had been abducted. Many parents found their message hard to believe. One woman, for example, was blind, and the rebels had abducted her only son and had slashed her back and burnt her as they separated her from her son who was clinging to her. As she heard Angelina speak about forgiveness, she asked, "Angelina, are you from a different planet? How can you tell us about forgiveness? Don't you know what the rebels have done to

9. Kampala 2008.

10. Angelina Atyam, sermon delivered at Park View Mennonite Church, Harrisonburg, Virginia, Sunday, June 15, 2008, http://www.pvmcsermons.com/.

11. Kampala 2008.

us?" This and other reactions of resistance, however, made her even more determined to share the gift of forgiveness. She went out to look for the mother of Rasca Lukwiya, the rebel commander, who she had learned was keeping Charlotte as his "wife" in the bush.

"And I went to this mother and told her, 'I am here to tell you that I have forgiven your son who is holding my daughter hostage. I have forgiven your clan, because I need to be free inside. I have also forgiven your tribe. And I want you to be free with me.'" The woman could not believe what Angelina was doing or saying. "She didn't find it very easy," Angelina remembers, "but in the end we embraced, and we wept. And we were reconciled. I felt like a very heavy weight was lifted from my soul, from my heart, so that I could go back and pray and call upon God and tell him what I want from him."[12]

As the parents of the Aboke girls continued to pray and share the gift of forgiveness they had experienced, even with the rebels, they at the same time threw themselves more determinedly into advocacy for the release not only of their own daughters, but of all the other abducted children. For this purpose, they launched an organization, the Concerned Parents Association (CPA), an advocacy and pressure group with three main objectives: (1) the immediate and unconditional release of all abducted children, (2) the peaceful resolution of the conflict in northern Uganda, and (3) the creation of an awareness of the plight of children in conflict.[13]

Thus over the next few years, Angelina Atyam, as co-founder and chairperson of the CPA, made numerous attempts to secure the release of the Aboke girls, spoke out against senseless war in northern Uganda, and extended the gift of forgiveness to the LRA. She met with the rebels and with different government leaders, including the president of Uganda, Yoweri Museveni. She traveled to Europe and the United States to call attention to the situation in Uganda. She petitioned the United Nations Assembly to intervene, and in 2002 she addressed the United Nations Security Council.

For her advocacy on behalf of children in northern Uganda, Angelina has received various honors and awards, including the 1998 United Nations Human Rights Prize. Significant as these recognitions are, it is important to remember the story that drives and sustains Angelina's activism. For

12. Kampala 2008.
13. CPA vision statement: http://www.uwyo.edu/girlmotherspar/info.asp?p=2253.

Angelina, the advocacy on behalf of children in northern Uganda and voiceless children elsewhere is the progressive working out of the gift of God's forgiveness that she and the other parents received following the tragic abduction of their daughters. It is this gift that Angelina and her fellow parents in CPA extend to their enemies, including the LRA, and the same gift that shapes their life of advocacy on behalf of children. Moreover, if the gift of God's forgiveness transformed Angelina from a generally quiet woman to an outspoken advocate on behalf of voiceless children, it also led her to sacrifice her own daughter Charlotte in view of a new and wider community, to which she had unknowingly become a midwife.

The Sacrifice of Charlotte

Soon, Angelina's outspoken crusades and advocacy began to irritate Kony and the LRA because of the national and international attention they were drawing. Eight months after Angelina's daughter disappeared, she received a message that an LRA commander wanted to meet with her. The LRA, it seemed, was ready to offer her a deal — the release of her daughter if she ceased her public-relations campaign. Angelina countered with an offer to do so if all the girls from St. Mary's were freed, but the LRA refused it.

Angelina's family was appalled that she had turned down the rebels' offer, but as she later reflected, "Getting my child back would be absolutely wonderful, but if I accepted the offer, I would be turning my back on all the other families. I'd destroy the new community spirit we had created — the hope of getting all the boys and girls back."[14]

This was not an easy decision for Angelina, who was quite aware of the horrific and unimaginable suffering that Charlotte was enduring in the bush. She knew, for instance, that Charlotte was regularly raped and used as a sex slave. Over the next few weeks she was haunted by the decision she had made. She not only agonized about Charlotte's well-being, she wondered and worried whether Charlotte would understand if she would ever be released. In the end, however, Angelina admits that she did not have much choice. "Some people thought I was crazy, but all those children had become my children."[15]

14. http://biography.jrank.org/pages/2895/Atyam-Angelina.html.
15. Bujumbura 2009.

Bearing the Sacrifice: Angelina's Journey with God

Still, it was a hard decision to make. Over the years, what would help Angelina accept and bear the sacrifice was the hope that one day Charlotte and the other girls would return. She prayed for Charlotte every day; she set an empty place at the table when the family ate and washed her clothes regularly and put them out to dry. Over and beyond these practices of hope, Angelina's deepening intimacy with God grounded and sustained her hope in her daughter's return. "I used to argue and wrestle with God everyday," she says.

Angelina remembers the particular night of July 19, 2004, as a night of such intense wrestling with God:

> I prayed and one day was again wrestling with God. And I sat on the floor and was telling God, "The Bible says you do not change, but seven years and seven months have gone by and I have not seen my daughter. In the Bible it says the seventh year is the year of freedom . . . Lord, are you changing in my situation?" I was wrestling with God . . . I wanted to ask God, "Jesus, when you went to see Martha and Mary, and you found Lazarus dead, why did you cry?" I asked him so many questions.[16]

Three days later, Angelina got a telephone call with the news that Charlotte had escaped. The girl who had been abducted at fourteen had become a young woman of twenty-two, with two children of her own fathered by Rasca Lukwiya. It was a joyous reunion. Angelina smiles as she tells the story. "She ran to meet me and I ran to meet her, and we couldn't talk. We just cried for a long, long, long time. She is the Lord's answer to my prayer."[17]

In the same way Angelina attributes Charlotte's return to God's miraculous intervention, Charlotte describes her escape as the work of God. She kept praying, she said, "I do not belong here, I can't fit in. God, please, please, please." By praying to God continually Charlotte was able to endure her ordeal in captivity and to keep hope in her freedom alive. As Angelina tells the story, the same night that Angelina was wrestling with God, Charlotte had a dream in which a voice told her that she would be reunited with

16. Atyam, Park View Mennonite Church sermon.
17. Atyam, Park View Mennonite Church sermon.

her family. Just walk to the left, the voice told her. The next day, there was an air raid on the camp by government forces. In the scuffle, Charlotte, carrying her two-year-old son on her back, followed what the voice had told her in the dream. She walked to the left and kept walking until she reached a village where a villager took her to the police station.

What the story of Charlotte's dream and subsequent escape confirms is that it was their relationship with God which sustained both Angelina and Charlotte through the ordeal. When her first son was born in the bush, Charlotte named him Rubangakene, a name that means "only God." The younger son's father had named him Vincent Otti, after the notorious rebel commander, Kony's deputy, but whom Kony has since killed. When they reunited, Angelina urged Charlotte to change the boy's name to "Miracle." Asked about the name, Angelina explains, "I saw the miracle of the living God when Charlotte was given back to me."[18]

It is this spiritual and theological lens that confirms Angelina's advocacy on behalf of children is not grounded simply in humanitarian ideals, but in her relationship with God. The full impact of this relationship would, even for Angelina, only emerge with time. For Angelina views her life and work as part of the journey of her deepening intimacy with God. The journey, which Angelina describes as "painfully beautiful," began with the tragic abduction of her daughter. It was this tragic event that first led her to discover the gift of God's forgiveness as a gift of healing of her sins and bitterness. Having received this gift of forgiveness herself, she was eager to share it with others and extend it even to the rebels. At the same time, this gift drew her into and later deepened and extended advocacy on behalf of abducted children. In the end, an activism that started with a concern only for her own biological child led to an expanded sense of family and a new community, for which she was now willing to sacrifice the same biological child.

Angelina's activism and advocacy, indeed her sacrifice, does not make sense outside this journey, which transformed a generally quiet woman into a fierce advocate on behalf of children, and a mother of six children into a mother of a new family that extends far beyond biological, clan, tribal, or national limits. When one puts the matter in this way, it becomes clear that Angelina stands within the same story and tradition as Abraham, and in fact, shares Abraham's unique call and promise. Like

18. http://mcc.org/news/news/article.html?id=378.

Abraham, who experienced the dramatic interruption of God's call not only to leave his own kinsfolk to become the father of a multitude but to sacrifice his own biological son Isaac, Angelina was also willing to sacrifice her own daughter in view of a new and expanded family.

Mama Angelina: Midwife to a New Future

Angelina is fondly referred to as "Mama Angelina," making the connection with Abraham even more striking. Many have rightly noted that Charlotte's abduction in 1996 transformed Angelina into an international advocate of children in northern Uganda. Although this is true, the far more radical transformation in Angelina's life is the transformation of the nurse-midwife into a midwife of a new family that stretches beyond northern Uganda. In addressing the UN Security Council in 2005, she noted, "There are hundreds of Charlottes in my country and beyond. . . . Every child is my child."[19]

Angelina has fond memories of her days as a midwife and speaks about them with tenderness. She talks about how she would massage the pregnant woman's stomach and speak to the child in the womb. She talks about her privilege as a midwife and the fact that she was always the first to see and hold the new child in her hands even before the mother saw her child, and the joy and special privilege she felt as she presented the newborn child to the mother. As chairperson and spokesperson of the CPA, Angelina similarly serves as a midwife for a new family birthed through forgiveness, offering peace and forgiveness as gifts that have to be massaged into birth, be tenderly received, and nurtured to life. Her own daughter Charlotte, together with her grandchildren, Rubangakene and Miracle, are only the first fruits and the first gifts of that new family.

A New Future: An Alternative to Fighting

Thus in Angelina's story one is able to catch a glimpse of a new future. This new future is not simply a return to civilized warfare, in which the weak, crippled, and children are protected during fighting. War and fighting,

19. http://ochaonline.un.org/cap2005/webpage.asp?Page=1180.

Angelina notes, are in and of themselves abominations, which not only make children's lives disposable, but involve a fundamental turning away from God: "Adults have become the first enemies of children. Children are not safe in their own homes. And we, the adults, send out children to fight wars because they are dispensable. We have turned against the very gift of God."[20]

The new future that Angelina dreams and talks about is a future beyond war, which begins with the acceptance of God's gift of forgiveness but extends to all aspects of human life and well-being. In service to this new future, CPA has extended their mission beyond the original three objectives to cover a host of programs that include support and counseling for the children who have escaped or been released, provision of school fees, relief and development programs through grassroots structures of parent and youth groups, teaching income-generating skills, and primary healthcare programs. It is this holistic vision of the new future that Angelina is driving at when she tells a gathering of Great Lakes leaders in Kampala: "I see a dream . . . I see green fields resplendent with all types of food. And I see children playing in those fields. I hear the joyful laughter of children playing, singing songs, and holding hands. There are Luo and Madi children; Acholi and Baganda children; black and white children playing together."[21]

This new future cannot be built on a story of "fighting." "You cannot overcome violence by violence," says Angelina, critically reacting to the Uganda government's Operation Iron Fist strategy of bombing out the rebels. On another occasion she adds: "And so, what do we gain when we kill them anyway? What do we gain as individuals? Some look at it as justice. I don't know. Me, I would like justice to preserve life, rather than taking away somebody's life — even if he's a witch, a murderer, a bad man like that."[22]

Neither can such a future be secured by our own strategic innovativeness. The new future is a gift grounded in God's forgiveness and reconciliation. "The Bible is telling us that Jesus gives us peace that surpasses human understanding. We need that peace — the peace that enables us to

20. Kristin Choo, "Uganda Mother Pleads for Abducted Children," *Women's E-News* (May 19, 2000): http://www.womensenews.org/article.cfm/dyn/aid/98/context/archive.

21. Kampala 2008.

22. Bujumbura 2009.

go out and reconcile to ourselves, to our neighbors, to everybody else in our communities."[23]

What Angelina and CPA represent therefore is an interruption to the competing sovereignties of Joseph Kony and the Uganda government, each built on a story of "fighting," each seeking to dominate northern Uganda, each seeking to control the bodies, minds, desires, and capacities of the Acholi, each bent on sacrificing the very people they seek to "liberate."

Conclusion: A Life from a Different Planet

In the gospel story of the anointing at Bethany, when the unnamed woman interrupted Jesus and his disciples and began to wash Jesus' feet and wipe them with her hair, she anticipated and interrupted the story of the Passion that was about to unfold. It drew attention to the reality of a community — the beloved community — that somehow stands "outside" the story of the powers through which Jesus' body was going to be handed over, tried, abused, and eventually crucified on the cross. We have already noted how the anointing at Bethany represents and illumines a different way of treating Jesus' body: an anointing, thus a "sacrifice" of a completely different type and logic, which is made possible by the story of love and forgiveness.

It is not that the anointing represents a more effective way of responding to the abuse of Jesus' body or of preventing the abuse of Jesus' body that was about to unfold. As a political or social strategy, the anointing at Bethany was very ineffective in stopping the battering of Jesus' body that was about to unfold.[24] Thus, it is not surprising that the guests at the

---

23. Atyam, Park View Mennonite Church sermon.

24. As we noted in chapter 1, attempts to recover forgiveness as a political strategy have grown in the wake of the South African Truth and Reconciliation Committee. See, e.g., Donald W. Shriver, *An Ethic for Enemies: Forgiveness in Politics* (Oxford: Oxford University Press, 1995); P. Digeser, *Political Forgiveness* (Ithaca, N.Y.: Cornell University Press, 2001); William Bole et al., *Forgiveness in International Politics: An Alternative Road to Peace* (United States Conference of Catholic Bishops Publishing, 2004). This is not the time to enter into a full discussion of this resurgent interest in forgiveness. One thing I often find misleading about this renewed interest, however, is that the attempts to offer forgiveness as a political strategy do not take into account the theology that makes it possible: the story in which it is grounded and the community that it shapes and whose social posture might set it at odds with the goals and purposes of political expedience. In most of these accounts, forgiveness is seen as a "useful" strategy that can be isolated from its religious roots; religion continues to

dinner table at Simon's house are indignant about the "scandalous waste" of resources that could have been better used to help the poor.

However, Jesus' response to their indignation is also quite telling: "leave her alone . . . the poor you will always have with you." That, I think, might be Jesus' way of saying that there will always be forms of politics that are built on stories that assume the sacrificing of the poor and the weak. Even though it is important to serve the poor, the beloved community gathered around the dinner table at Simon's house is also to be a community that exemplifies a different way of imagining and treating the bodies of the poor, a way of investing their lives on behalf of and for the poor and weak. The call of the community is also to be a community that responds to the systems that abuse the poor and weak not on the terms of those systems, but in a way that is odd, a way that is "out of place," and thus interrupts those systems by illuminating a different story and thus a different social possibility.

In the same way, Angelina and CPA do not offer the most effective way of stopping the rebel madness of Kony and LRA. For instance, Pastor Sam Childers, a former U.S. mercenary who, armed with AK-47s, hunts down the LRA rebels into the bush to rescue children (his orphanage at Nimule has over 150 rescued children) may be far more effective.[25] However, Angelina and the CPA resist the assumption that the only way to secure a future in northern Uganda is to fight Kony on his own terms. Angelina's story displays a radical alternative to "fighting," and the possibility of a different order within the madness of war. The story of her life and work stands within and helps to birth into existence a new reality that is totally out of place within the competing sovereignties of war and terror.

This makes the reaction quite telling of the woman who, upon hearing Angelina's call for forgiveness, wondered if she was from a different planet. Angelina and the story of CPA reveal the gifts that allow Christians to live in the world as if they are from a different planet. In fact, just like Taban, what drives Angelina and the CPA is an ecclesiological vision of a

---

be narrated as a source of something external to itself, as a motive either for killing or forgiving. For an account of forgiveness that locates it within its biblical and theological context in a way that illumines its personal, social, and historical possibilities similar to what I develop here, see L. Gregory Jones, *Embodying Forgiveness: A Theological Analysis* (Grand Rapids: Eerdmans, 1995).

25. On Sam Childers and his *East African Angels* organization, see http://www.angelsofeastafrica.org and http://www.machinegunpreacher.org/.

community whose calling is to "be in the world and yet not of this world" (John 17:15-16) and to be the recipient of God's precious gift of a new creation that Paul talks about in 2 Corinthians 5:17-18: "So, for anyone who is in Christ, there is a new creation. The old order is gone, the new is here. All this is from God, who has reconciled us to himself through Christ and has given us the ministry of reconciliation." Paul then adds in verse 20: "So we are ambassadors for Christ, it is as though God were appealing through us."

Angelina and the CPA serve as ambassadors of God's forgiveness and reconciliation, showing how such an extravagant display of self-sacrificing love can interrupt the world shaped by the likes of Kony. Through their embodiment of service, advocacy for the weak, and midwifery of the gentle gifts of forgiveness, Angelina and CPA illumine the possibility and reality of a new creation made possible by the story and politics of forgiveness.

CHAPTER 9

Gathering the Fragments of a New Future: Maggy Barankitse and Maison Shalom

When it was evening, the disciples came to him and said, "This is a deserted place, and the hour is now late; send the crowds away so that they may go into the villages and buy food for themselves." Jesus said to them: "They need not go away; you give them something to eat." They replied: "We have nothing here but five loaves and two fish." And he said, "Bring them here to me." Then he ordered the crowds to sit down on the grass. Taking the five loaves and the two fish, he looked up to heaven, and blessed and broke the loaves, and gave them to the disciples, and the disciples gave them to the crowds and all ate and were filled; and they took up what was left over of the broken pieces, twelve baskets full. And those who ate were about five thousand men, besides women and children.

Matthew 14:15-21 (NRSV)

We need to uproot the sprout from which the hatred grew and festered . . . we need to create a system in which the hatred, however ferocious, no longer exists. We need to invent a way of living without hate.

Maggy Barankitse

Five Loaves and Two Fish

In the story of the feeding of the crowds, told in varying detail by all four Gospel writers, Jesus and the disciples find themselves in what seems to be a hopeless situation. They are not only in a deserted place, but they are surrounded by large crowds of mostly sick and hungry men, women, and children, and the hour is "getting very late." In many ways, this is the story of Africa, a continent marginalized from the global systems of power, whose centers in New York, London, and Paris increasingly view Africans as nameless and desperate "crowds" of hungry, sick, and poor mouths to be fed — in a word, as a problem. Many within these centers have given up on Africa. It is too late, they think. Africa cannot be saved. It is a hopeless continent.[1]

In the gospel story, the disciples respond to the situation pragmatically: "send the crowds away so that they may go into the villages and buy food for themselves." The recommendation makes sense since it is based on a realistic assessment of the resources at hand: "We have nothing here but five loaves and two fish." However, one can also see reflected in the disciples' realism an implicit assumption that the *specific* need for food is beyond what they or Jesus can do anything about. Jesus, the disciples assume, has a *spiritual* message for the crowds — that is why they come to *listen* to him. When it comes to such material needs like food, Jesus and the disciples can do very little. The crowds must live by the same economic rules as everyone: they must go to villages and buy food for themselves.

This is what makes Jesus' response in the gospel story even more telling: there is no need to send the people away, "You yourselves give them something to eat." One can read Jesus' response in many ways: as a sign of compassion, or as an occasion for another miracle. I, however, read it as a form of resistance. Through his response, Jesus resists the spiritualization of his ministry. His ministry is not simply about a spiritual message to be listened to and later applied. The Good News that Jesus proclaims is a material vision, which involves a reordering of such material realities as geography, time, food, bodies, and communities. That is why Jesus' statement only makes sense in the context of what follows: he *asks* the disciples what

---

1. See *The Economist*, May 13, 2000, in which Africa is blatantly depicted as the "hopeless continent." A more recent issue of *The Economist* (February 24-March 2, 2001) paints a similar picture of gloom with its cover story, "Africa's Elusive Dawn." For a journalistic account of the same pessimism about Africa, see Keith Richburg, *Out of America: A Black Man Confronts Africa* (New York: Basic Books, 1997).

they have; he *orders* everyone to sit on the *grass;* he *takes* the *loaves* and *fish;* he *looks* up to *heaven;* he *blesses, breaks,* and *gives* it out . . . with the effect that everyone *eats* and has their *fill,* and twelve *baskets* of leftover *fragments* were *gathered.*

The more one attends to these material details, not only do the Eucharistic overtones (took, blessed, broke, and gave) of the story become evident, but also the fact that Jesus' response is a full-fledged social vision — a social vision that is radically different from the one assumed by the re-alism of the disciples' suggestion to send the people away to the villages to buy food for themselves. This is why the story of five loaves and two fish is a story of two competing social visions. There is on the one hand the story of scarcity ("we do not have enough"). It is the story that from the begin-ning defines and frames the way the situation is viewed as occurring in a "deserted place," with "large crowds," and "getting late." In other words, it is this story of scarcity that suggests not only a sense of desperation, but also the disappearance of community ("send the crowds away"). On the other hand, there is the performance of Jesus that not only resists the "real-ism" of the disciples, but provides an alternative to it. However, what I find particularly interesting about the account of Jesus' performance is the way it reframes and shapes the very description of what is at stake. Where the scattering of community seems to be the wise and pragmatic thing to do, Jesus orders a gathering of the crowds (let people sit down); where initially the location is described as a desolate place, we later have a lush field (peo-ple are ordered to sit down "on the grass"); where there was scarcity (only five loaves and two fish), there is now not only enough (everyone had their fill) but a superabundance (twelve baskets of leftover fragments).

This story is therefore not simply the story of the miracle of "multi-plication." It is a drama of competing stories — specifically, a Eucharistic alternative to the desperation that comes from scarcity. Thus, the story of five loaves and two fish provides a good outline of the multifaceted mis-sion and ministry of the church. The calling and mission of the church is to reproduce and make real the miracle of the five loaves and two fish — a mission that among other things involves resisting the forms of politics that lead to the disappearance of community; it involves ordering material realities like space, food, and bodies; it is about shaping grassroots com-munities grounded in the story of God's bounteous love; it is about gath-ering scattered fragments into baskets — and here the twelve baskets rep-resent the twelve tribes of Israel, foreshadowing the new Israel, God's new family that is beyond boundaries of race, nation, tribe, and geography. For that is the other significant detail in the story of five loaves and two fish: whereas the Synoptic Gospels simply note the fact that twelve baskets of leftover pieces were collected, in John's version, the disciples are specifically commanded by Jesus to "gather the fragments left over, so that nothing will be wasted" (John 6:12). The story of five loaves and two fish offers a good outline of what it means to be church and what it means to say that the church is a Eucharistic community.

That is what makes the story of five loaves and two fish such a powerful one for Africa: it is a counter-narrative to the story of *la politique du ventre,* the political and economic imagination that shapes modern Africa. As our analysis in chapter three confirmed, it is a story that not only leads to the disappearance of community, but to the senseless waste of Africa through all forms of violence, tribalism, corruption, poverty, and the desperation of "mere survival." Like the disciples, one can stand in that story and try to come up with so-called realistic solutions, but these are the old formulas of social ethics. What the pressing challenge of daring to invent the future calls for is taking leave of this foundational narrative and standing in a different story that reproduces and makes real the politics of five loaves and two fish. This is what Marguerite Barankitse and her ministry of Maison Shalom in Burundi have done.

Maggy Barankitse: A Call to Love and a Future Beyond Hatred

Burundi is a nation shaped by contradictions. It is one of the most beautiful countries in Africa and, given its rolling green hills, mountains, and lush valleys, it is often referred to as "the Switzerland of Africa." But this beautiful country is also one of the poorest — ranked third poorest by the Global Economic Index, with an average annual income of less than $150. Also, even though the close to seven million Burundians speak the same language and share the same cultural traditions, they self-identify as Hutu (85 percent), Tutsi (14 percent), or Twa (1 percent). In order to understand this story of ethnicity and the social history of hatred that has shaped Burundi, one must examine Burundi's colonial past. Just like Rwanda, its neighbor to the north, Burundi was originally part of German East Africa, but became a Belgian colony after Germany lost World War I. Using the same Hamitic mythology as Rwanda, which viewed the Tutsi as superior non-natives and "natural born leaders," the colonialists affirmed Tutsi privilege (making the Tutsi their natural allies) while setting up a system of political and economic administration that marginalized the majority Hutu and Twa populations. Unlike in Rwanda, Burundi's independence in 1962 left the Tutsi minority in power, yet the hatred between ethnic groups set the imaginative framework for Burundi's life after independence, which has been marked by political instability and numerous takeovers and massacres, notably in 1965, 1972, 1988, 1991, and 1993. These massacres, although not on the scale of the 1994 Rwanda genocide, have pitted Hutu against Tutsi in a series of revenge attacks and counterattacks. In this context of civil war, ethnic hatred, and revenge massacres, Maggy Barankitse received her call to establish Maison Shalom.[2]

Maggy Barankitse

Born of Tutsi parents in a village outside Ruyigi in 1956, Maggy lost her father when she was six years old. Maggy's mother brought her up with her brother. Later, as a teacher, Maggy battled the discrimination that reigned between the two ethnic tribes, the Tutsis and Hutus. One day, a young girl who had been raped, thrown out of her home by her family, and excluded from her school came to see her. Maggy took her and her baby in and helped her get back to school. However, this gesture caused Maggy to lose her job as a teacher. She left to study in Switzerland on a scholarship before returning to Ruyigi to become secretary to the bishop.

Widespread ethnic violence between Hutu and Tutsi factions was triggered when Burundi's first democratically elected president, a Hutu, was assassinated in October 1993 after only a hundred days in office. More than 200,000 Burundians perished in the ensuing civil war, which lasted for almost twelve years. UNICEF estimates that during this period 10 to 20 percent of the population fled to neighboring countries or lived in refugee camps at the border. The civil war created more than 600,000 orphans and

2. Unless otherwise stated, the source for Maggy's story, including the direct quotations reproduced here, are personal interviews carried out during the Duke Center for Reconciliation Gatherings of the Great Lakes Initiative in Bujumbura (January 12-16, 2009) and at Ruyigi (January 17-19, 2009), hereafter Bujumbura 2009 and Ruyigi 2009 respectively. I am grateful for my colleague Stephanie Wheatley, who conducted part of the interview at Ruyigi.

7,000 children soldiers, and left 5,000 children in the streets and 200 children in prison; 19 percent of Burundi's children died before the age of five.[3]

When the civil war began in October 1993, Maggy was working as a secretary at the bishop's house in Ruyigi. She had already adopted seven children — four Hutus and three Tutsis — and although the situation was becoming increasingly dangerous, she refused to separate them. With the political situation deteriorating, a number of Hutu adults and children hid at the bishop's palace in Ruyigi. On Sunday morning, October 24, Tutsi assailants armed with clubs, machetes, and rocks attacked the palace. Maggy tried to intervene, but they knocked her aside and tied her to a chair in the courtyard, then slaughtered seventy-two people before her eyes and set the building on fire. Miraculously, Maggy's seven children survived the massacre by hiding in the sacristy. After the massacre, one of the attackers freed her in exchange for the keys to the storeroom. Bribing the rebels with money, Maggie managed to save another twenty-five Hutu children from the burning building and hide them in the cemetery. Then as night fell, she went to get help from a German aid worker, Martin Novack, who provided them with a place to stay.

In remembering the events of that day, Maggy recalls the extraordinary courage and resolve that came to her as an unexpected gift. The gift, she now recognizes, was the gift of her calling:

> I felt this incredible resistance inside me, like strength. . . . As soon as I knew that my children had survived, I felt a strong will to live. I could think of one thing and only one thing: taking care of them; raising them beyond this hatred and the bitterness that I came to see in their eyes.[4]

Thus while the tragic events of October 1993 affirmed Maggy's determination to take care of the orphans as a religious call, they also clarified her calling to a bigger vision than merely providing care for the orphans. The bigger vision was to raise the children "beyond this hatred and bitterness that I came to see in their eyes." In order to appreciate the significance of this vision in shaping Maison Shalom, it is important to explore more fully these two complementary aspects of Maggy's calling.

3. United Nations Office for Humanitarian Aid and UNICEF, 2003.

4. Christel Martin, *La haine n'aura pas le derniere mot: Maggy la femme aux 10000 enfants* (Paris: Albin Michel, 2005), unpublished translation by Trent Dailey-Chwalibog and David Dimas, 47.

Called by Love

When Maggy speaks about her call, she notes that it is not first and foremost a call to look after children. The call was also Maggy's discovery of her own relationship and intimacy with God. This was a new experience, Maggy notes, and amounted to a realization that her own life is intimately connected to God's love. That is why Maggy describes her call as a mystical experience through which her life was drawn into the story and reality of God's love:

> I always felt called to a mission, but I did not know exactly what that mission was — until then. I was always afraid of failing, of not having the strength to do what I needed to do, of being unfaithful to myself. I was afraid of being judged. Before it was me, Maggy, that helped a few children; but in 1993, after such great pain, I felt the call to leave it all behind and count on God's mighty power. I devoted myself entirely to their service. I was driven by this inexplicable strength; I had not eaten anything in two days, but I wasn't the least bit hungry. I had plenty of energy. I had never felt closer to God than on that day. I was completely helpless, but strengthened by love. I was exhausted, but there wasn't the slightest bit of despair on my face. What is really beautiful is that our heart can always go there; always.[5]

Maggy's newly rediscovered relationship with God liberated her from her fear, but also raised her beyond herself to a new place and a new story, into which she now wished to invite others. Her relationship with God released not only a sense of audacity in Maggy, but also a realization that in taking care of the children, something bigger was at stake. This new story was not only bigger than her life, but bigger than the story of Burundi. It was as if a kind of new allegiance — a new claim on her life bigger than her Tutsi or Burundian identity — was revealed. Later, as Maggy listened to Nelson Mandela's inauguration address in 1994 as the first elected black president in South Africa, this same sense of new identity grounded in God's love was confirmed. At his inauguration, Mandela said,

> Our deepest fear is not that we are inadequate. Our deepest fear is that we are powerful beyond measure. It is our light, not our darkness that

---

5. Martin, *La haine*, 88-89.

most frightens us. We ask ourselves, who am I to be brilliant, gorgeous, talented, fabulous? Actually, who are you *not* to be? You are a child of God. Your playing small does not serve the world. There is nothing enlightened about shrinking so that other people won't feel insecure around you. We are all meant to shine, as children do. We were born to make manifest the glory of God that is within us. It's not just in some of us; it's in everyone. And as we let our own light shine, we unconsciously give other people permission to do the same. As we are liberated from our own fear, our presence automatically liberates others.[6]

These words, especially the reminder, "you are a child of God. Your playing small does not serve the world," reminded Maggy not only of her newly rediscovered identity, but of the ambitious invitation into a story bigger than taking care of orphans. This bigger, expansive story of God's love explains not only how Maison Shalom came to be, but also Maison Shalom's growth and accomplishments.

In the beginning, 25 children whose parents had been killed settled in Martin Novack's house; after one year, there were 100, then 500, and then more than 10,000. So Maggy began to look for land, and she thought, "Why don't I use my parents' land?" Thus Maison Shalom was born in Ruyigi, in Maggy's home village. Maggy believed these children needed a home where they could grow up in a family with love, security, and education. So she started setting up houses for the children to live in together as a family. In time she set up businesses that the children own together and run, including a salon, a tailor and seamstress shop, and a mechanic school called the Garage of Angels. Here, former child soldiers, street children, and war orphans learn skills and earn a living. Over the years she added a library, a tailoring school, language classes, a computer school, and to prove that the children deserved more than just survival, she built them a cinema and even a swimming pool. With time, Maggy's work has expanded beyond Ruyigi. She has founded four children's villages around the country, as well as a center for children in the capital, Bujumbura. By 2008, an estimated 30,000 children had already benefited from Maison Shalom either directly or indirectly.

When asked about this expansive vision of Maison Shalom, Maggy

6. As cited in Martin, *La haine*, 114. These words attributed to Mandela were never actually spoken by him. They come from Marianne Williamson's *A Return to Love* (New York: Harper Collins, 1992), 190-91.

repeats her observation that Maison Shalom is not merely about the children, but that it is first and foremost a story about God's love: "God gives us so much energy," she said; "we are not to become satisfied with mediocrity." That is why Maggy also insists that Maison Shalom is not an orphanage. Whereas orphanages focus on providing "services" for the children, Maison Shalom gives them a home and a family — and even this is not an end in itself, but a reminder of who they already are: "God's family: princes and princesses, all destined to live in a place."[7]

A Future beyond Hatred

For Maggy something bigger than taking care of the orphans was at stake: "I could think of one thing and only one thing: taking care of them; raising them beyond this hatred and the bitterness that I came to see in their eyes."[8] In the tragic massacre of October 1993, Maggy had witnessed the depth to which the story of ethnic hatred and revenge had brought her country: "I saw humanity reduced to its absolute worst: crushed, denied, destroyed . . . nothing could console me. I did not know how to cry anymore." Maggy's call, therefore, was to restore the vision of humanity. She "wanted to shine joy's light on the darkness, where inhumanity lives and thrives."[9]

This call to repair the image of humanity that hatred had shattered led her to look more critically at Burundi society. "We are crazy," she noted. "We are not afraid to kill one another. We have accepted hatred because of ethnicity and have forgotten the most noble gift of belonging to the family of God."

Once Maggy started naming ethnicity as a lie, she was also now more clearly able to see how the lie, like a malignant cancer, had metastasized and infected all aspects of Burundian society, even becoming a cultural pattern:

> In a country where vengeance has practically become cultural, the desire for reconciliation was a relative challenge. Here everyone who asks for forgiveness loses honor. . . . The desire for vengeance is like a substitute for dignity (it forms identity). The notion of responsibility in

7. Ruyigi 2009.
8. Martin, *La haine*, 47.
9. Martin, *La haine*, 47.

our country was never personal. Everyone was responsible for the committed crime against someone in their clan. Likewise if someone is humiliated, the entire clan shares the shame. *Umuryambura atukisha umuryango;* one who eats taboo food brings shame to the entire family — this spirit of solidarity requires that an individual feels they need to avenge for anyone in their family, clan.[10]

Thus the African values of community and solidarity had themselves been subverted to serve the story of hatred and revenge. In fact, to say that vengeance had become a substitute for dignity meant that vengeance had become integral to the very identity of the Burundi people. Indeed, the culture of revenge had become so pervasive that Christianity in Burundi had not been able to break it. Instead, the practice of Christianity had accommodated itself to this lie, giving rise to a "practical hypocrisy."

> October 24 showed me just how superficial the practice of Christianity in our country had become. It had no effect on many . . . this is what allowed the massacre to take place, even in a sacred place, by people who were Christians. What kind of Christianity did they practice?[11]

Against this background, Maggy came to see her mission as one of healing Burundi society. She speaks of having two sick relatives, Burundi society and the church, both of whom need healing. "I wanted to break the cycle of hatred, to interrupt this chain of vengeance that was silently transmitting itself from generation to generation."[12] To do so, Maggy knew that the challenge was not simply one of advocacy to stop the killing, or even merely reconciliation between ethnic groups.

> We need to uproot the sprout from which the hatred grew and festered . . . we need to create a system in which the hatred, however ferocious, no longer exists. We need to invent a way of living without hate.[13]

The challenge as Maggy understood it required raising the children beyond the story of ethnicity. This meant inviting and raising the children

---

10. Martin, *La haine,* 149-50.
11. Bujumbura 2009.
12. Bujumbura 2009.
13. Martin, *La haine,* 81.

into the new story of God's love, which Maggy had rediscovered as a far more truthful account of who we are.

Maison Shalom and the Politics of Love

According to Maggy, love is our true identity. Love is the dignity that God gives each person in creation. Each person is created out of love as God's child, and is meant to live in the house of God as a member of God's family. Thus, love is not only our identity; it is our unique vocation: "Love is the most beautiful calling of human beings. We are created out of love and to love."[14]

Maggy's hope was for Maison Shalom to become not simply an example of the identity and calling of God's love, but also the seed for a new culture — and indeed a new future founded on the story of love. As she says, "I would like for Burundi to give birth to a new generation who will carry the light of love and forgiveness to all the surrounding hills."[15]

But how is the story of love able to shape a new identity and a new future in a country that has been shaped by so many years of ethnic hatred? What does that future look like? How exactly would the story of love be able to undermine and uproot the entrenched patterns of hatred and desire for revenge that have themselves become a culture? What are the decisions, actions, and patterns of living through which the new future can become a reality? What does its everyday politics look like? In order to get a sense of the culture and future that the story of love is able to shape, we need to attend to at least four gifts that came to characterize Maggy's life as well as the life of Maison Shalom: resistance, innovation, forgiveness, and revolution.

A Rebel for Love

Saying "Yes to love" has made Maggy a rebel. The first indication of this claim is Maggy's determination to live outside the conventional bound-

---

14. Speech at the 49th International Eucharistic Congress, Quebec, Canada, June 21, 2008," http://www.ecdq.tv/en/videos/, hereafter Eucharistic Congress.
15. Martin, *La haine*, 149.

aries of Burundi culture. "I am Tutsi and the Tutsis thought I was a traitor," she says, "whereas the Hutus took me for a spy. Everyone distrusted me. I was searched wherever I went. The NGOs and religious hierarchy thought I was at best naïve, and probably crazy. After all, I was neither married nor a nun."[16]

Maggy attributes her own rebelliousness in part to her upbringing under the key influence of her mother, Therese, who was a strong and independent woman. Widowed in 1962 at the age of twenty-four, Maggy's mother refused to remarry one of her late husband's brothers, as was customary. Not only did she refuse to leave her house, but she demanded part of the family estate, which for a wife in Burundi is not allowed. Maggy's mother was also a woman with strong Christian convictions, which she passed on to Maggy. In her eyes, the words of Christ were not only true, they were only ever worth anything when put into practice. When one day Maggy came home and told her that children at school were asking her why there were only two children in her family, Maggy's mother told her: "No, you are not only two; all the other children are your brothers and sisters." Maggy took that to heart. But one day when she invited a girl who had lost her parents to her home, Maggy's uncles protested and kicked the little girl out. That was when, according to Maggy, she began to see the lies (and hatred) within her own family.

Maggy's rebelliousness had already been shaped as a rebellion against the lies that she saw not only in her family, but also within the church. She tells of an incident in 1972, when a number of children at her Catholic school lost their parents in a massacre, but school went on "as usual" without even a mention of the children's parents who had been killed, nor Mass at the church to pray for them. Maggy could not understand. "How come we did not have mass for the children's parents and yet 'we are one family'?" she later asked the priest.

What these and many stories reveal is that for Maggy learning to say Yes to love meant learning to say No to hate. But this also meant living a life of constant vigilance against what Maggy now repeatedly refers to as the "lies" of ethnic hatred — lies that had become so naturalized that they had come to be unquestioningly accepted as "our way of life." This meant living an unconventional life of resistance, which involved a willingness to "betray" her people in view of a higher loyalty. That was, in fact, Maggy's

---

16. Bujumbura 2009.

fate. At the bishop's residence in 1993, her attackers accused her of "betraying us" by adopting Hutu children and hiding Hutus, even though she herself was Tutsi. Her punishment was that they would kill all the Hutus before her.

What makes Maggy's rebelliousness possible, shapes her various tactics of resistance, and even sustains her through the loneliness of being outside the cultural mainstream, is her faith in God and steadfast conviction that hate must never have the last word.

"Love Has Made Me an Inventor"

Maggy also says love has made her an inventor. This is perhaps the most comprehensive description that Maggy uses to describe the innovativeness of Maison Shalom. First, Maggy has developed her work in Burundi on a day-to-day basis, without any big structures and without big strategic planning. On the other hand, Maggy is determined about her dreams and goals for Maison Shalom, although she likes to poke fun at Western donors when they ask her for a "strategic plan." The Western preoccupation with strategic planning, Maggy quips, reflects a lack of confidence in God. "My plan", she says, "is only five letters of the French alphabet: A-M-O-U-R; in English only four: L-O-V-E."[17] So for Maggy to say love has made her an inventor means that her innovativeness is grounded in the clarity and simplicity of her vocation. The clarity of this goal makes improvisation not only possible but the hallmark of life in Maison Shalom, especially in its early days. "We invented and improvised. . . . Nothing was planned. It was adversity that taught us how to face this all."[18]

Innovativeness also meant being open to new opportunities, and a readiness, at times, to go against the grain.

> Every morning, we have to be inventive. When we discovered that the region we wanted to base our program to the east declared a red zone, that same morning we went north. When we couldn't go north anymore we would change direction. At times we would work like mad people in the way ambulances wouldn't obey a single rule in traffic.[19]

17. Bujumbura 2009.
18. Martin, *La haine*, 141.
19. Martin, *La haine*, 141.

The image of the ambulance cutting through traffic reflects Maggy's ability to navigate the institutional frameworks of her society. Being an inventor meant that she had to learn to shape Maison Shalom in a territory controlled by powers over which she had no control. She also had to learn to navigate the institutional structures of her Catholic church, of traditional society, and of nation-state bureaucracies (military, police, and government) to serve the children — through persuasion, advocacy, cajoling, and even outright manipulation.

Learning to navigate institutional frameworks has also meant learning to sift through her social, cultural, and religious heritage, saying No to some and Yes to others, rejecting some, adopting others, reevaluating some, and even modifying others as a way of creating a whole new culture for the children grounded in the story of love. In the process, Maggy and the children often found themselves having to play out new roles, and even invent new language. It was within these circumstances that the name Maison Shalom came to be adopted. Maggy and the children did not want to call it "Amahoro," the Kirundi word for peace. The children remembered hearing the word "amahoro" from the lips of the killers. Those who had killed their parents and relatives had done so apparently in the name of "amahoro." By adopting the name Maison Shalom, they wanted to reinvent the very meaning of "peace," a word that had become profoundly marred by the lie of ethnic hatred.

Being an inventor also meant learning to use whatever was at hand, and weaving together what might appear to be disparate or contradictory strands and traditions, as a way of inventing a new future for the children. In this way, Maison Shalom became a patchwork community that brought together not only children from different ethnicities and countries, but also different traditions: "I was trying to take everything beautiful in every culture, be it from mine or Western [culture]. But it was above all my faith that helped me have another perspective. Faith maintained me above every moment and all atrocities."[20] The weaving together, therefore, was not random or haphazard; it was guided and shaped by the vision of a new community and a new future, which she drew from her Christian faith and particularly the story of God's love, which she had rediscovered. That is what allowed Maggy to "say yes to the gift of life, and no to death; yes to love and no to hatred." As she notes, "saying no to fraternal hatred requires an energy that is

20. Martin, *La haine,* 151.

superior to simple human strength. My heart was always encouraged by that phrase in the Bible: 'I am with you always until the end of time.'"[21] Maggy's innovativeness is, in the end, an aspect of her trust in God's providence.

> We were completely overwhelmed, but *somehow*, we pushed on and survived. There was much more need than we could ever meet. Every day hundreds of people arrived. It would not end. Right at the moment when the situation was so grave, aid arrived, and seeing this sign reminded me that I should not give up hope. Similar signs would come every time I would begin to lose hope. In 1997, under the embargo, when I used up the last can of milk a container arrived. And it was like that all the time. *Somehow, we pushed on.*[22]

This sense of *somehow* confirms that love made Maggy an inventor not so much because of her own gifts of creativity and genius, but because of God's bounteous resourcefulness, in which she is grounded and out of which she discovers each day new gifts, new possibilities, new friendships, and new miracles. Inventing the future is not simply a task; it is a gift to be received. In this connection, Maggy has received many gifts to help her establish and maintain Maison Shalom. Her friends supported her from Europe. The church came to her side when French Catholic relief services donated the first vehicle and Belgian and German Caritas organizations got in touch; other NGOs heard about Maison Shalom and also took the initiative to help. This is what sustains Maggy's confidence that Maison Shalom will carry on even after her.

> There are always miracles in the Shalom House because I believe in love. I believe that nobody can stop me. I compare the Shalom House to a train that God conducts. Nobody can stop this train. He will still move it — because God is God. There will be some cars that will stop. But He will continue to gather Congolese, Rwandese, Europeans, saying, "Come my children and build my dream."[23]

Accordingly, God's dream is the dream of a new generation, a new family, a new community, and a new "tribe" beyond Hutu, Tutsi, and Twa.

---

21. Martin, *La haine*, 151.
22. Martin, *La haine*, 151.
23. Ruyigi 2009.

The children of Maison Shalom confirmed this dream when, asked by a journalist recently whether they were Hutu or Tutsi, the children responded, "No, we are Hutsitwacongozungu."[24]

No Future without Forgiveness

Even though ethnic hatred is deeply entrenched in the imagination of Burundi, Maggy's work is driven by the conviction that hatred will never have the last word. A new future of love is still possible even to those who have killed. However, moving from hatred to love requires more than a simple decision. It requires a total reversal "at the very core of oneself," which is only made possible by the gift of forgiveness. This gift of forgiveness allows one to rediscover one's true identity and one's true calling, which is love.

Because Maggy knew that revenge, like acid in a metallic container, eats away and eventually destroys the one that carries it, from the very start she encouraged the children to live with forgiveness. Even then, she admits, the full potential of forgiveness and the reality of the future it unveiled only emerged with time — a lesson she learned mostly from the children themselves. She tells the story of Justine, who was nine years old in 1993 when Maggy took her in, after a neighbor killed her parents and her sister and used a machete on her head.

> I decided to rebuild the house of the parents and to trust them to re-take their original village. Justine told me, "No ma'am. I think we will call the man who killed my parents and show him the burned house to make reconciliation." I said, "We call this killer?" She said, "Yes, of course. Because I want to rebuild first the heart, not the house. Because I will tell him what he must do for us." I said, "But it's very dangerous for you, Justine." She said, "No. I want to *live*. Because if I hate him, I can't live. Because the hatred stops me from continuing to live." And I accompanied her and then she said to this killer, "I want to ask you to ask me for forgiveness. I am able to forgive you." And the man began to [blush]. He said, "You forgive me? You forgive me child?" She said, "I forgive you. I accept. Because you can't give me back my father, my mom, my sister, I ask you to become my father." And he said, "Yes. I accept." They became friends. They rebuilt the house together. They

24. Burundi 2009.

were neighbors. Three years ago, the man became very ill. And Justine went to take care of this man and then I saw Justine when we went to the funeral. She made flowers [for him] and everybody there was crying. Justine was crying when her father died, when this killer died. And when I visited him [before he died], he said to me, "Thank you, Maggy. Because now I am dying like human person, not like a killer. Your forgiveness gave me back hope, love, life." And this is what the children taught me — it's new life.[25]

Justine's story is one of many in which the children showed an incredible capacity for forgiveness. Granting forgiveness to those who hurt them or who killed their parents or relatives released the children from the burden of hatred and therefore allowed them to live into a new future. It also offered an opportunity to the offenders to rediscover their true identity as children of God.

How we can look at the killers, not like killers only, but like our brothers, like the children of God. Even though they had killed, they are still the children of God. And God on the cross gives them life. Because you remember when the thief asked pardon from God, from Jesus, "Remember me when you will be in paradise." And he says, "This evening you will be with me in paradise." This is what we Christians forget because we want to judge, we want to punish, we don't want to give life to our brothers. When we forgive, we give life, to others, but also to ourselves. Because the person who doesn't forgive does not exist. You know, when you refuse to forgive, you stop living. And it's during these 15 years that I have learned all this.[26]

What Maggy has learned, mostly from children, is not only the possibility for forgiveness, but the realization that there really can be no future without forgiveness. The children's lives and stories reveal the kind of future that the gift of forgiveness makes possible. That is the reason, Maggy notes, that it is really the children who have created the spirit of Maison Shalom: "they build my heart. They give me hope. They show me love, and what love is."[27]

25. Ruyigi 2009.
26. Ruyigi 2009.
27. Opus Prize Video, http://www.opusprize.org/winners/08_Barankitse.cfm.

A Revolution of Love

The new future of love that forgiveness makes possible is a future on a grand scale. To this end, Maggy speaks about the new future as a revolution of love, which would be able to transform all of Burundi society and beyond. In this respect, Maggy is driven by the same revolutionary madness as Thomas Sankara and by the same ambitious dream for a completely new society, which involves a total reconversion at all levels. But if, as we noted, Sankara's revolutionary madness lacked the crucial elements of memory, community, and story to sustain it, the story of God's love that grounds Maggy's madness is based on the conviction that the new future is not a static product but a journey that takes time. In this way, like Bishop Paride Taban who hopes to "fight tribalism in a small way," Maggy speaks about the small steps and small candles that shape the revolutionary future of love. There is always much more to be done, she admits, many more needs than one can touch. "But like Mother Teresa says, it is better to light a candle than to curse the darkness."[28] Maggy thus understands her daily work as one of lighting small candles to fight the darkness and ignite a revolution of love. Thus during the years of the war, the simple everyday life of the children through activities like playing, going to school, and celebrating birthdays in the middle of the civil war allowed Maison Shalom to be a witness to a new future beyond the war.

Maggy is therefore very proud as she takes us around the Ruyigi Center, or City of Angels, which includes a library, boutique, hair salon, tailoring school, the cinema hall, and the swimming pool. "You see," she says, "I decided to build the cinema and swimming pool here when the war was going on, to say no to war; no to killing."[29] The cinema and swimming pool (as well as all the other activities at City of Angels) point to a reality bigger than themselves, to a story beyond them. They are not an end in themselves, nor are they simply "income generating projects." Rather, they are spaces for socialization into a new future. As an alternative to the war, the cinema is a socialization into the story of rest and God's Sabbath. And the swimming pool, Maggy says, "is like the baptism."[30]

Thus the ambitious and extravagant display of the cinema and the

28. Ruyigi 2009.
29. Ruyigi 2009.
30. Ruyigi 2009.

swimming pool become "signs" and confirmations of God's bounteous love. These signs show "that all the possibilities that exist in God exist in each and for each person. We are kings and queens, we are all destined to live in a palace, and each one of us deserves the best."[31] It is this connection between palace and place, between heaven and earth, between the future and the now, between revelation and history that baptism establishes and names. In doing so, baptism sacralizes the "rough ground," as Éla called it, of our mundane existence, and names this rough ground as the site and theater of God's extravagant love. This explains the extravagant display of a swimming pool and a cinema even for orphans, even in a place like Ruyigi. If the revolution of love takes shape through such ordinary acts of "lighting a candle to fight the darkness," it requires the display of the outrageous extravagance and abundance of its promises. Thus in Maggy, we find the same extravagant "waste" we encountered with Angelina Atyam and within the story of the anointing at Bethany. As we noted, this extravagant display reveals the genuine sacrifice *(sacra-facere)* of Africa. It is this extravagance and this excess that makes sacred — thus making possible the simple, ordinary activities like playing, going to school, and the celebration of birthdays.

Crafting a New Future: A Eucharistic Praxis

Maggy's roles as both rebel and inventor, the dynamic interaction between resistance and innovativeness in her life, and her constant No to hatred and Yes to love make Maison Shalom at once a social critique and alternative to the culture of hatred. This also makes Maison Shalom very Eucharistic. For like in the gospel story of the five loaves and two fish, it is the dynamic interaction between Jesus' words, "No — there is no need to send the crowds away" and "Yes, you give them something to eat yourselves" that transforms what had been imagined as a desperate situation into a feast of abundance. That, to be sure, is the same dynamic possibility that is made available every day through the gift of Eucharist, and the reality that Maggy's life and Maison Shalom illuminate.

31. Martin, *La haine*, 12.

Eucharist as Spirituality

When asked about what kept her going, Maggy responded: "it is prayer that keeps me going. The Eucharist is my source of true courage."[32] Maggy attends Mass regularly and receives the Eucharist, and at six o'clock every evening, Maggy withdraws and spends an hour in front of the Blessed Sacrament in the chapel next to her home. During this time, in silence, meditation, prayer, and interior dialogue, Maggy says, she rediscovers her vocation as she is healed, consoled, and strengthened. It is particularly during this time, Maggy says, that she is rejuvenated, feels fully herself again, and even becomes young. And so, like a little girl, in her chapel, Maggy writes small notes to God, which she places by the tabernacle where the Blessed Sacrament is kept. Maggy's small notes cover a wide range of concerns, needs, and celebrations. Sometimes it is a list of her complaints against God, another time her wish list or a name of a child who needs special attention. Sometimes, Maggy says, she ends a list with an "asap — please."[33] She notes,

> Every morning we become new, because God creates anew. And every time we go to Communion — Eucharist — [we pray,] "Make us new." We go like this: [*stretches hands out to receive*]. And when I go and take, I know that God cleans my sins; God gives me another life, and then I can celebrate life all the day, all the night.[34]

Eucharist therefore is for Maggy not only a source of intimacy with God or of courage and strength; it is the celebration of our identity as God's children. It is the remembrance of our identity as God's children — as princes and princesses. That is why Eucharist is what we are called to be about (*eucharistia*: thanksgiving = celebration). "Life," she noted, "is a feast that God gives. We must celebrate life — even in death." Thus at Rema Hospital in Ruyigi, as Maggy takes us around the new hospital facility that includes a nurses' training school, nutrition unit, surgical wards, and some of the most spacious and cleanest bathrooms in an African hospital, she is particularly proud to show us a room that was being designed as a funeral parlor. Here, she noted, "after the body has been cleaned, it is dressed up and laid out for viewing by the relatives." In a country where

32. Bujumbura 2009.
33. Bujumbura 2009.
34. Ruyigi 2009.

death has become so casual and where people die anonymously, Maggy's provocative decision to set up a funeral parlor is quite powerful. "Even in death," she notes, "the dignity which God gives us must be allowed to shine, to be celebrated and named."[35] From the funeral parlor Maggy leads us a short distance to the chapel, which is just outside the hospital gate. "From the funeral parlor," she says, "the family and community can bring their loved one here to say farewell and give the gift of life back to God."

A Spirituality That "Includes Everything"

This same Eucharistic theology permeates and informs all the other activities and programs at Maison Shalom. Some bishops came to Maison Shalom and wanted to know whether Maison Shalom was a religious congregation or an NGO, and inquired about its spirituality. Stammering, Maggy answered them, "Ours is spirituality that includes everything."[36]

Eucharist is indeed a spirituality that includes everything. Just as the story of the five loaves and two fish is at once a social critique and a new social alternative, at once material and concrete, so too is the Eucharist a way of saying no to hatred and yes to love, which includes everything in life — food, health, spirituality, relationships, community, identity — everything. That is why, Maggy insists, in spite of IMF and World Bank statistics that show Burundi as the third least developed country, Burundi is not a poor country. "What a disgrace that our country receives food from outside. Look how rich our land is," Maggy points out to me as we drive through the lush countryside on the way to Ruyigi in January 2009. "We live under a lie. It disgusts me," she added.

Thus the various activities at Maison Shalom — the hair salon, the garage of angels, the farm, the swimming pool and the cinema hall — not only reveal the lie of "poverty" but illumine the possibilities, indeed the abundance, that are available in Burundi. These possibilities are part of the "everything" of a Eucharistic spirituality. It is this spirituality that she invited the bishops and other delegates at the 2008 Eucharistic Congress to rediscover. We must rediscover, she told the delegates, "the true mystery of the Eucharist," and "have the audacity to be crazy with the Eucharist, and

35. Ruyigi 2009
36. Eucharistic Congress.

take it outside our chapels and parishes into the world, into the villages and market places." "The Eucharist," she added, "is not found in your writings; the Eucharist is not found in your pastoral letters; not in the convents; the Eucharist is US. The Eucharist is in the market places."[37]

She confirmed the same conclusion as she and I drove through the countryside on the way to Ruyigi. "The Eucharist," she said, pointing, "is about that woman growing peas and cabbages; it is about the boy herding the goats." The Eucharist offers the lens to see this woman's life not as a poor and worthless statistic, nor first and foremost as a Hutu or Tutsi, but as a child of God, a princess, and God's unique gift. In other words, Eucharist makes sacred her ordinary life that has been dismissed as "hopeless" and invests in it productive forms of communal and social engagement, which transform her otherwise forlorn existence into gifts of flourishing abundance. Eucharist is not only an internal spirituality; it is a social praxis. Maison Shalom is a provocative demonstration plot of the claim that Eucharist is a spirituality, indeed politics, that covers everything.

Gathering Fragments

There is another sense in which Maison Shalom reveals and illumines a Eucharistic theology and praxis and thus a unique ecclesiology, namely, in the gathering of fragments. The majority of the children Maggy gathers into Maison Shalom are orphans, former child soldiers, and street children. Many are called "bastards" or "illegitimate" children. The majority have been abandoned and discarded. The story of Dieudonné best captures Maggy's commitment to gather these abandoned and discarded children. And since it is such a telling and powerful story, it is helpful to reproduce it with full details as Maggy told it to us:

> I remember I was on the street and I saw so many bodies because the military had killed many people . . . and I stopped and tried to take those bodies in my car in order to give them dignity. And when I was taking those bodies I found one man with a baby on his back. Because they killed him with a grenade. The man died, but when I took the baby, I found that the mouth was gone, but he was still alive because

37. Eucharistic Congress.

his heart was beating. And I said, "What must I do?" I took this baby (he was only 4 months old) — but unfortunately, the hospital had Tutsi military who took over the hospital and I was afraid to stay because this baby was a Hutu.

And I began to lie and to the doctors who were in the military I said, "My children went to play in this Tutsi camp and the Hutu rebels came and put a grenade (I lied) and look at my child, he lost the mouth and part of his tongue!"

And the military asked me, "What's the name?"

I said, "Dieudonné." It's the gift of God.

And he said to me, "We can't save your child. Go over there. In ten minutes he will die."

And I was there, waiting, nobody wanted this baby, even the nurses, and I told the nurses, "Look, I will give blood or other, I know this child will be saved."

They said, "Go away. You are tricked."

And I said, "No." I said to the nurses, "One day I will build a hospital where Hutu, Tutsi, Congolese, other will come."

And I went with this child, thinking that he would die. But he didn't die. I was there every morning trying to put stitches in his nose. And keep feeding this child. Nobody wanted this child because it was so horrible to look at this Dieudonné.

Even in the meeting I put him on my back and hid his face, going to the meeting to UNICEF and others.

Even in the church people said, "Look at this crazy woman. She lost her mind."

And one day, after two years with Dieudonné — traveling with this baby, and everybody saying, "Look, he's punished," and him saying, "My family doesn't want me" — a German journalist came to make a report at Maison Shalom. They reported on Dieudonné. And then some families decided to take him for medical care and they rebuilt his mouth. During three years he was in the hospital in Germany and then I returned to take back Dieudonné.

Today he is fourteen years old.[38]

There is also the story of Chloe, who was seven when her father was killed in 1972. She was thirteen years old when she met Maggy, and almost

38. Ruyigi 2009.

seventeen when she lost her mother and Maggy took her in as a daughter of Maison Shalom. "But Chloe was a Hutu, a Protestant, and came from the South, a culmination of all that the local Ruyigi administration despised. Imagine, in all my excitement (of taking her in) I didn't even notice the tension I created around me and amongst my colleagues."[39]

Gloriose's story is similar but reveals another crucial aspect about Maggy's commitment to gathering children who are discarded. On October 22, 1993, Gloriose, a young thirteen-year-old Tutsi, watched her parents die before her in the hills of Butezi. Her two little sisters were able to escape the massacres, but Gloriose was kidnapped by the killers. After having been raped for weeks, she was finally abandoned in her house. The attackers left for Tanzania where they sought refuge. She was pregnant, but she did not yet know it. It was the "old mothers" (Hutus) that brought her first to Butezi, then to Ruyigi to Maggy where her sisters were already. In Burundi, a young woman that is pregnant but not married is rejected by her family, and even more so if she was raped by a man of the other ethnicity. The rapists know this well and use it as a weapon. When Gloriose gave birth in August of 1994 to a little girl, they named her Inamahoro, "child of peace."[40]

Maggy also likes to tell the story of her driver, Geraldo, who was a child rebel soldier. He stopped Maggy at a roadblock and ordered her out of her car, and ordered her to kneel down. Maggy refused, saying that she only knelt down before God. Then she noticed the boy had a rosary around his neck. Maggy added, "But I will kneel down to pray if you kneel down with me." The boy hesitated. Maggy then asked him: "Why do you carry a gun and a rosary? The two you know do not go well together?" Then Maggy made the boy an offer: "If you give the gun back and come with me, I will give you something better to do." The boy abandoned his weapon. He came with Maggy and is now Maggy's driver.[41]

Through these and other children's stories, Maggy and Maison Shalom confirm and make real the gospel story of five loaves and two fish. In the story, after all ate and had their fill, twelve baskets of fragments were collected. As I noted at the beginning, in John's version of the story, the gathering of fragments is in response to Jesus' explicit command: "gather

---

39. Martin, *La haine*, 87.
40. Martin, *La haine*, 95-96.
41. Ruyigi 2009.

the fragments left over, so that nothing will be wasted" (John 6:12). As the stories of Glorise, Chloe, Dieudonné, and Geraldo confirm, Maggy is doing precisely that. But the fact that, at least in John's Gospel, gathering fragments is an explicit command by Jesus, it reveals a crucial mission of the church — to be a community committed to the gathering of the vulnerable, broken (fragmented), rejected, easily discarded, yet most precious gifts of God's creation, "so that nothing [and no one] is wasted."

Like Bishop Taban and Angelina Atyam, Maggy's Maison Shalom is driven by an ecclesiastical vision. Maggy's life and work exemplify not only the story of God that shapes the future, but that the task, gift, and art of crafting this new future is what it means to be a church. That is why, in the final analysis, Maggy's Maison Shalom is primarily about proclaiming the gospel, which is the ministry of the church — it is not about the programs and projects; it is about the mission. Maggy attended the third Gathering of the Great Lakes Initiative, hosted by the Duke Center for Reconciliation at Club du lac Tanganyika in Burundi in January 2009. Asked why she had adjusted her busy schedule to respond to our late invitation to be at the gathering, she answered: "Even though I was so busy, I know my first mission is not to take care of children, it's to announce the gospel . . . to announce the good news. . . . This message doesn't belong to me. It's my vocation. . . . I want to tell to all those people that evil will never take the last word. It's always the love."[42]

Conclusion: Hatred Will Never Have the Last Word

We have taken time to tell Maggy's story as a spiritual and theological journey, because without this theological framework, Maggy's Maison Shalom would not exist or be what it is today. It is her faith that explains the social critique as well as the alternative to the social history of ethnic hatred that Maison Shalom is. In her Kirundi language, Maggy's maiden name Barankitse means "they have made me crooked." The name seems to be an appropriate reminder of what Maggy's life has come to be about: a life of struggle against the history and the many lies that keep twisting — making crooked — Maggy's life and the life of others in Burundi. Maggy has spent her life pushing back against the forces of lies, ethnicity, and hatred. It is as

42. Ruyigi 2009.

if Maggy is determined to prove that her name, Barankitse, will never have the last claim on her life.

In this, she has succeeded greatly. For the first thing one notices about Maggy is her natural beauty, grace, and irrepressible laugh. All these qualities radiate a mystery about Maggy's life: it is the ability, in the midst of hatred, to say Yes to love; it is the celebration of life even amidst ruin, the patience built up from years of struggle against hatred, and the confidence of someone who knows that victory against those forces has already been secured. The mystery that Maggy's beauty and joy radiates is the mystery of a world beyond hatred; it is the mystery of her faith, which according to Maggy is nothing but the story of God's love, by which we are created as God's children. This is the mystery she rediscovered in the hatred of the events of October 1993, but a mystery that has come to sustain her confidence that hatred will never have the last word. "I am a woman of conviction," she told us. "I believe that evil will never, ever have the final word. I have been through terrible things." She paused, tellingly, before she continued: "But I have also understood great joy."[43]

The great joy that Maggy speaks about is the confidence that evil will never have the last word. For her work with Maison Shalom, Maggy has received various international awards and honors. In 2004, she received the Four Freedoms Award from the Franklin and Eleanor Roosevelt Institute, and the Voices of Courage Award from the U.S.-based Women's Commission for Refugee Women and Children. Her other awards include the World's Children's Prize (2003), the Spanish Committee for Aid to Refugees' Juan Maria Bandrés Prize for Asylum Rights Advocates (2003), the North-South Prize (2000), The Nansen Refugee Award (2006), as well as the French government's Human Rights Prize (1998). In 2004, she was awarded an honorary doctorate by the Catholic University of Louvain in Belgium, and more recently (2008) received the $1 million humanitarian award by the Opus Prize Foundation.

All these awards and recognitions validate the success of Maggy's dream and work with Maison Shalom. No awards, however, are able to confirm the truth of Maggy's conviction that evil will never have the last word as well as the words of Justine, whose story we have already mentioned. In January 2001, Maison Shalom organized a huge party to celebrate the construction of eighty-five houses for the children. Many digni-

43. Ruyigi 2009.

taries were invited, including the minister of social development, the Belgian ambassador, representatives of UNICEF, the World Food Program (WFP), the United Nations Development Program (UNDP), the apostolic pronuncio, and the bishops. In the gardens of Maison Shalom, the children played the drums, danced, and sang for the guests. Justine came to give a speech. At one point in her speech, she addressed Maggy:

> Maggy, you often repeated to us that one day we will find our own homes, our identities. Oma, your dreams have become a reality. Oma, you cried like a mother for seven years. This is the moment to console yourself and to dry your tears. We learned from you to respect and forgive those who killed our parents, who looted our goods, who violated our rights, or who physically and morally beat us.[44]

Calling on the adults present to change their "irresponsible behavior" and to awaken their conscience, Justine continued: "Maggy gave us love and the grace with which we can overlook our sad experiences. She was not obliged to do it. We ourselves were not part of her family. If I hadn't found her, I myself would in time have become a killer."[45]

Justine's story and words, "If I hadn't found her, I myself would in time have become a killer" — words that could be echoed by many of Justine's friends at Maison Shalom — confirm that Maggy's dream of a new future in Burundi, founded on the story of love, has already become a reality. Justine and her friends at Maison Shalom are, so to say, the first harvest of Maggy's crazy hope — the victory of love over hatred.

There could be no better argument and proof of Paul's claim "If anyone is in Christ, he is a new creation" (2 Cor. 5:17) than this. A journalist who had been following Maggy's life and work with Maison Shalom over the years, at first with a lot of reservations, recently told Maggy: "that secret — saying that it's God who's carrying the world — I am starting to believe it."[46]

---

44. Martin, *La haine*, 155.
45. Martin, *La haine*, 155.
46. Eucharistic Congress.

Conclusion

No, I am not a dreamer. It is real.

Maggy Barankitse

So, what do Taban, Angelina, and Maggy have in common? First, they are all "crazy." Taban noted that when asked to lead the prayer at the signing of the Comprehensive Peace Agreement for Southern Sudan, President Omar al-Bashir turned in his seat and said, "It is that mad and stubborn bishop." The old woman, who upon hearing Angelina speak about forgiveness, asked, "Angelina, are you from a different planet?" Angelina herself admits that when she refused the rebels' deal and let them keep her daughter if they were not willing to release the other girls, "people thought I was crazy, but all the other children had also become my children." And Maggy admits, "Love has made me crazy." All three share Thomas Sankara's revolutionary madness, grounded in his observation that "you cannot carry out fundamental change without a certain amount of madness." All three share the same rascality that we noted about Taban, which is the stubbornness of nonconformity, the willingness to turn one's back on old formulas.

But as their stories indicate, their stubbornness makes it possible to invent the future. In other words, their willingness to say No to hatred, violence, or tribalism and their Yes to a future of love, peaceful coexistence, and forgiveness is the audacity that makes both their lives and work possible. This is what makes their lives and work both a critique of the current social history and an alternative to it. They are constantly pushing the limits of the present, the conventional, and what appears to be normal and "realistic" in order to reveal the future they are inventing and living.

However, to say that they invent the future is misleading, because all three are clear that the future is not of their own making; it is the future that God has promised for God's people, into which they themselves have been invited. Thus Angelina, Taban, and Maggy constantly draw attention to God's story as foundational to their lives and work. That is the source of the incredible energy, vision, and strength that drives them, but at the same time they feel powerless, because they are being led. Angelina, in refusing the rebels' deal, confessed, "I did not have much choice; all the other children had become my children." Taban attests to the same sense of powerlessness when he says many times, "I feel like a blind man, being led by God." Maggy confirms the same out-of-control experience when she says, "I believe that nobody can stop me. I compare the Shalom House to a train that God conducts. Nobody can stop this train. He will still move it — because God is God. There will be some cars that will stop. But He will continue to gather Congolese, Rwandese, Europeans, saying, 'Come my children and build my dream.'" Given this overwhelming sense of God's story within which Taban, Angelina, and Maggy locate their lives and work, it is not surprising that their daily lives are characterized by the disciplines of prayer, penance, silence, meditation, and Mass, through which their relationship with God is constantly remembered, affirmed, renewed, and deepened.

Accordingly, the three reveal a holistic sense of the future shaped by God's story. That is why what Taban is doing in Kuron or Angelina with CPA is not merely advocacy or development. Maggy's Maison is not an "orphanage," nor even a humanitarian or relief agency. They understand themselves as living out a story, which involves but is not limited to advocacy, economics, relief, agriculture, healthcare, education, and cooperative associations. What they are doing involves all aspects of human life. Maggy's remark about the Eucharist as a spirituality that "covers everything" is a true depiction of the holistic social, economic, political, and theological entrepreneurship all three exemplify. In fact, that they all share Maggy's Eucharistic spirituality, which "includes everything," confirms that they are able to move beyond what Éla referred to as the sociological burden of religion into a form of Christian social praxis that involves reordering geography, history, economics, politics, time, communities, relationships — in short, everything. Given this "everything," their stories confirm that the gospel does not have a social message (from which to draw implications), but that the gospel *is* a social message.

Moreover, the fact that the Eucharistic spirituality that Maggy, Angelina, and Taban all relate to (no doubt in varying ways) "includes everything" does not render it a kind of ephemeral relationship that "wafts above the everyday." Rather, Eucharist makes for concrete engagement with and in particular histories and geographies. The fact that all three are deeply engaged in very specific locations — Taban in Kuron, Angelina in Bobi and surrounding districts, and Maggy in Ruyigi — not only confirms that geography and history matter, but that relocation and incarnational activism are essential marks of the church committed to a new future in Africa. Only through its presence and ministries grounded in local places is the church able to proclaim the gospel message: "*Today* salvation has come to *this* house."

But Taban, Angelina, and Maggy also confirm how the good news of the gospel is at the same time an interruption of the social history shaped by tribalism, poverty, violence, and hatred. This is what makes the proclamation a *fresh* interruption, and this is what is refreshing about the lives and work of Taban, Angelina, and Maggy. In each of their stories, one can see how a history of ethnic hatred can give way to a future of forgiveness, peaceful existence, and a revolution of love. That is why their stories not only illumine the shape of a new future, but also reveal a fresh and redemptive sacrifice of Africa. If the social history of Africa's modernity assumes and enacts the sacrificing of Africa, especially the weak, children, women, and the poor, then Taban, Angelina, and Maggy interrupt it with their extravagant attention, advocacy for, and gathering of those discarded ones. This extravagant attention makes sacred the lives of the discarded and reveals them to be what they are — God's precious children, the unique sacrifice *(sacra-facere)* of the God who "dwelt among us."

That is indeed not only a unique sacrifice, but also a unique form of madness, made possible by a unique story. For if the story that shapes modern Africa is grounded in a story of lies, whose effect has been to shape patterns of madness (tribalism, violence, plunder, corruption, ethnicity) that *waste* the lives of Africans, what Angelina, Taban, and Maggy reveal is a different type of madness — one that *saves* the very lives that have been wasted. This type of madness is grounded and made possible by a story, the story of the God of creation and redemption revealed in Scripture.

This story is not independently given, but is discovered and renewed through concrete practices through which the story is remembered and made present. Taban, Angelina, and Maggy's revolutionary madness reveals different aspects not only of the Christian foundational story, but of the church in its historical, incarnational, and Eucharistic existence. Taban, Angelina, and Maggy represent different aspects of this ecclesiology, of a fresh vision of the church in Africa, engaged in very concrete and dynamic ways in the mundane and everyday tasks of crafting the temporal, social, geographical, and practical implications of that story. This is what constitutes the politics of that story. Accordingly, Maggy, Angelina, and Taban not only reveal the politics of the Christian story; they show that that politics requires and depends on a particular vision of the church. Angelina, Taban, and Maggy not only confirm that the church is essential to the search for a new future in Africa; they reveal the type of church that is able to both engage the future as a task (to be invented) and receive it as a fresh gift, the promise of God's new creation.

To the extent that Maggy, Taban, and Angelina's revolutionary madness is grounded in the story of God, their stories reveal an entirely new world that God's story makes possible in Africa. A good way to capture this conclusion is to look at Christel Martin's description of his first meeting with Maggy:

> In January 1999, I came in on a little inland plane from PAM ('World Aid Program') on Ruyigi's dusty runway. Two doctors from the MSF Belgique came with me. I caught a ride in their car headed into town to the guesthouse where I had the privilege of staying. The only thing they said to me as they dropped me off was "that's her" and pointed to Maggy. She was standing in front of the house, slightly keeping a watch over the shoulder, and giving a few orders. She insisted that the entire place, everything be kept spotless. Her outfit was brightly colored. I remember that she seemed gigantic to me — with her open arms, and that look on her face like she wanted to hug everything, even the horizon. I was taken back by her laughter and energy, seeing this female extrovert amongst a group of people that are so reserved. Because of her words and powerful voice, I could feel her unexpected inward nature; it was profound. It was like the entire universe was held inside one person.[1]

---

1. Christel Martin, *La haine n'aura pas le derniere mot: Maggy la femme aux 10000 en-*

"It was like the entire universe was held inside one person." This is true not only of Maggy, but of Taban and Angelina. Each of their lives and their work holds an entire universe, the "different world right here" to which Jean-Marc Éla pointed. With the stories of people like Taban, Angelina, and Maggy, we are able not just to dream about this new world and this new future in Africa, but to experience its reality. What Maggy says about her hope for a new generation in Burundi can also be said about God's new future in Africa: "No, I am not a dreamer. It is real."[2]

---

fants (Paris: Albin Michel, 2005), unpublished translation by Trent Dailey-Chwalibog and David Dimas, 48.

2. Opus Prize Video, http://www.opusprize.org/winners/08_Barankitse.cfm.

Index